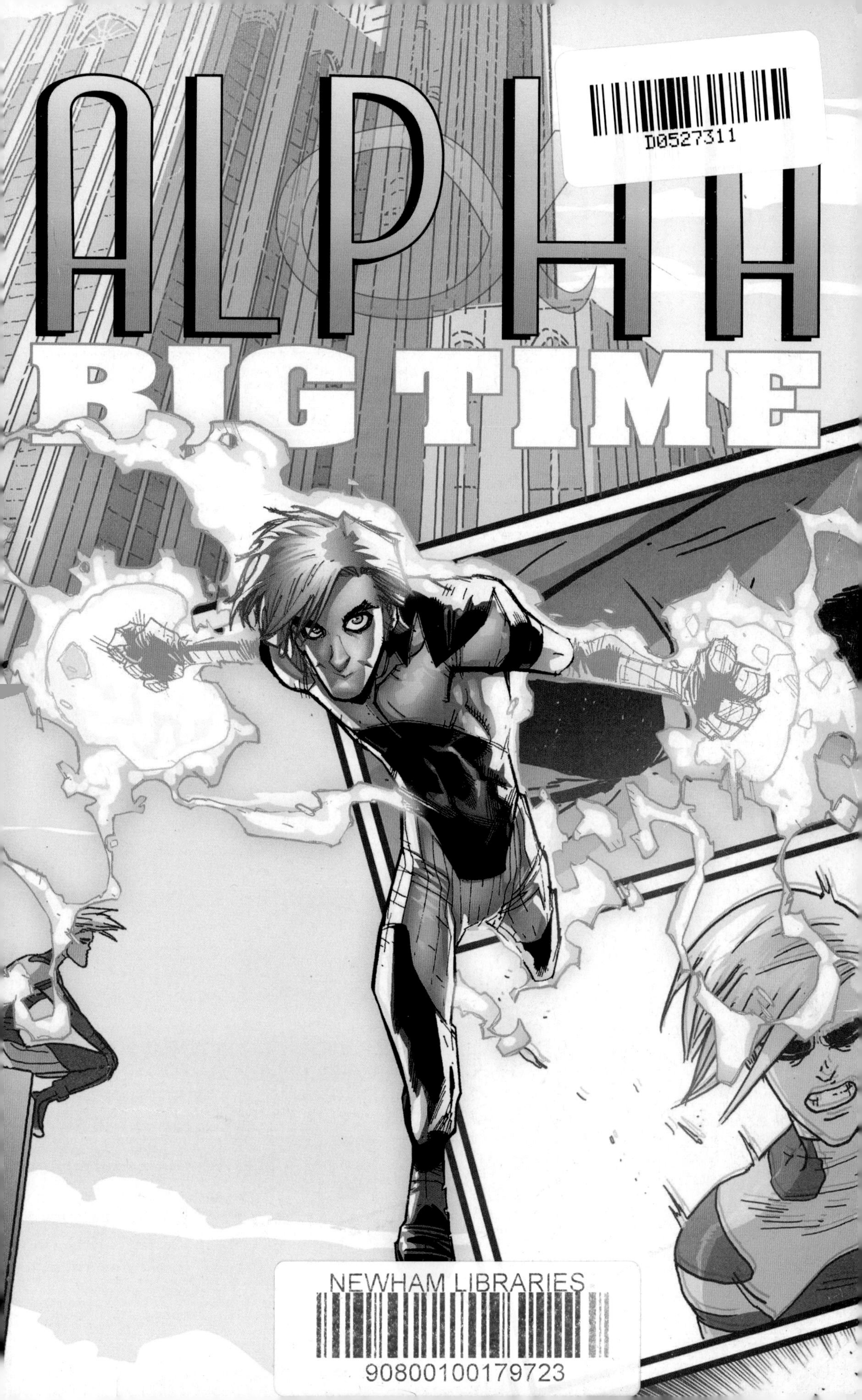
ALPHA
BIG TIME

WRITER
JOSH FIALKOV

ARTIST
NUNO PLATI

COLOR ART, #4: **JOHN RAUCH** • LETTERER: **VC'S JOE SABINO**
COVER ARTISTS: **HUMBERTO RAMOS** & **EDGAR DELGADO**
EDITOR **TOM BRENNAN** • SENIOR EDITOR: **STEPHEN WACKER**
SPECIAL THANKS TO **DAN SLOTT**

COLLECTION EDITOR & DESIGN: CORY LEVINE • ASSISTANT EDITORS: ALEX STARBUCK & NELSON RIBEIRO
EDITORS, SPECIAL PROJECTS: JENNIFER GRÜNWALD & MARK D. BEAZLEY
SENIOR EDITOR, SPECIAL PROJECTS: JEFF YOUNGQUIST • SVP OF PRINT & DIGITAL PUBLISHING SALES: DAVID GABRIEL
EDITOR IN CHIEF: AXEL ALONSO • CHIEF CREATIVE OFFICER: JOE QUESADA
PUBLISHER: DAN BUCKLEY • EXECUTIVE PRODUCER: ALAN FINE

ALPHA: BIG TIME. Contains material originally published in magazine form as ALPHA: BIG TIME #1-5. First printing 2013. ISBN# 978-0-7851-8387-7. Published by MARVEL WORLDWIDE, INC., a subsidiary of MARVEL ENTERTAINMENT, LLC. OFFICE OF PUBLICATION: 135 West 50th Street, New York, NY 10020. Copyright © 2013 Marvel Characters, Inc. All rights reserved. All characters featured in this issue and the distinctive names and likenesses thereof, and all related indicia are trademarks of Marvel Characters, Inc. No similarity between any of the names, characters, persons, and/or institutions in this magazine with those of any living or dead person or institution is intended, and any such similarity which may exist is purely coincidental. **Printed in the U.S.A.** ALAN FINE, EVP - Office of the President, Marvel Worldwide, Inc. and EVP & CMO Marvel Characters B.V.; DAN BUCKLEY, Publisher & President - Print, Animation & Digital Divisions; JOE QUESADA, Chief Creative Officer; TOM BREVOORT, SVP of Publishing; DAVID BOGART, SVP of Operations & Procurement, Publishing; C.B. CEBULSKI, SVP of Creator & Content Development; DAVID GABRIEL, SVP of Print & Digital Publishing Sales; JIM O'KEEFE, VP of Operations & Logistics; DAN CARR, Executive Director of Publishing Technology; SUSAN CRESPI, Editorial Operations Manager; ALEX MORALES, Publishing Operations Manager; STAN LEE, Chairman Emeritus. For information regarding advertising in Marvel Comics or on Marvel.com, please contact Niza Disla, Director of Marvel Partnerships, at ndisla@marvel.com. For Marvel subscription inquiries, please call 800-217-9158. **Manufactured between 6/21/2013 and 7/29/2013 by** QUAD/GRAPHICS ST. CLOUD, ST. CLOUD, MN, USA.

10 9 8 7 6 5 4 3 2 1

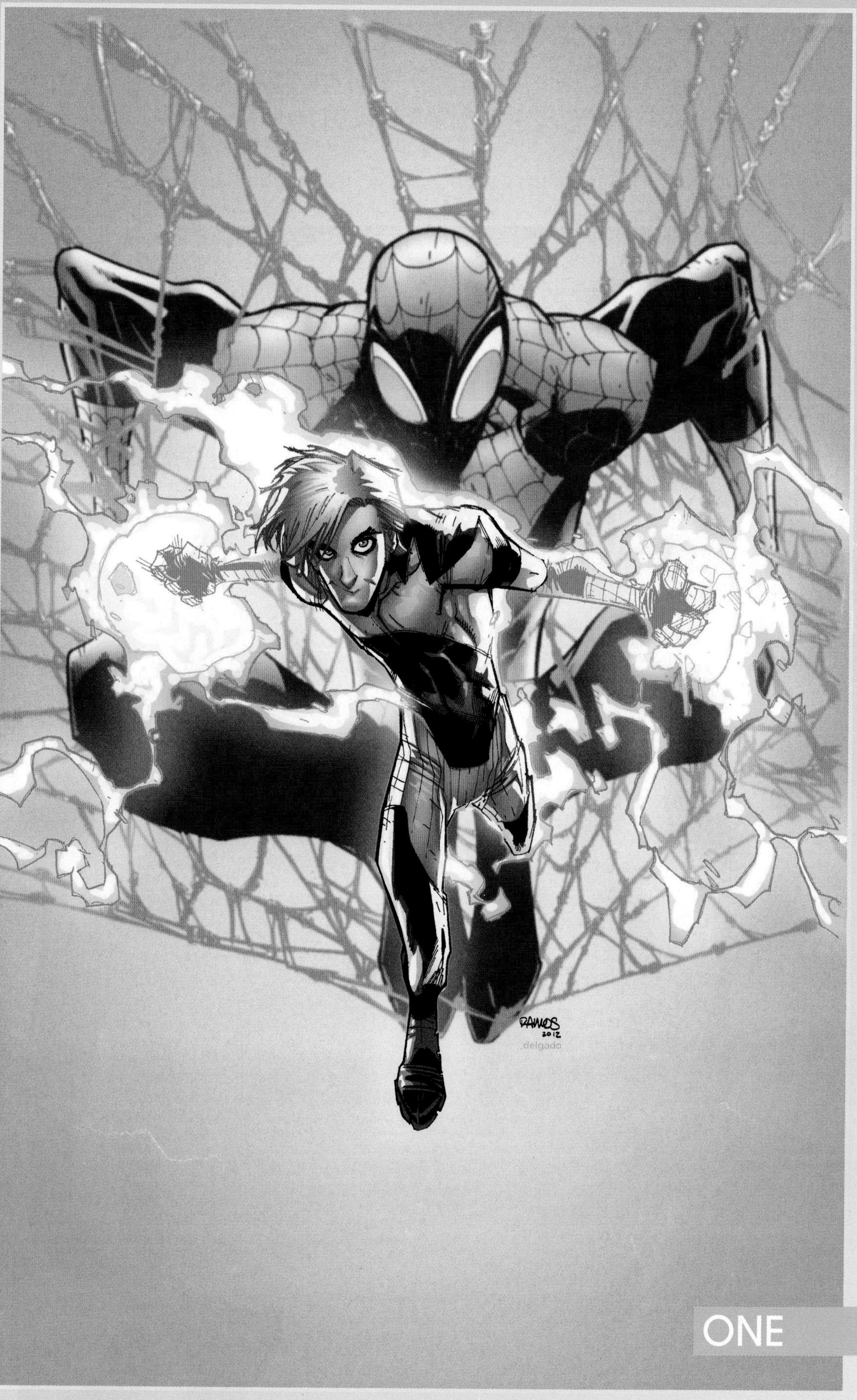
RAMOS 2012
delgado

ONE

HEY, MY NAME'S *ANDY MAGUIRE*. AND THAT'S ME. OR, IT *WAS* ME.

SEE, MY HIGH SCHOOL TOOK A FIELD TRIP TO *HORIZON LABS*, THIS NERD THINK TANK BACK HOME IN NEW YORK. ONE OF THE NERDS, SOME TIGHT-WAD NAMED *PETER PARKER*, RAN AN EXPERIMENT.

IT WENT WRONG, I GOT CAUGHT UP IN IT AND *BOOM!* I HAD SUPERPOWERS.

I WAS A *SUPER HERO.* THEY CALLED ME *"ALPHA."* PRETTY AWESOME, RIGHT?

EXCEPT IT *WASN'T* AWESOME. I MEAN, I COULD DO *ANYTHING*--FLY, LIFT CARS OVER MY HEAD, YOU NAME IT.

BUT I COULD ONLY USE *ONE* POWER AT A *TIME*, BUT WHATEVER, I WAS *FAMOUS*! I HAD *MONEY*, AND *FRIENDS*, AND *EVERYTHING*!

AND THEN IT WENT TO MY *HEAD*. AND I GOT RECKLESS. AND PEOPLE ALMOST GOT *KILLED*.

THANKS TO ME.

SO PARKER AND THE *"AMAZING"* SPIDER-MAN SHUT ME DOWN. THEY CREATED A DEVICE THAT *DEACTIVATED* MY POWERS.

I GUESS I DESERVED THAT.

THAT WAS MY STORY.

UNTIL NOW.

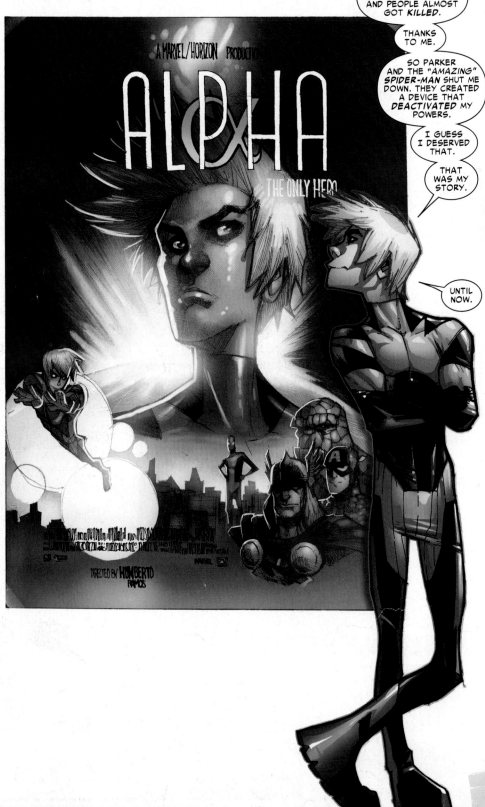

A MARVEL/HORIZON PRODUCTION

ALPHA

THE ONLY HERO

DIRECTED BY HUMBERTO RAMOS

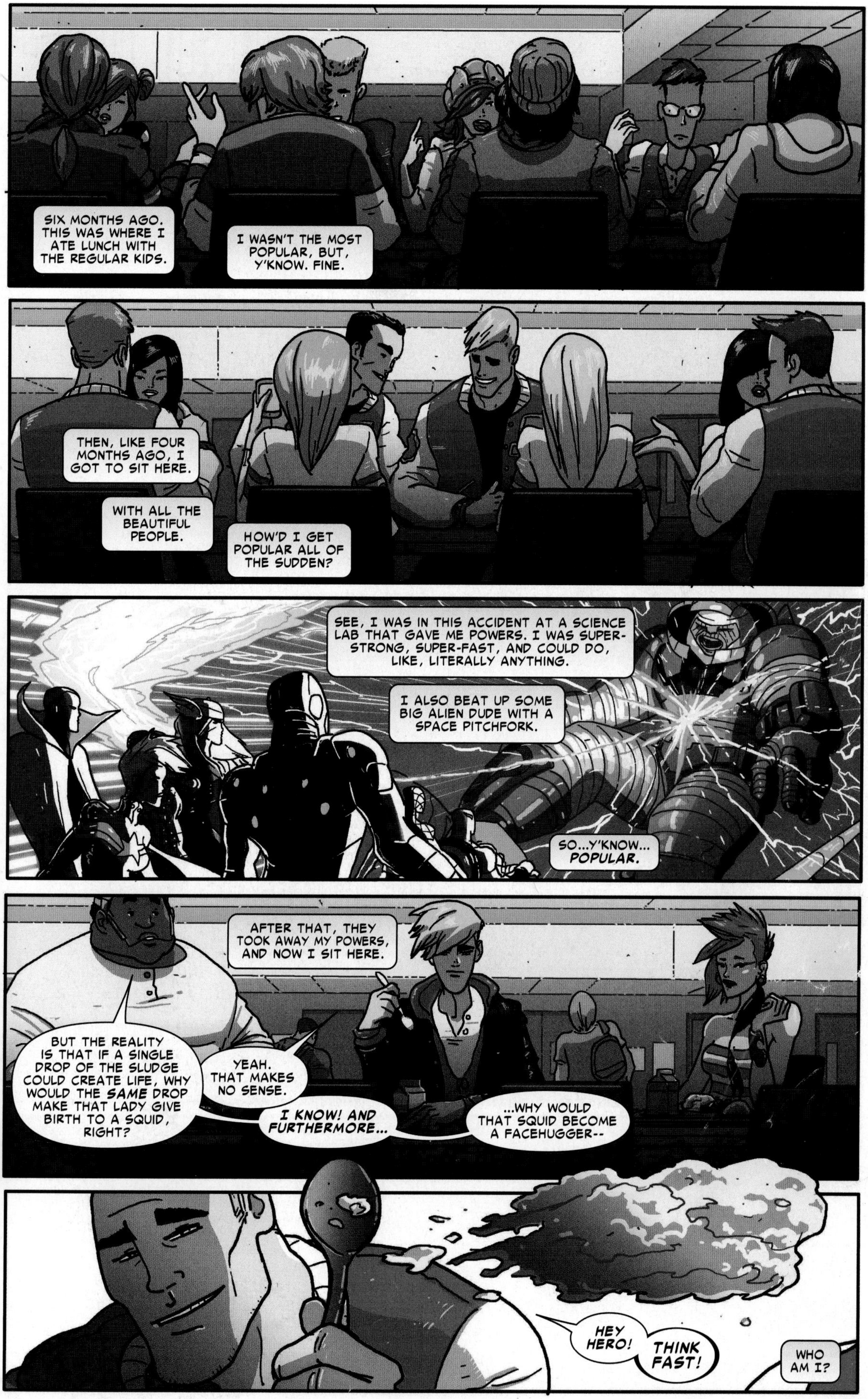
SIX MONTHS AGO. THIS WAS WHERE I ATE LUNCH WITH THE REGULAR KIDS.
I WASN'T THE MOST POPULAR, BUT, Y'KNOW. FINE.
THEN, LIKE FOUR MONTHS AGO, I GOT TO SIT HERE.
WITH ALL THE BEAUTIFUL PEOPLE.
HOW'D I GET POPULAR ALL OF THE SUDDEN?
SEE, I WAS IN THIS ACCIDENT AT A SCIENCE LAB THAT GAVE ME POWERS. I WAS SUPER-STRONG, SUPER-FAST, AND COULD DO, LIKE, LITERALLY ANYTHING.
I ALSO BEAT UP SOME BIG ALIEN DUDE WITH A SPACE PITCHFORK.
SO...Y'KNOW... POPULAR.
AFTER THAT, THEY TOOK AWAY MY POWERS, AND NOW I SIT HERE.
BUT THE REALITY IS THAT IF A SINGLE DROP OF THE SLUDGE COULD CREATE LIFE, WHY WOULD THE SAME DROP MAKE THAT LADY GIVE BIRTH TO A SQUID, RIGHT?
YEAH. THAT MAKES NO SENSE.
I KNOW! AND FURTHERMORE...
...WHY WOULD THAT SQUID BECOME A FACEHUGGER--
HEY HERO!
THINK FAST!
WHO AM I?

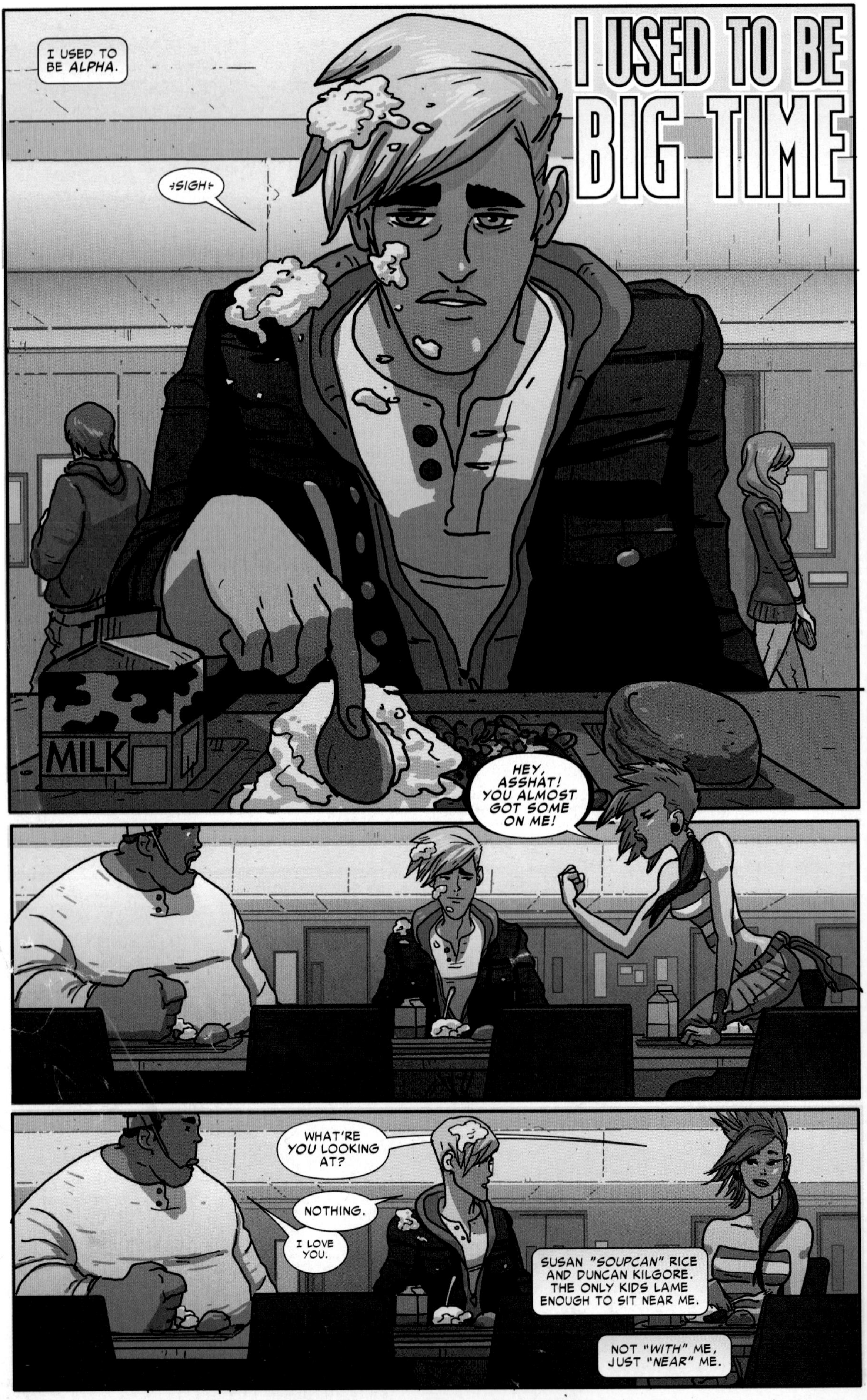
I USED TO BE BIG TIME
I USED TO BE ALPHA.
-SIGH-
MILK
HEY, ASSHAT! YOU ALMOST GOT SOME ON ME!
WHAT'RE YOU LOOKING AT?
NOTHING.
I LOVE YOU.
SUSAN "SOUPCAN" RICE AND DUNCAN KILGORE. THE ONLY KIDS LAME ENOUGH TO SIT NEAR ME.
NOT "WITH" ME, JUST "NEAR" ME.

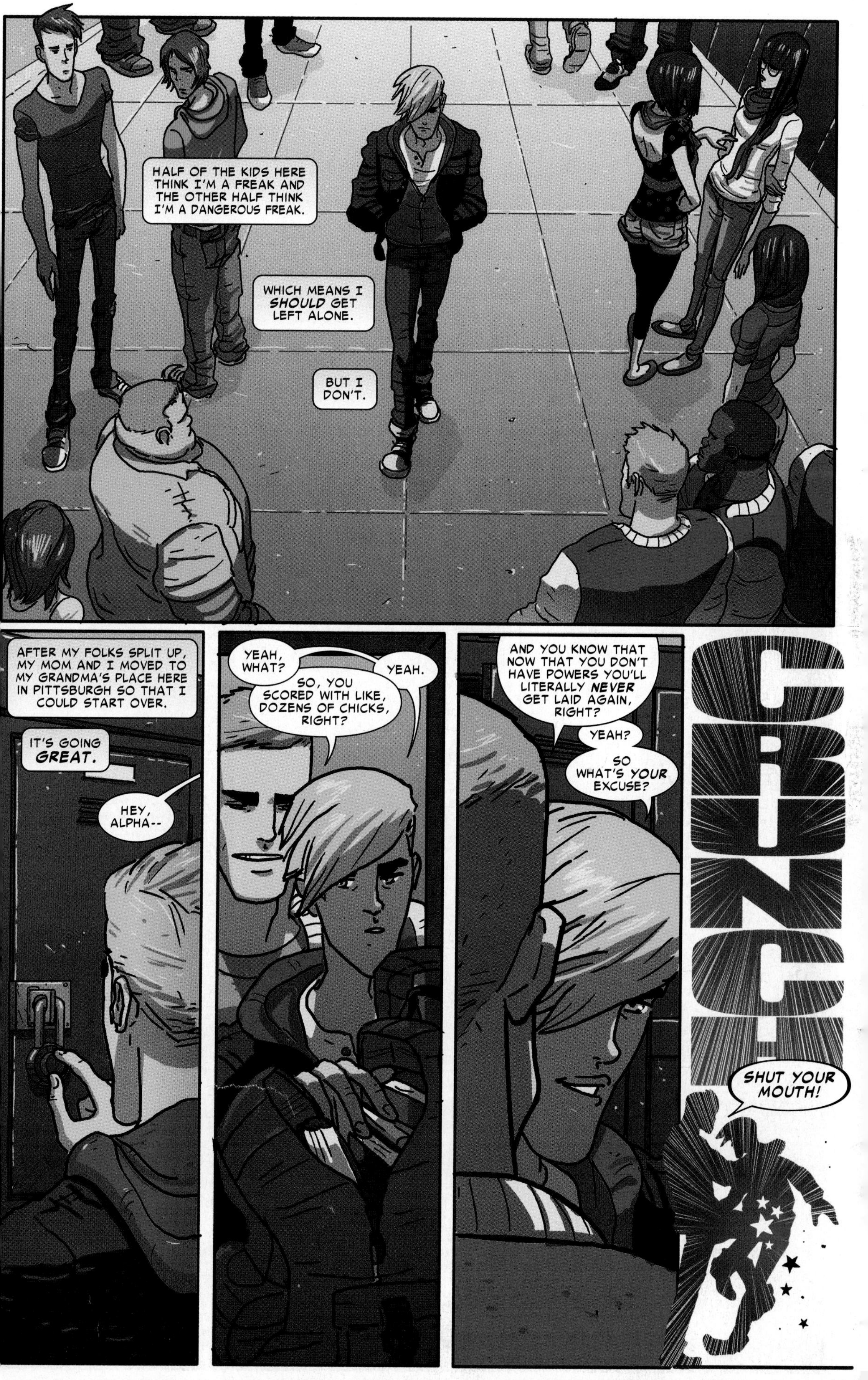

HALF OF THE KIDS HERE THINK I'M A FREAK AND THE OTHER HALF THINK I'M A DANGEROUS FREAK.
WHICH MEANS I SHOULD GET LEFT ALONE.
BUT I DON'T.
AFTER MY FOLKS SPLIT UP, MY MOM AND I MOVED TO MY GRANDMA'S PLACE HERE IN PITTSBURGH SO THAT I COULD START OVER.
IT'S GOING GREAT.
HEY, ALPHA--
YEAH, WHAT?
YEAH.
SO, YOU SCORED WITH LIKE, DOZENS OF CHICKS, RIGHT?
AND YOU KNOW THAT NOW THAT YOU DON'T HAVE POWERS YOU'LL LITERALLY NEVER GET LAID AGAIN, RIGHT?
YEAH?
SO WHAT'S YOUR EXCUSE?
CRUNCH!
SHUT YOUR MOUTH!

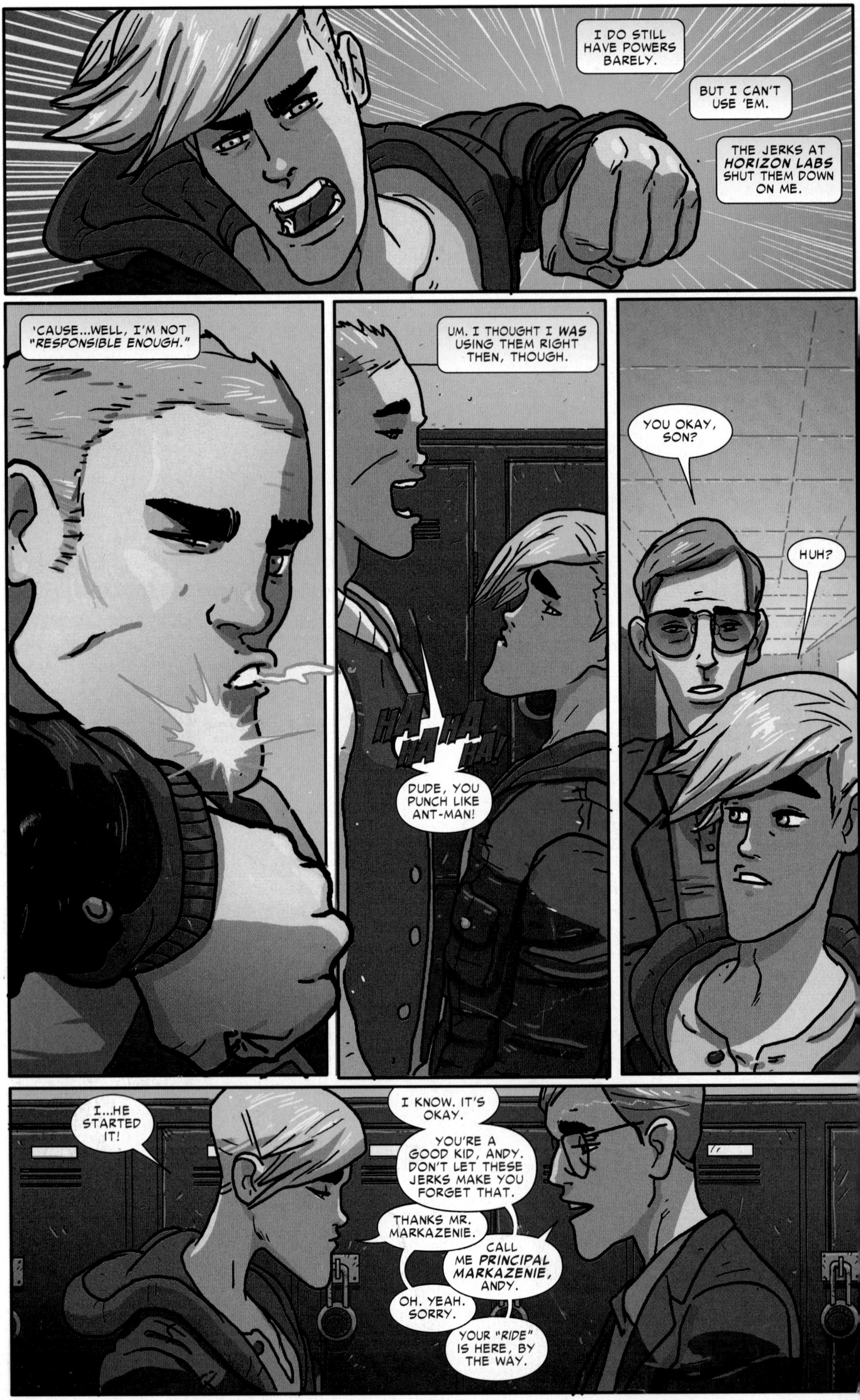

I DO STILL HAVE POWERS BARELY.
BUT I CAN'T USE 'EM.
THE JERKS AT *HORIZON LABS* SHUT THEM DOWN ON ME.
'CAUSE...WELL, I'M NOT "*RESPONSIBLE ENOUGH.*"
UM. I THOUGHT I *WAS* USING THEM RIGHT THEN, THOUGH.
HA HA HA HA HA!
DUDE, YOU PUNCH LIKE ANT-MAN!
YOU OKAY, SON?
HUH?
I...HE STARTED IT!
I KNOW. IT'S OKAY.
YOU'RE A GOOD KID, ANDY. DON'T LET THESE JERKS MAKE YOU FORGET THAT.
THANKS MR. MARKAZENIE.
CALL ME *PRINCIPAL MARKAZENIE,* ANDY.
OH. YEAH. SORRY.
YOUR "*RIDE*" IS HERE, BY THE WAY.

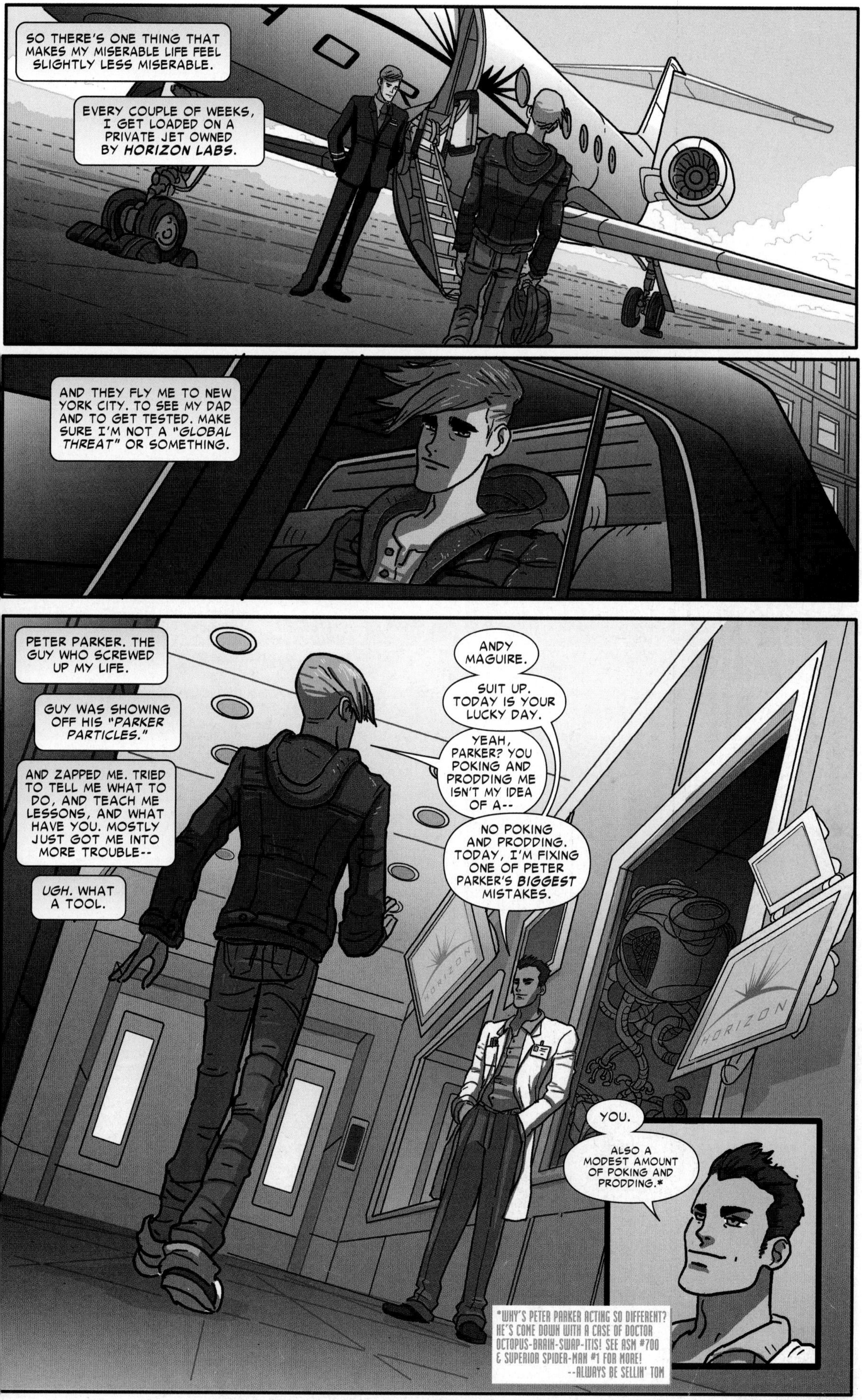
SO THERE'S ONE THING THAT MAKES MY MISERABLE LIFE FEEL SLIGHTLY LESS MISERABLE.
EVERY COUPLE OF WEEKS, I GET LOADED ON A PRIVATE JET OWNED BY *HORIZON LABS*.
AND THEY FLY ME TO NEW YORK CITY. TO SEE MY DAD AND TO GET TESTED. MAKE SURE I'M NOT A "*GLOBAL THREAT*" OR SOMETHING.
PETER PARKER. THE GUY WHO SCREWED UP MY LIFE.
GUY WAS SHOWING OFF HIS "*PARKER PARTICLES*."
AND ZAPPED ME. TRIED TO TELL ME WHAT TO DO, AND TEACH ME LESSONS, AND WHAT HAVE YOU. MOSTLY JUST GOT ME INTO MORE TROUBLE--
UGH. WHAT A TOOL.
ANDY MAGUIRE.
SUIT UP. TODAY IS YOUR LUCKY DAY.
YEAH, PARKER? YOU POKING AND PRODDING ME ISN'T MY IDEA OF A--
NO POKING AND PRODDING. TODAY, I'M FIXING ONE OF PETER PARKER'S *BIGGEST* MISTAKES.
HORIZON
HORIZON
YOU.
ALSO A MODEST AMOUNT OF POKING AND PRODDING.*
*WHY'S PETER PARKER ACTING SO DIFFERENT? HE'S COME DOWN WITH A CASE OF DOCTOR OCTOPUS-BRAIN-SWAP-ITIS! SEE ASM #700 & SUPERIOR SPIDER-MAN #1 FOR MORE! --ALWAYS BE SELLIN' TOM

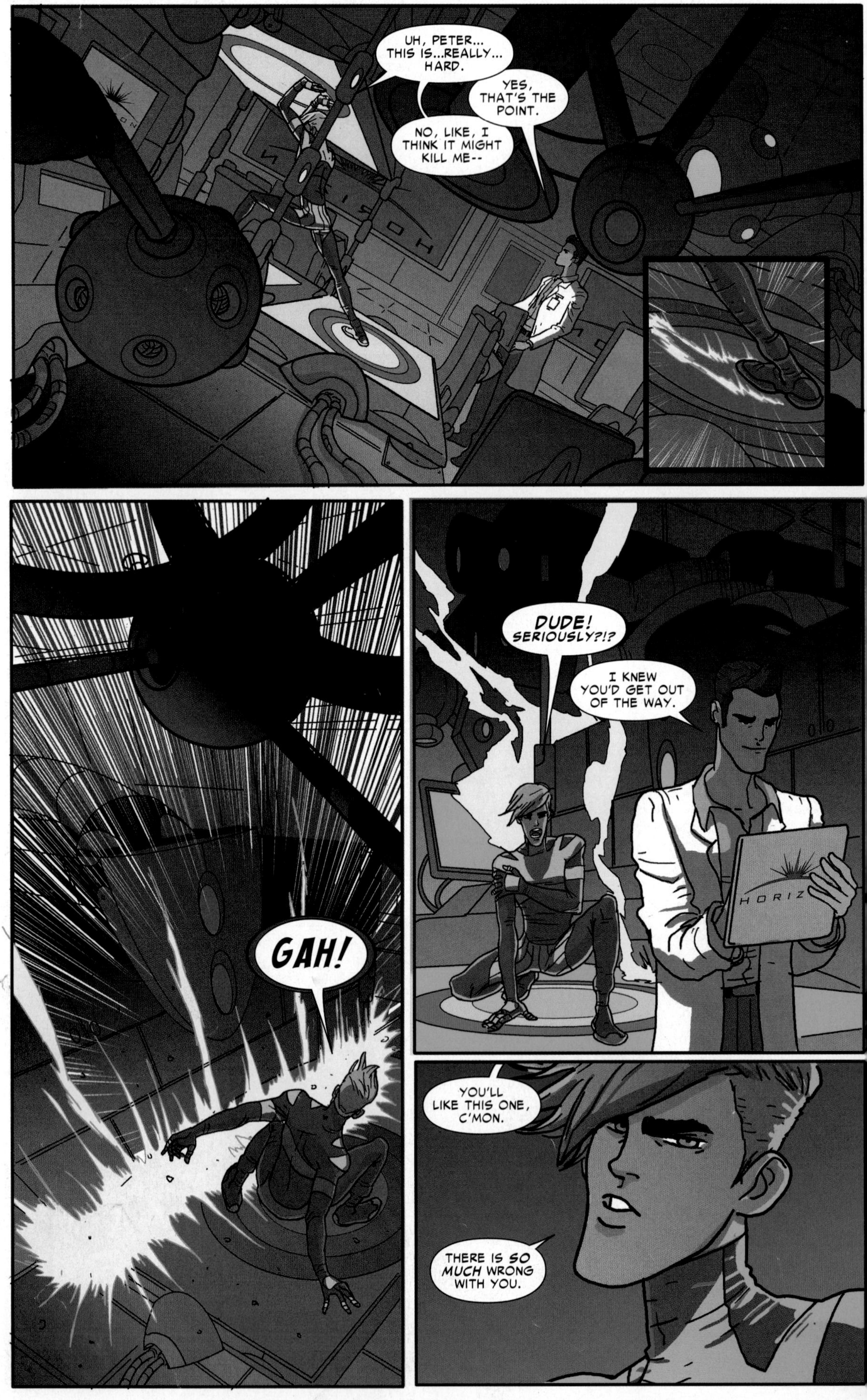
UH, PETER... THIS IS...REALLY... HARD.
YES, THAT'S THE POINT.
NO, LIKE, I THINK IT MIGHT KILL ME--
GAH!
DUDE! SERIOUSLY?!?
I KNEW YOU'D GET OUT OF THE WAY.
HORIZ
YOU'LL LIKE THIS ONE, C'MON.
THERE IS SO MUCH WRONG WITH YOU.

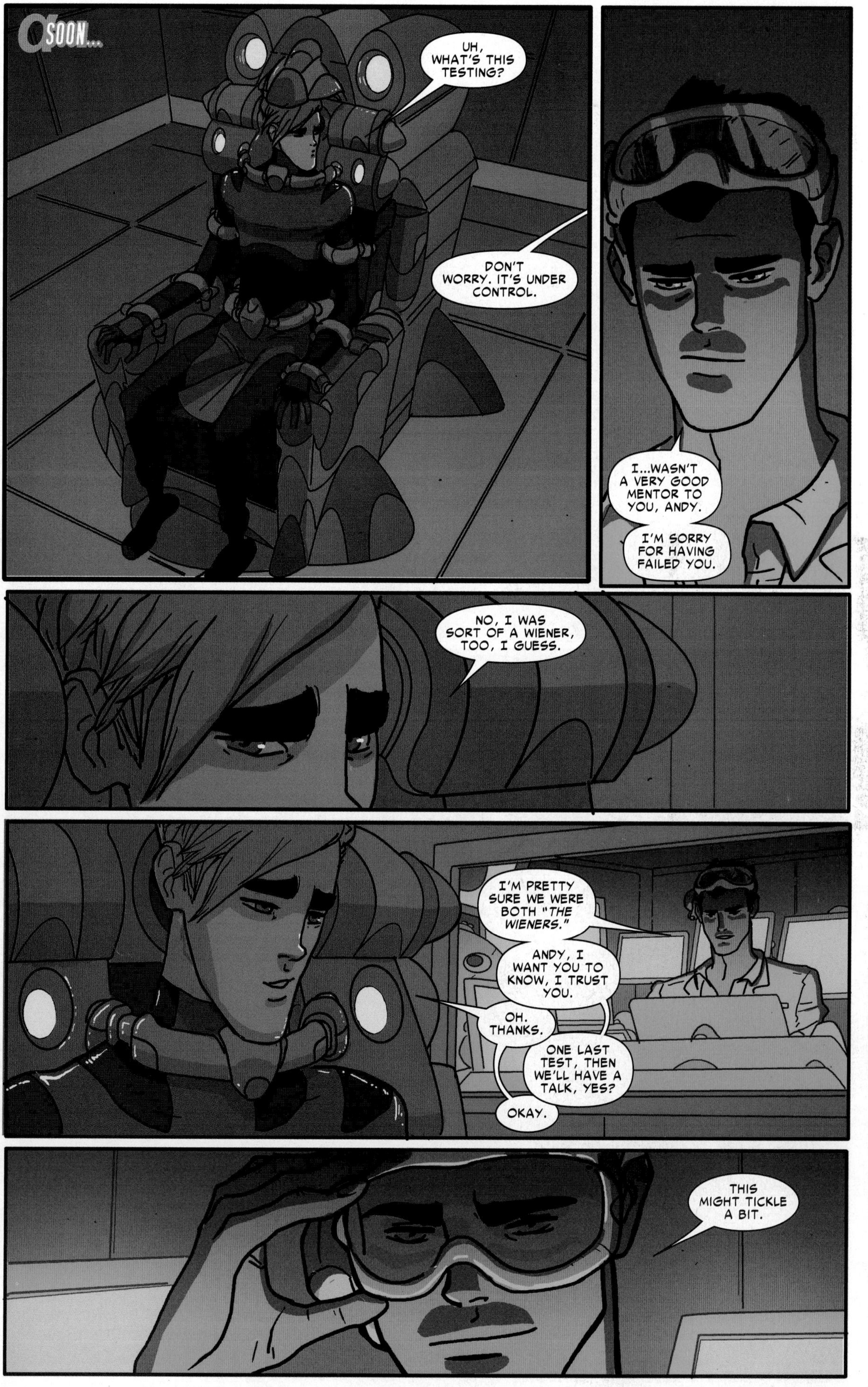
SOON...
UH, WHAT'S THIS TESTING?
DON'T WORRY. IT'S UNDER CONTROL.
I...WASN'T A VERY GOOD MENTOR TO YOU, ANDY.
I'M SORRY FOR HAVING FAILED YOU.
NO, I WAS SORT OF A WIENER, TOO, I GUESS.
I'M PRETTY SURE WE WERE BOTH "THE WIENERS."
ANDY, I WANT YOU TO KNOW, I TRUST YOU.
OH. THANKS.
ONE LAST TEST, THEN WE'LL HAVE A TALK, YES?
OKAY.
THIS MIGHT TICKLE A BIT.

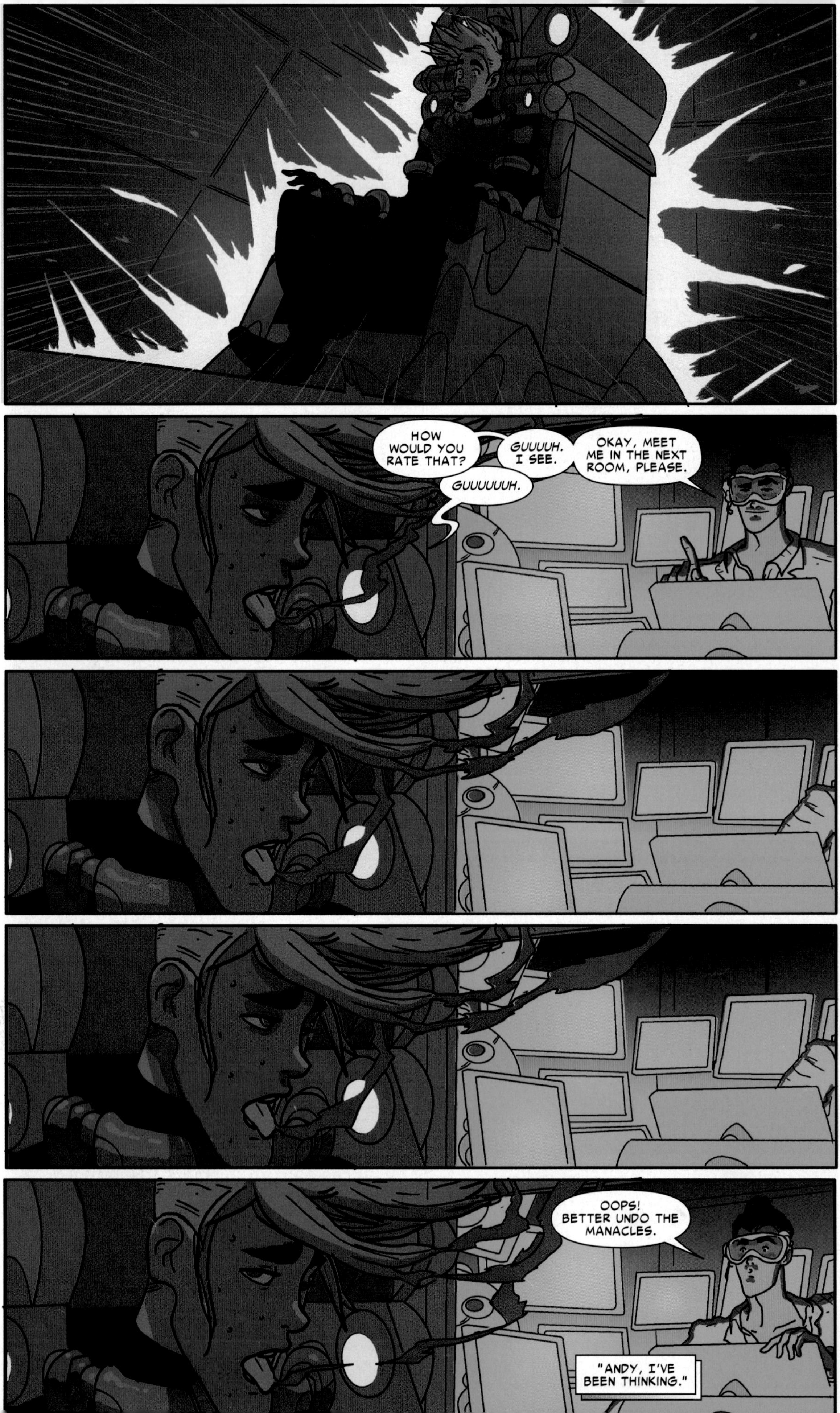
HOW WOULD YOU RATE THAT?
GUUUUH. I SEE.
GUUUUUUH.
OKAY, MEET ME IN THE NEXT ROOM, PLEASE.
OOPS! BETTER UNDO THE MANACLES.
"ANDY, I'VE BEEN THINKING."

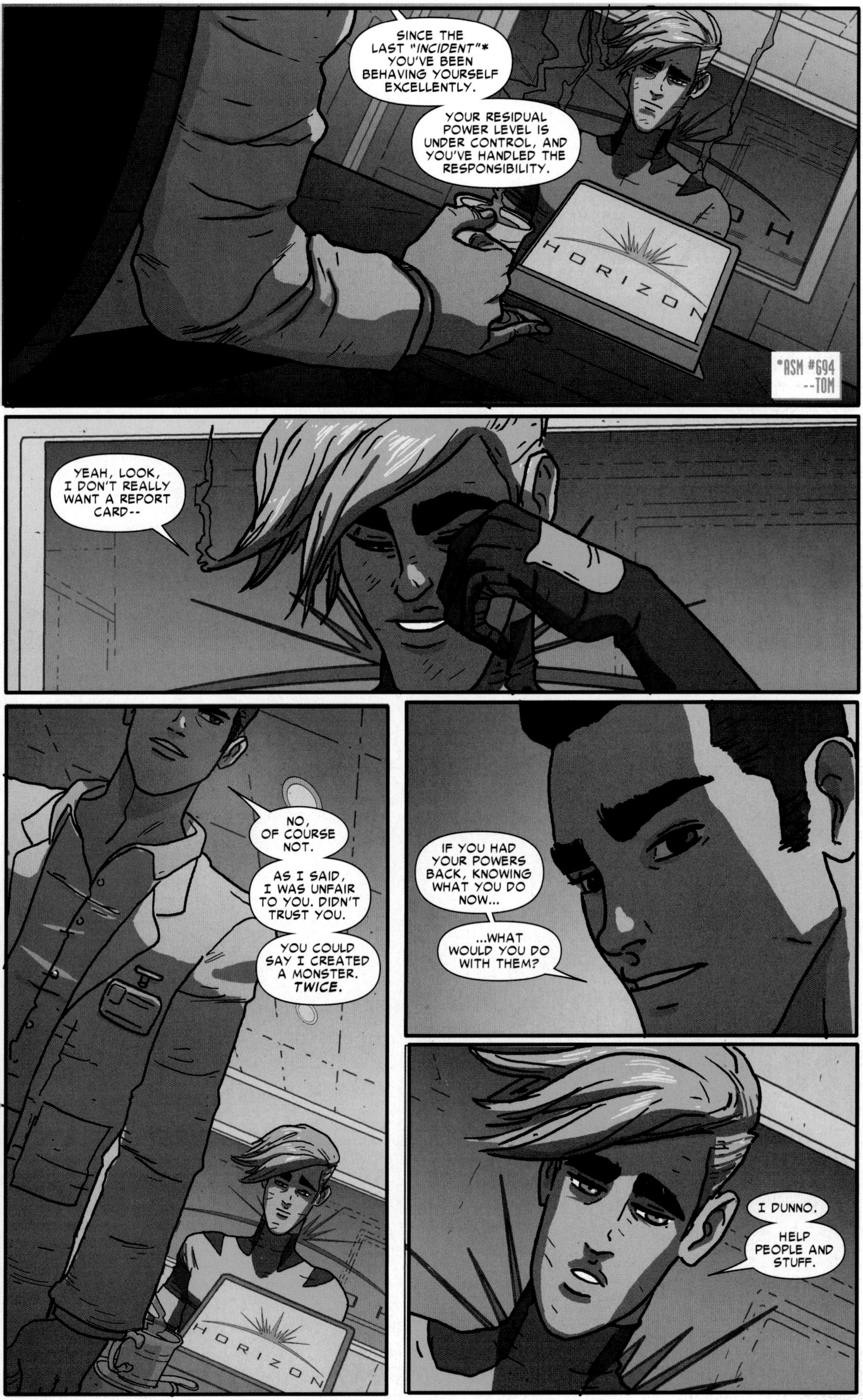
SINCE THE LAST "INCIDENT"* YOU'VE BEEN BEHAVING YOURSELF EXCELLENTLY.
YOUR RESIDUAL POWER LEVEL IS UNDER CONTROL, AND YOU'VE HANDLED THE RESPONSIBILITY.
HORIZON
*ASM #694 --TOM
YEAH, LOOK, I DON'T REALLY WANT A REPORT CARD--
NO, OF COURSE NOT.
AS I SAID, I WAS UNFAIR TO YOU. DIDN'T TRUST YOU.
YOU COULD SAY I CREATED A MONSTER. TWICE.
HORIZON
IF YOU HAD YOUR POWERS BACK, KNOWING WHAT YOU DO NOW...
...WHAT WOULD YOU DO WITH THEM?
I DUNNO.
HELP PEOPLE AND STUFF.

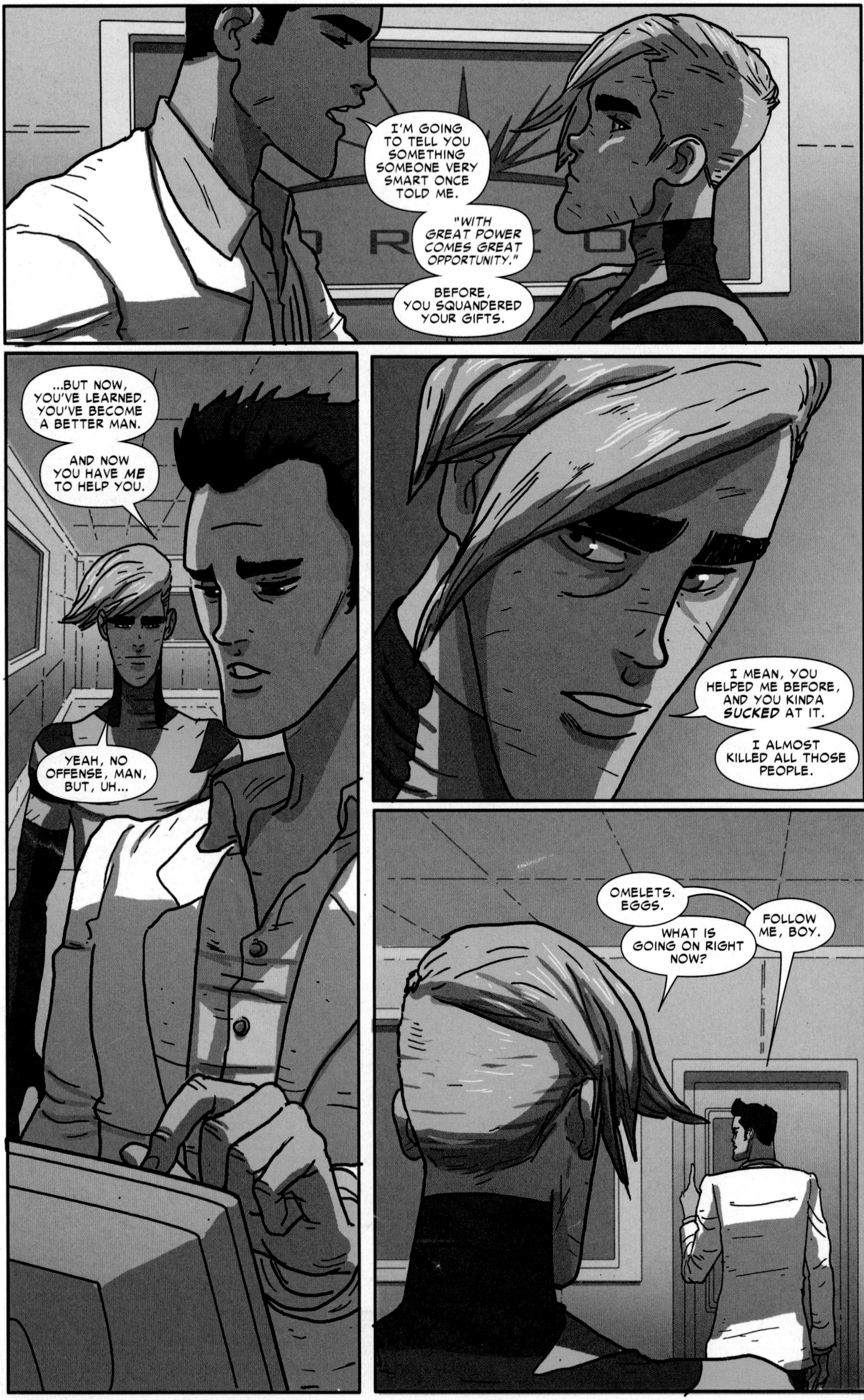
I'M GOING TO TELL YOU SOMETHING SOMEONE VERY SMART ONCE TOLD ME.
"WITH GREAT POWER COMES GREAT OPPORTUNITY."
BEFORE, YOU SQUANDERED YOUR GIFTS.
...BUT NOW, YOU'VE LEARNED. YOU'VE BECOME A BETTER MAN.
AND NOW YOU HAVE *ME* TO HELP YOU.
YEAH, NO OFFENSE, MAN, BUT, UH...
I MEAN, YOU HELPED ME BEFORE, AND YOU KINDA ***SUCKED*** AT IT.
I ALMOST KILLED ALL THOSE PEOPLE.
OMELETS. EGGS.
FOLLOW ME, BOY.
WHAT IS GOING ON RIGHT NOW?

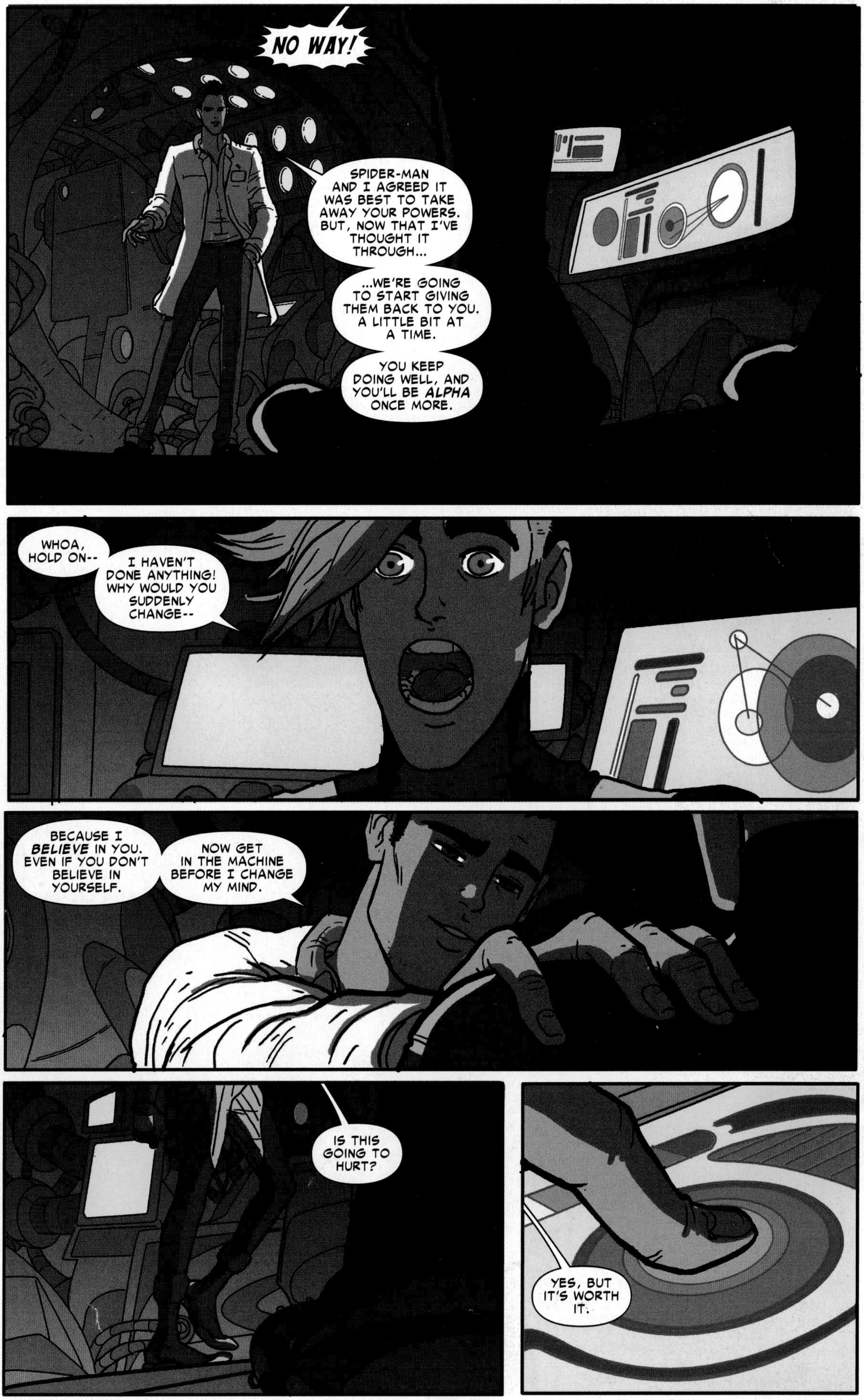
NO WAY!
SPIDER-MAN AND I AGREED IT WAS BEST TO TAKE AWAY YOUR POWERS. BUT, NOW THAT I'VE THOUGHT IT THROUGH...
...WE'RE GOING TO START GIVING THEM BACK TO YOU. A LITTLE BIT AT A TIME.
YOU KEEP DOING WELL, AND YOU'LL BE *ALPHA* ONCE MORE.
WHOA, HOLD ON--
I HAVEN'T DONE ANYTHING! WHY WOULD YOU SUDDENLY CHANGE--
BECAUSE I *BELIEVE* IN YOU. EVEN IF YOU DON'T BELIEVE IN YOURSELF.
NOW GET IN THE MACHINE BEFORE I CHANGE MY MIND.
IS THIS GOING TO HURT?
YES, BUT IT'S WORTH IT.

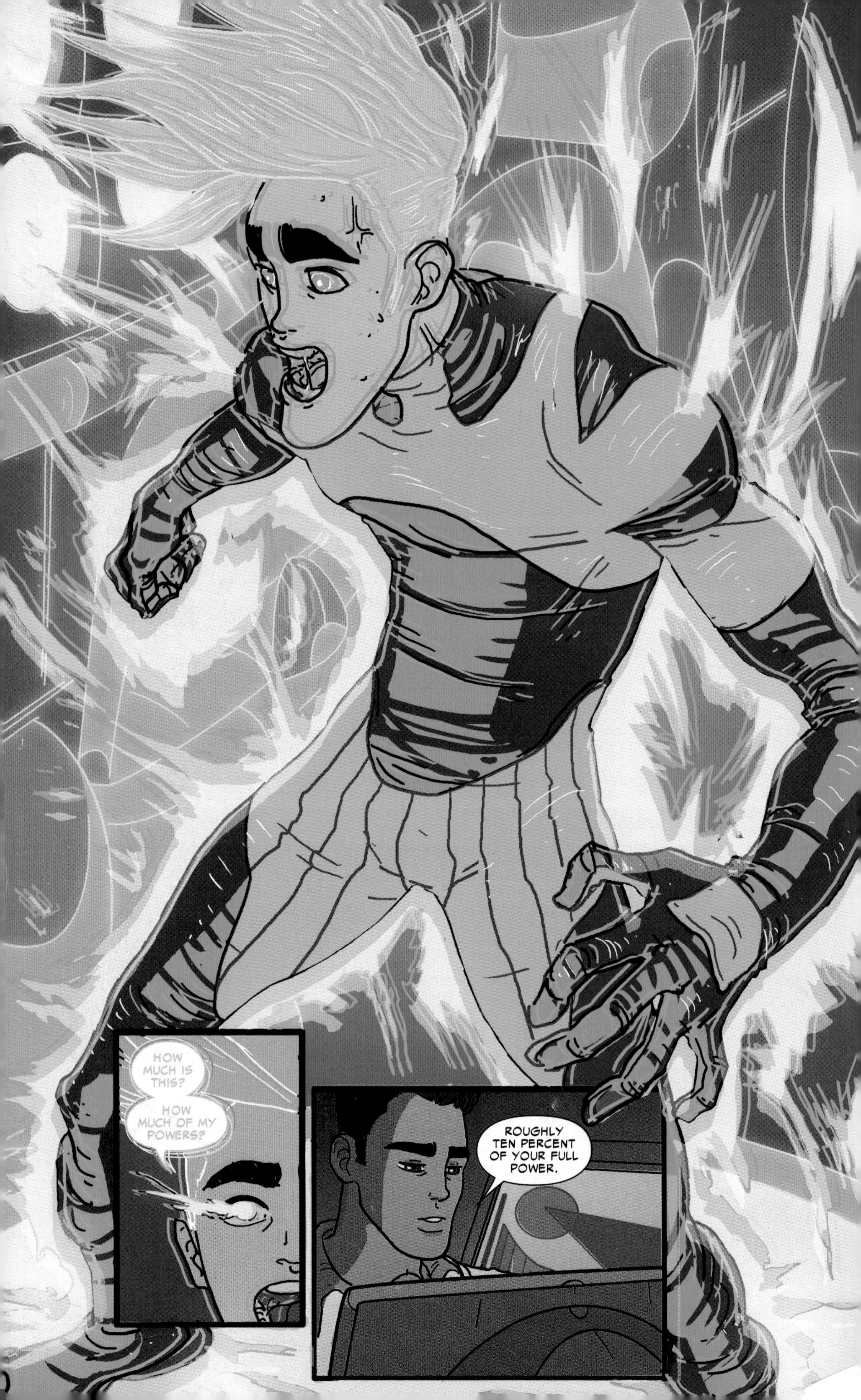
HOW MUCH IS THIS?
HOW MUCH OF MY POWERS?
ROUGHLY TEN PERCENT OF YOUR FULL POWER.

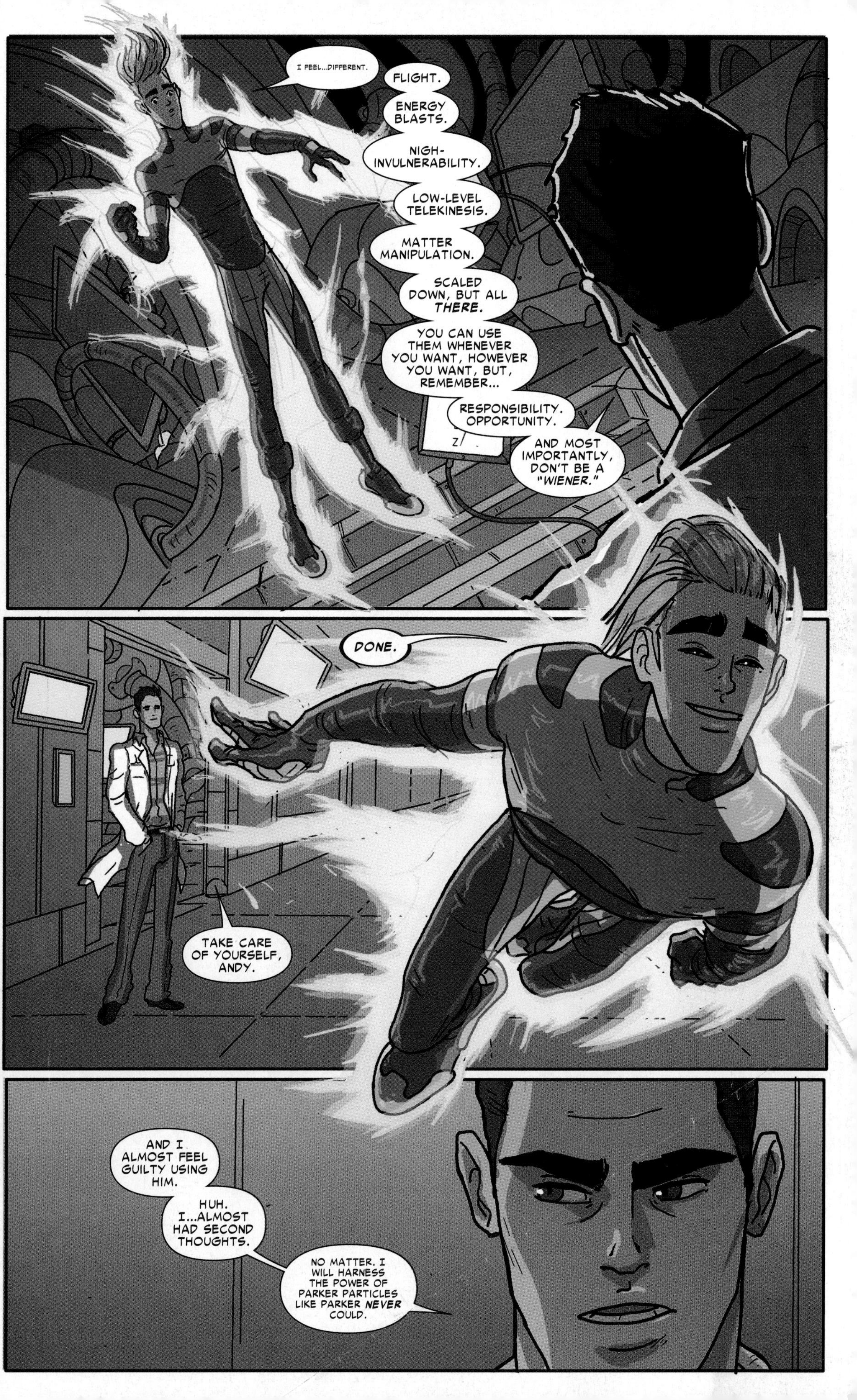
I FEEL...DIFFERENT.
FLIGHT.
ENERGY BLASTS.
NIGH-INVULNERABILITY.
LOW-LEVEL TELEKINESIS.
MATTER MANIPULATION.
SCALED DOWN, BUT ALL *THERE.*
YOU CAN USE THEM WHENEVER YOU WANT, HOWEVER YOU WANT, BUT, REMEMBER...
RESPONSIBILITY. OPPORTUNITY.
AND MOST IMPORTANTLY, DON'T BE A "*WIENER.*"
DONE.
TAKE CARE OF YOURSELF, ANDY.
AND I ALMOST FEEL GUILTY USING HIM.
HUH. I...ALMOST HAD SECOND THOUGHTS.
NO MATTER. I WILL HARNESS THE POWER OF PARKER PARTICLES LIKE PARKER *NEVER* COULD.

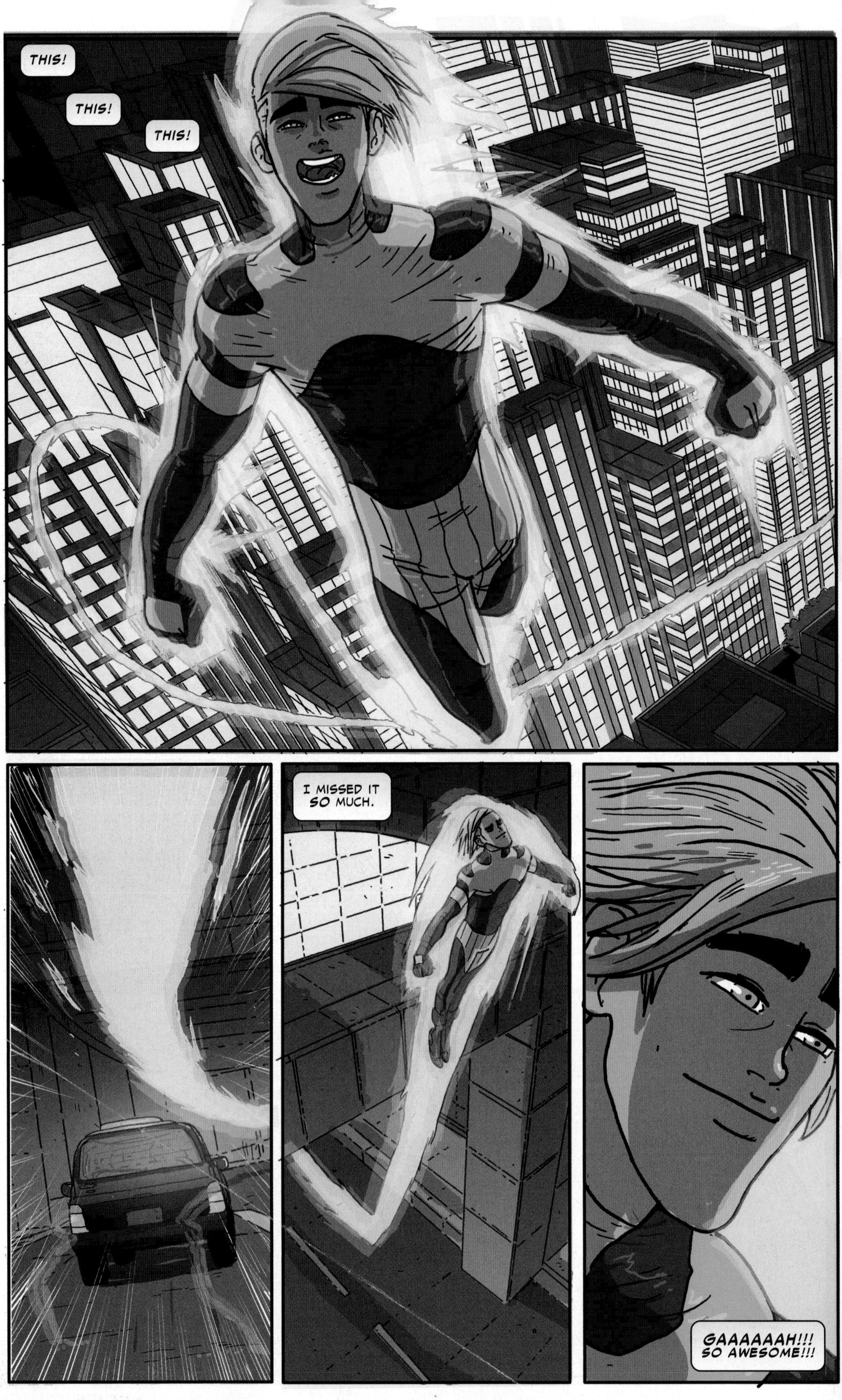
THIS!
THIS!
THIS!
I MISSED IT SO MUCH.
GAAAAAAH!!! SO AWESOME!!!

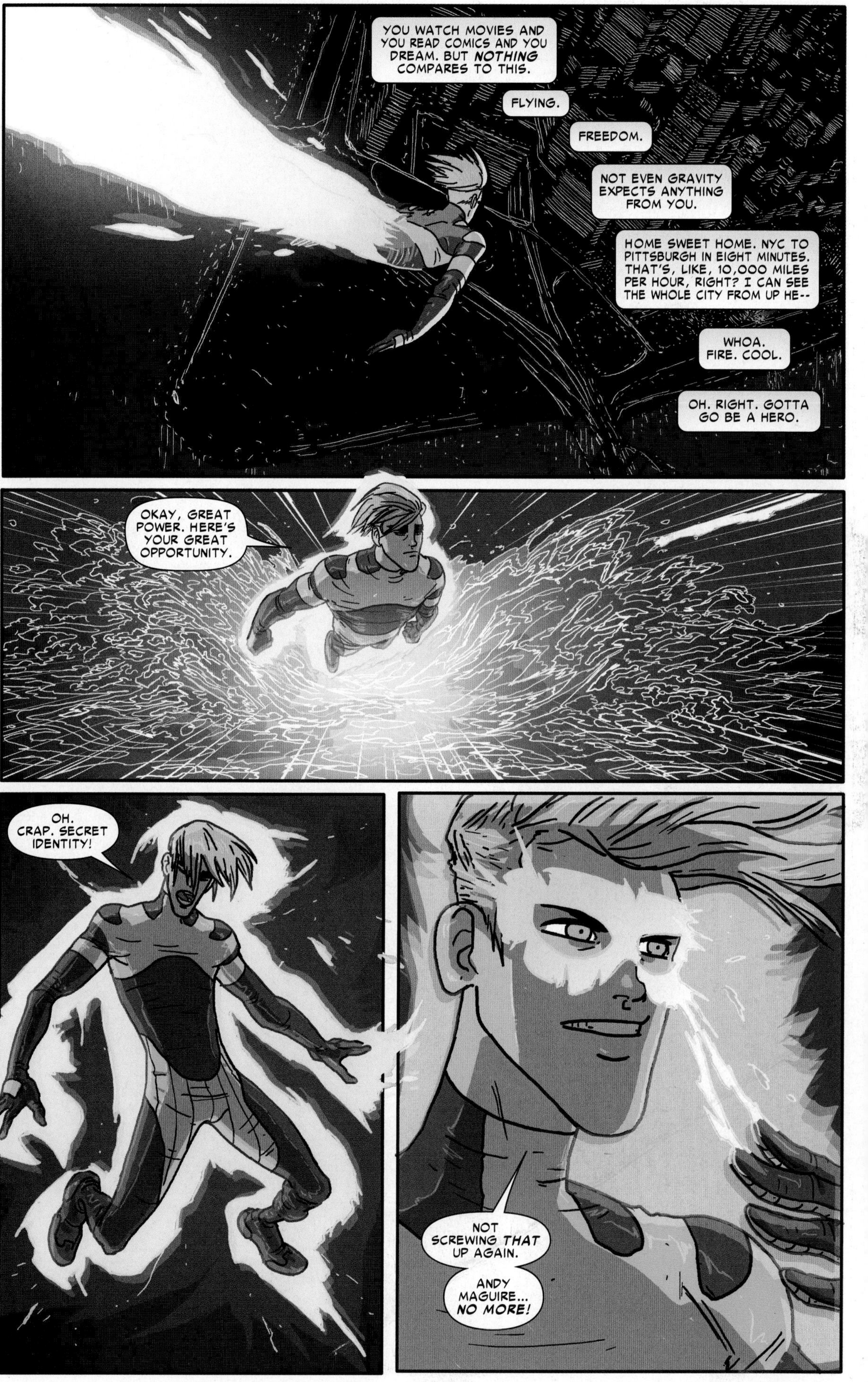
YOU WATCH MOVIES AND YOU READ COMICS AND YOU DREAM. BUT *NOTHING* COMPARES TO THIS.
FLYING.
FREEDOM.
NOT EVEN GRAVITY EXPECTS ANYTHING FROM YOU.
HOME SWEET HOME. NYC TO PITTSBURGH IN EIGHT MINUTES. THAT'S, LIKE, 10,000 MILES PER HOUR, RIGHT? I CAN SEE THE WHOLE CITY FROM UP HE--
WHOA. FIRE. COOL.
OH. RIGHT. GOTTA GO BE A HERO.
OKAY, GREAT POWER. HERE'S YOUR GREAT OPPORTUNITY.
OH. CRAP. SECRET IDENTITY!
NOT SCREWING *THAT* UP AGAIN.
ANDY MAGUIRE... ***NO MORE!***

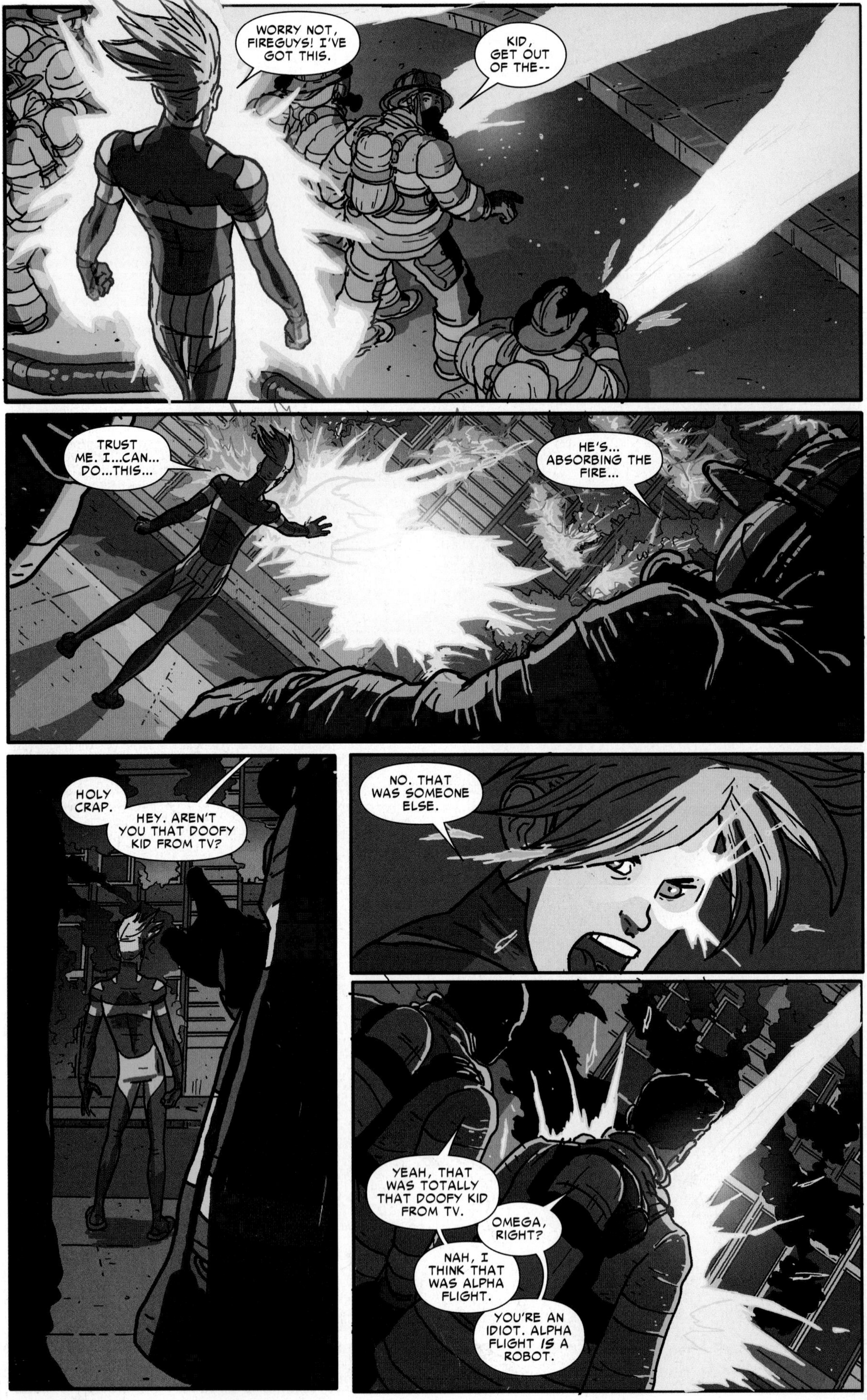
WORRY NOT, FIREGUYS! I'VE GOT THIS.
KID, GET OUT OF THE--
TRUST ME. I...CAN... DO...THIS...
HE'S... ABSORBING THE FIRE...
HOLY CRAP.
HEY. AREN'T YOU THAT DOOFY KID FROM TV?
NO. THAT WAS SOMEONE ELSE.
YEAH, THAT WAS TOTALLY THAT DOOFY KID FROM TV.
OMEGA, RIGHT?
NAH, I THINK THAT WAS ALPHA FLIGHT.
YOU'RE AN IDIOT. ALPHA FLIGHT IS A ROBOT.

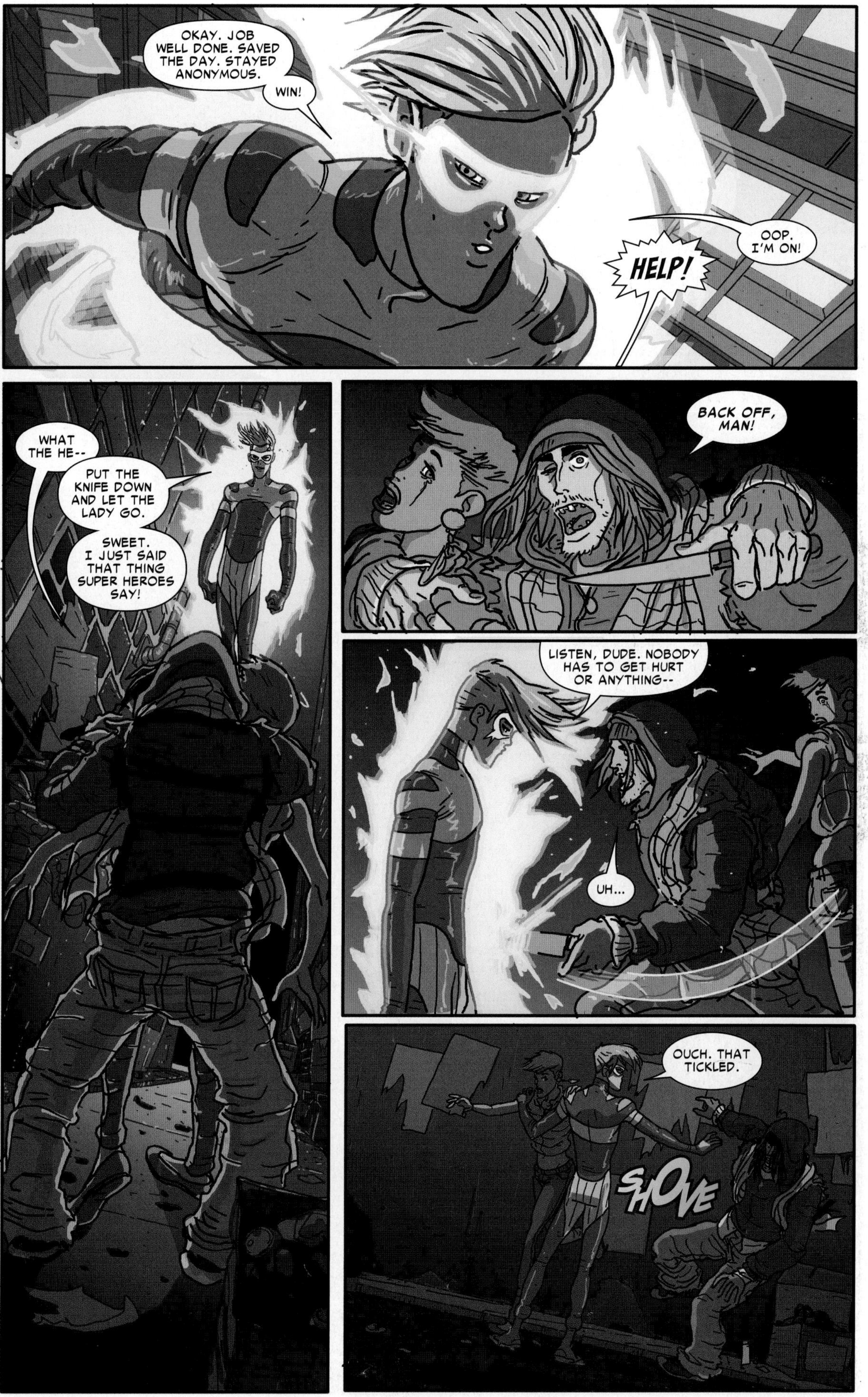

OKAY. JOB WELL DONE. SAVED THE DAY. STAYED ANONYMOUS.
WIN!
HELP!
OOP. I'M ON!
WHAT THE HE--
PUT THE KNIFE DOWN AND LET THE LADY GO.
SWEET. I JUST SAID THAT THING SUPER HEROES SAY!
BACK OFF, MAN!
LISTEN, DUDE. NOBODY HAS TO GET HURT OR ANYTHING--
UH...
OUCH. THAT TICKLED.
SHOVE

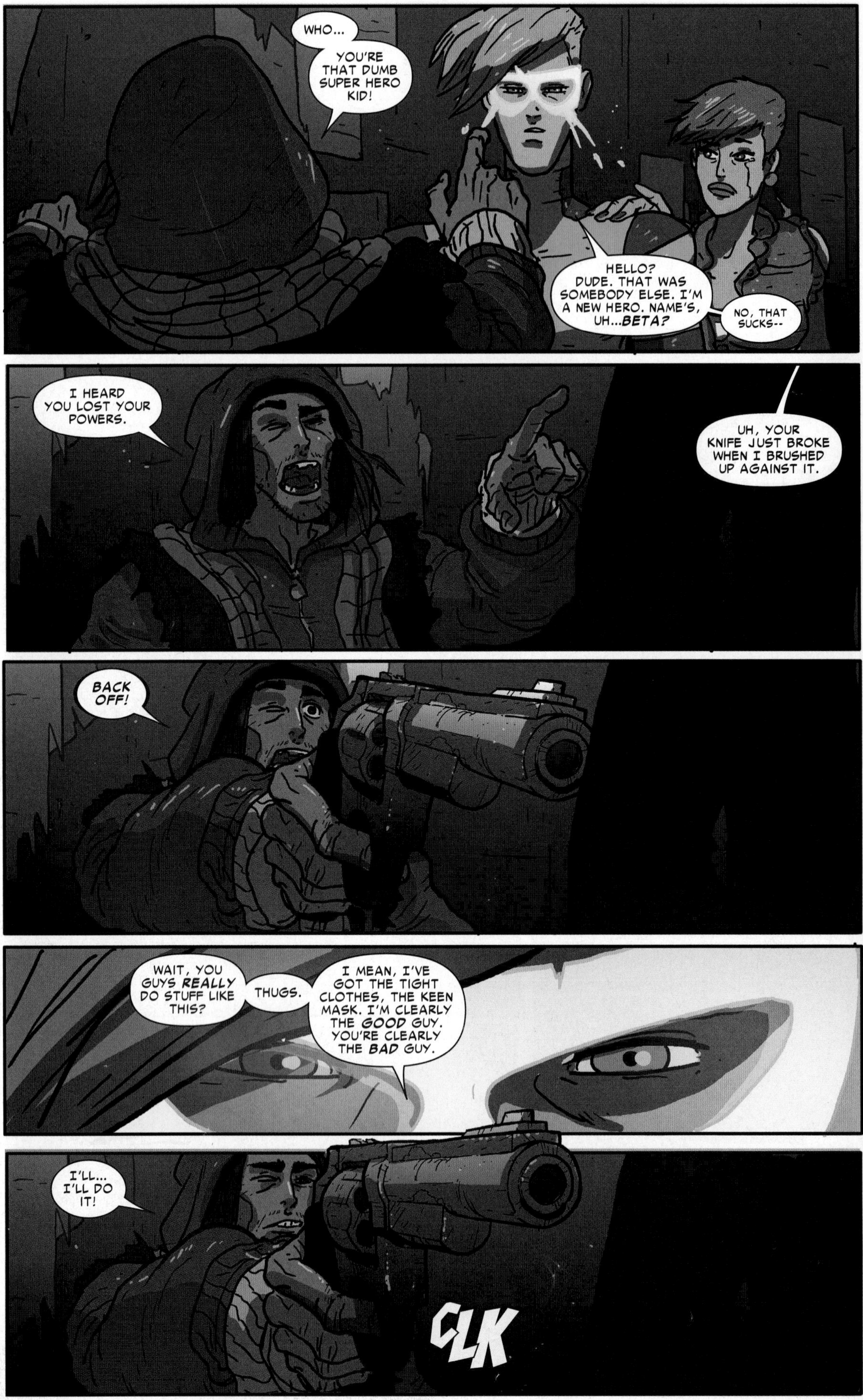
WHO...
YOU'RE THAT DUMB SUPER HERO KID!
HELLO? DUDE. THAT WAS SOMEBODY ELSE. I'M A NEW HERO. NAME'S, UH...BETA?
NO, THAT SUCKS--
I HEARD YOU LOST YOUR POWERS.
UH, YOUR KNIFE JUST BROKE WHEN I BRUSHED UP AGAINST IT.
BACK OFF!
WAIT, YOU GUYS REALLY DO STUFF LIKE THIS?
THUGS.
I MEAN, I'VE GOT THE TIGHT CLOTHES, THE KEEN MASK. I'M CLEARLY THE GOOD GUY. YOU'RE CLEARLY THE BAD GUY.
I'LL... I'LL DO IT!
CLK

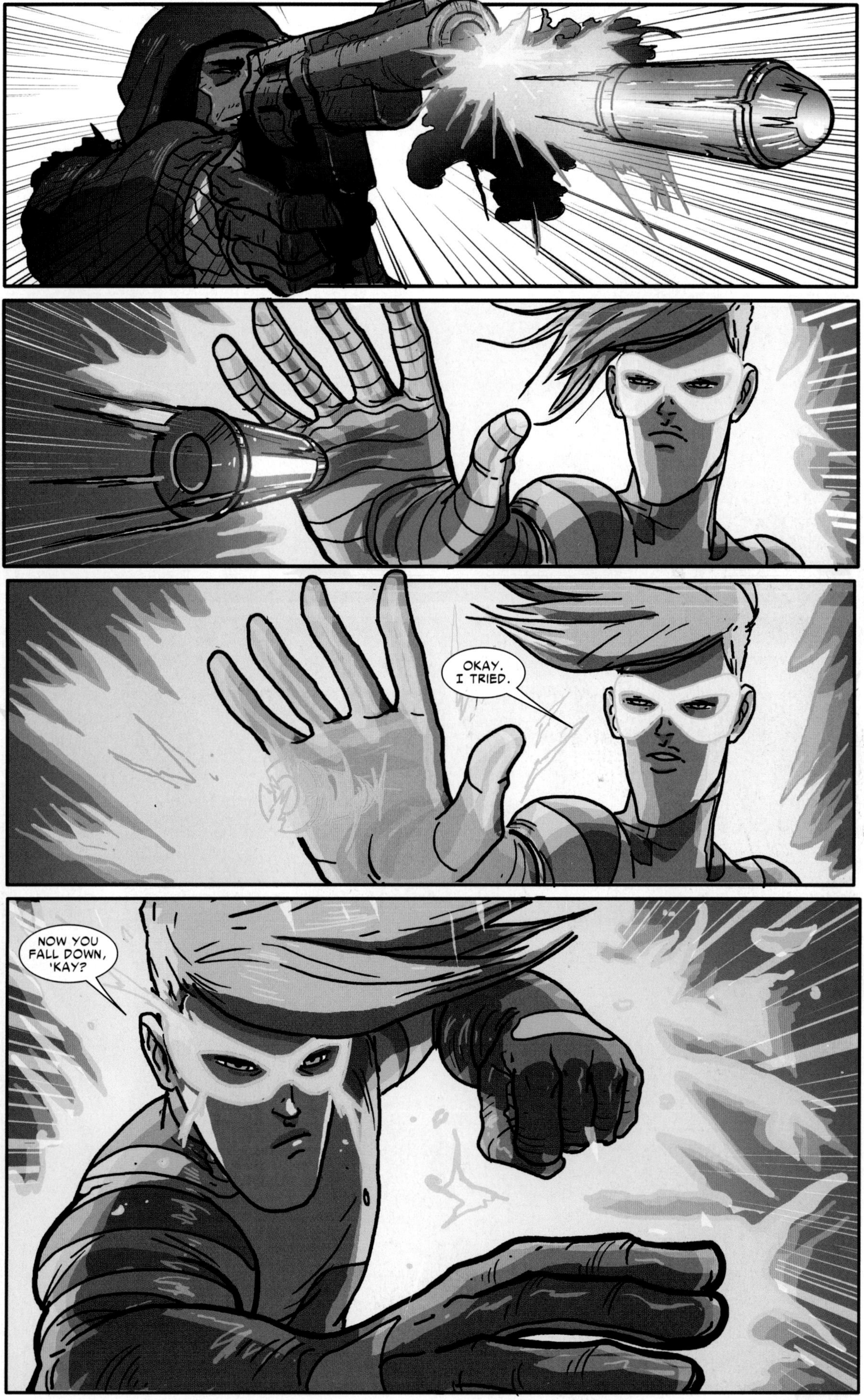
OKAY. I TRIED.
NOW YOU FALL DOWN, 'KAY?

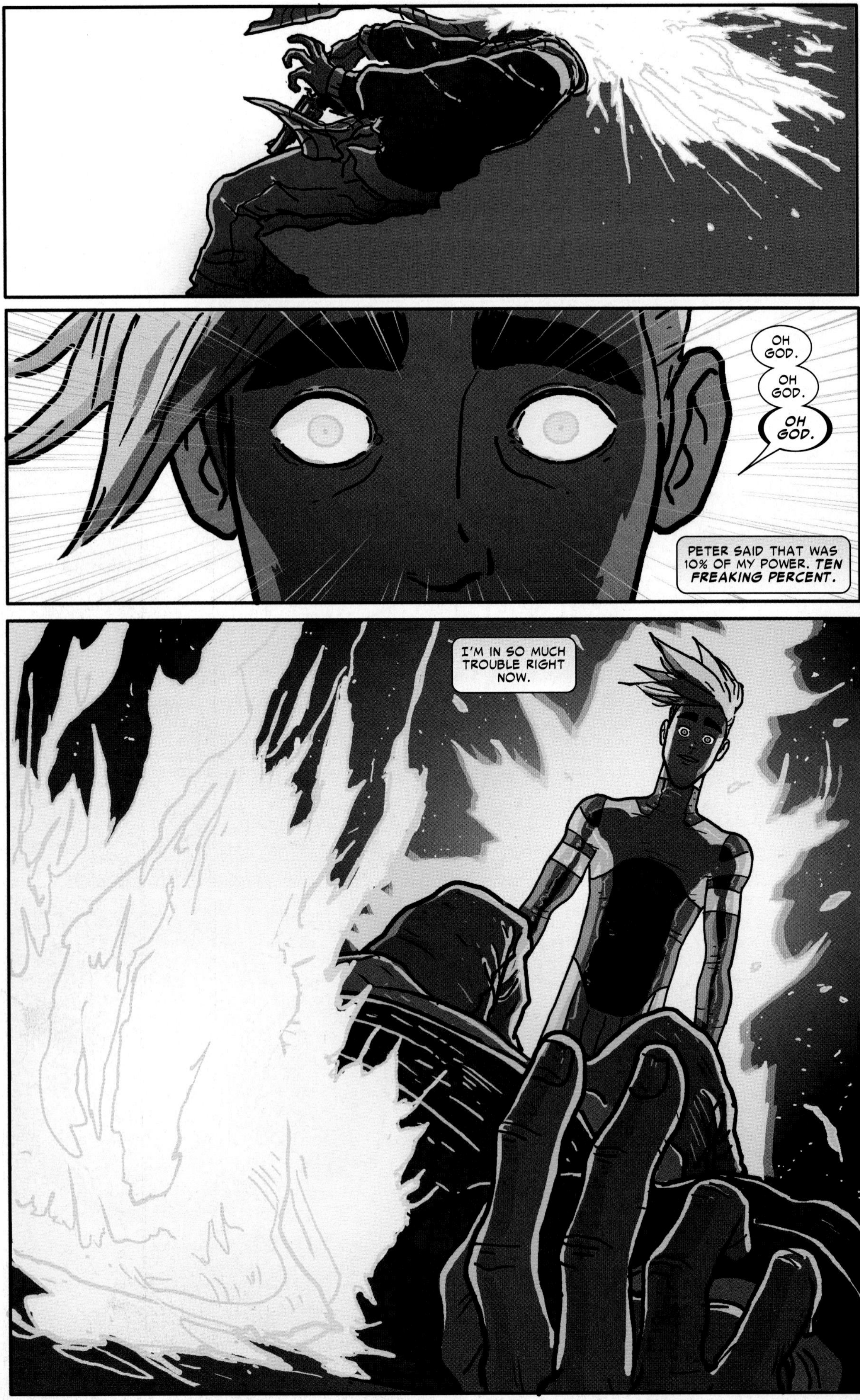
OH GOD.
OH GOD.
OH GOD.
PETER SAID THAT WAS 10% OF MY POWER. TEN FREAKING PERCENT.
I'M IN SO MUCH TROUBLE RIGHT NOW.

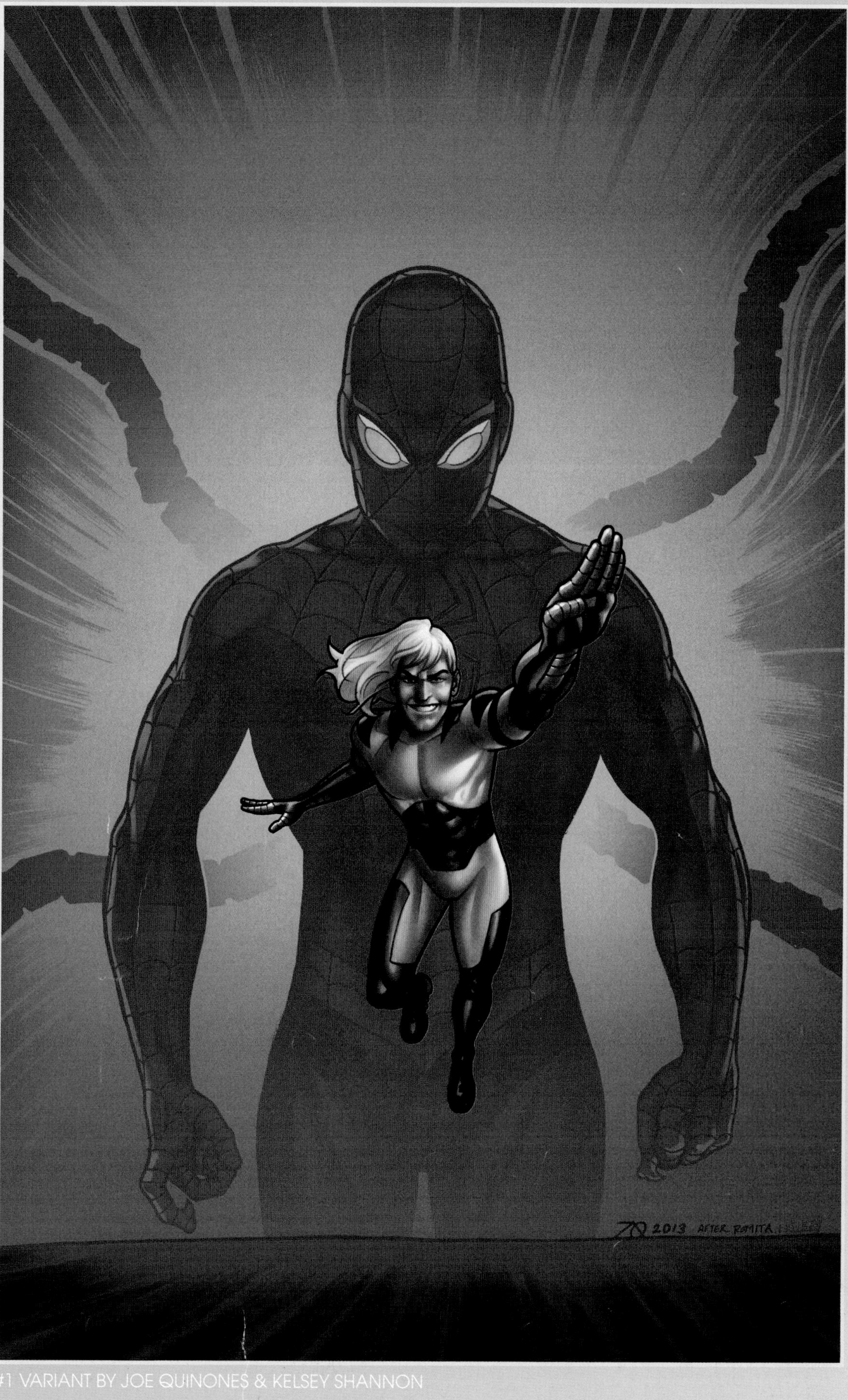
2013 AFTER ROMITA

#1 VARIANT BY JOE QUINONES & KELSEY SHANNON

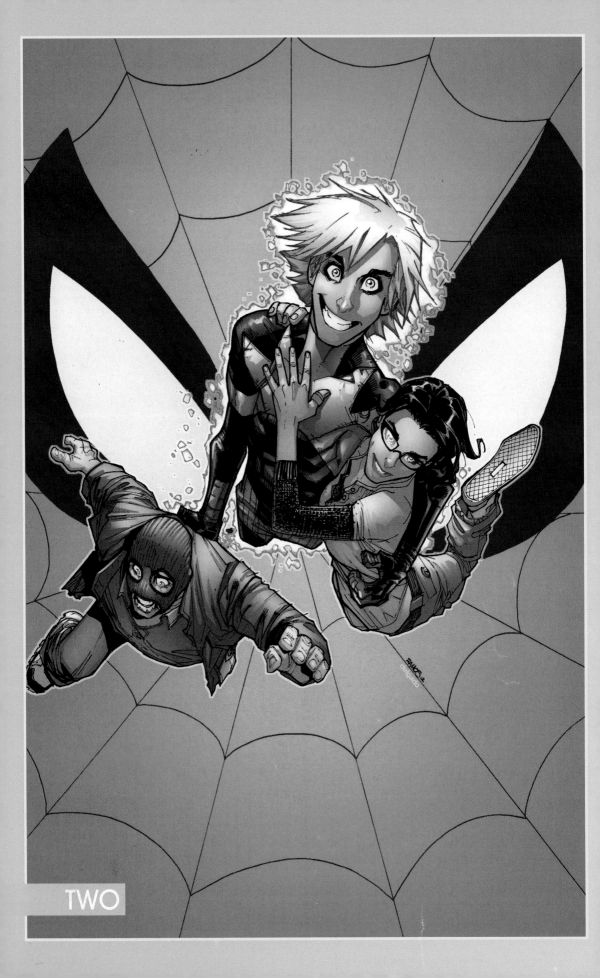

TWO

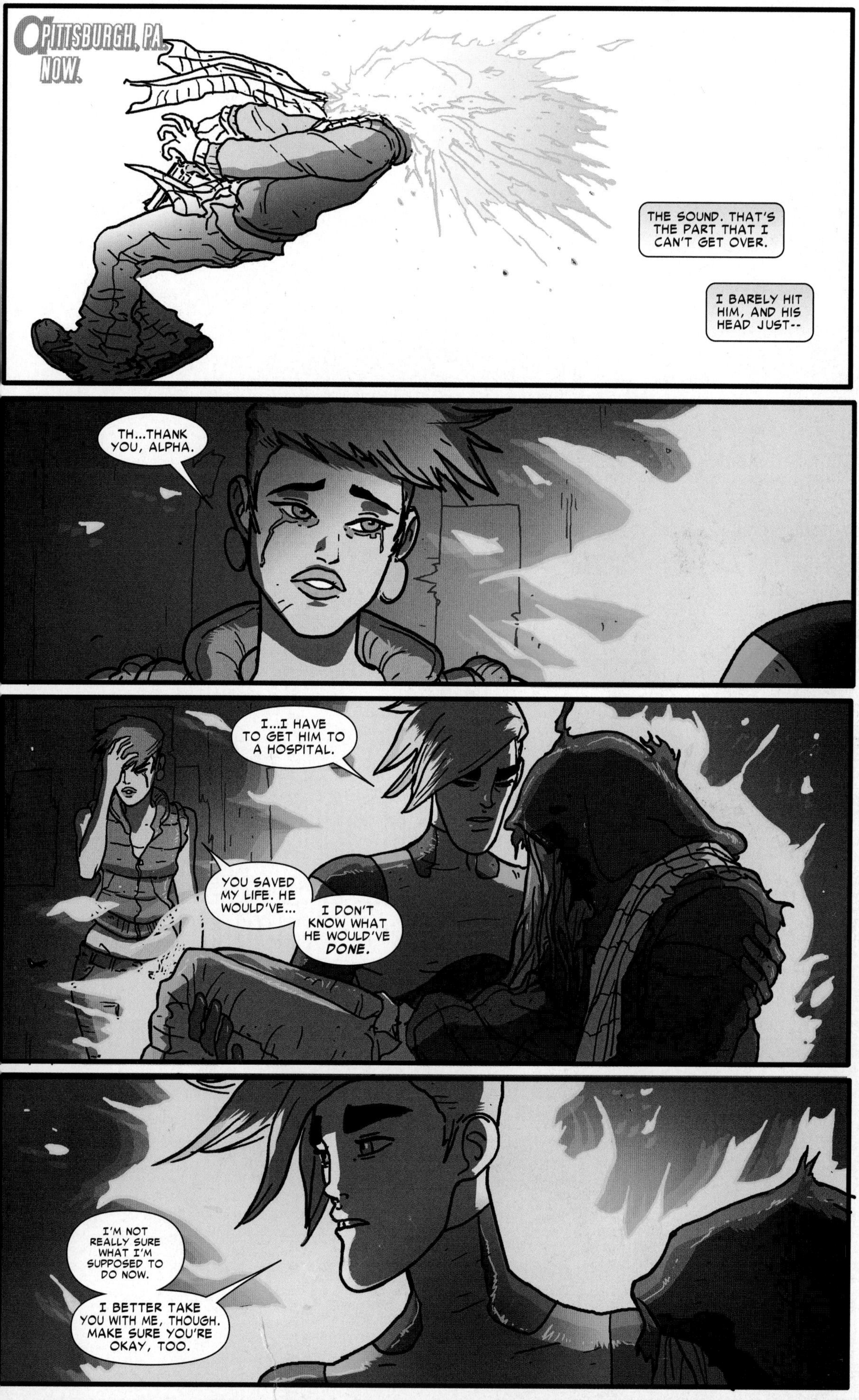
PITTSBURGH, PA.
NOW.
THE SOUND. THAT'S THE PART THAT I CAN'T GET OVER.
I BARELY HIT HIM, AND HIS HEAD JUST--
TH...THANK YOU, ALPHA.
I...I HAVE TO GET HIM TO A HOSPITAL.
YOU SAVED MY LIFE. HE WOULD'VE...
I DON'T KNOW WHAT HE WOULD'VE DONE.
I'M NOT REALLY SURE WHAT I'M SUPPOSED TO DO NOW.
I BETTER TAKE YOU WITH ME, THOUGH. MAKE SURE YOU'RE OKAY, TOO.

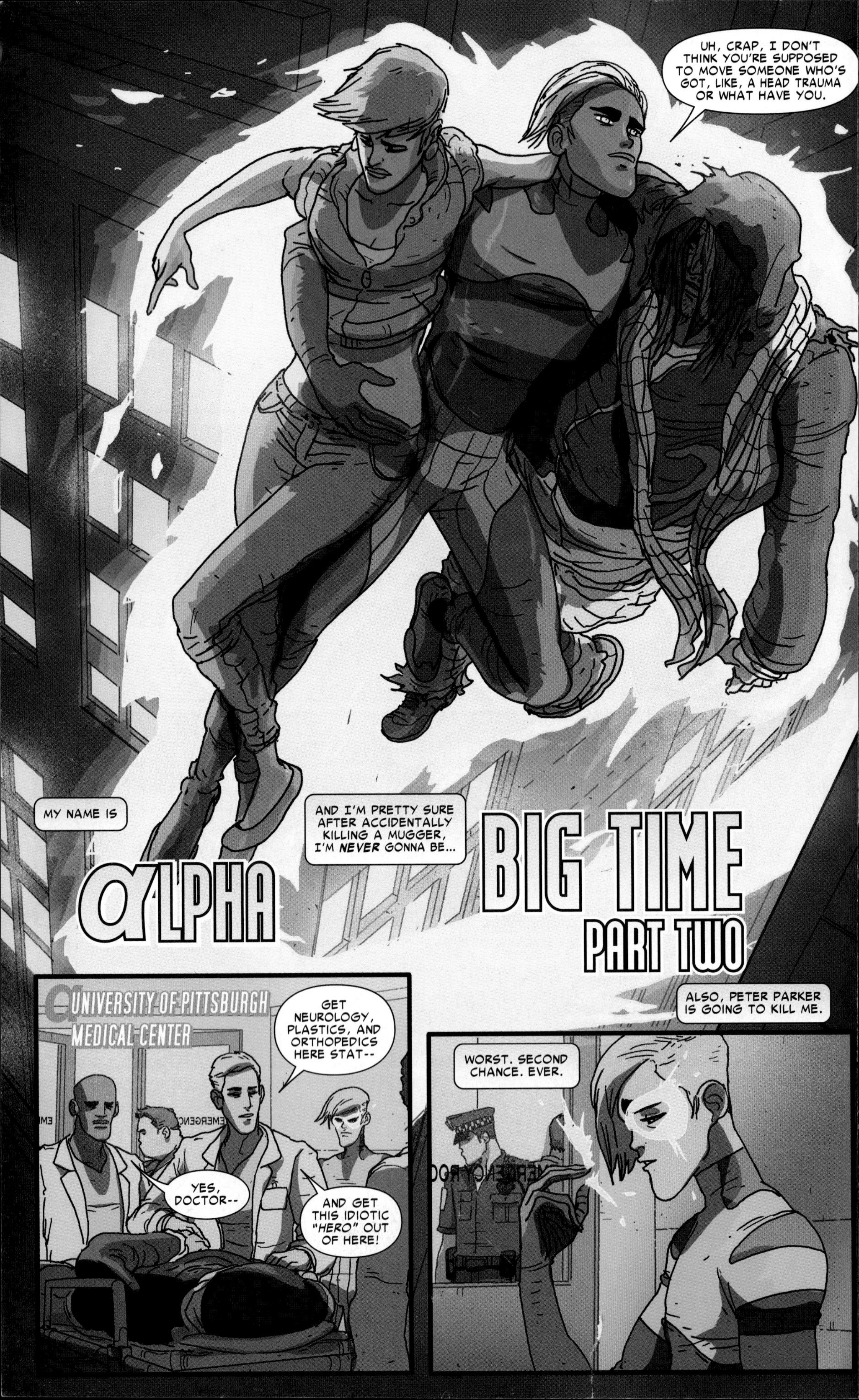
UH, CRAP, I DON'T THINK YOU'RE SUPPOSED TO MOVE SOMEONE WHO'S GOT, LIKE, A HEAD TRAUMA OR WHAT HAVE YOU.
MY NAME IS
ALPHA
AND I'M PRETTY SURE AFTER ACCIDENTALLY KILLING A MUGGER, I'M NEVER GONNA BE...
BIG TIME
PART TWO
UNIVERSITY OF PITTSBURGH MEDICAL CENTER
GET NEUROLOGY, PLASTICS, AND ORTHOPEDICS HERE STAT--
YES, DOCTOR--
AND GET THIS IDIOTIC "HERO" OUT OF HERE!
ALSO, PETER PARKER IS GOING TO KILL ME.
WORST. SECOND CHANCE. EVER.

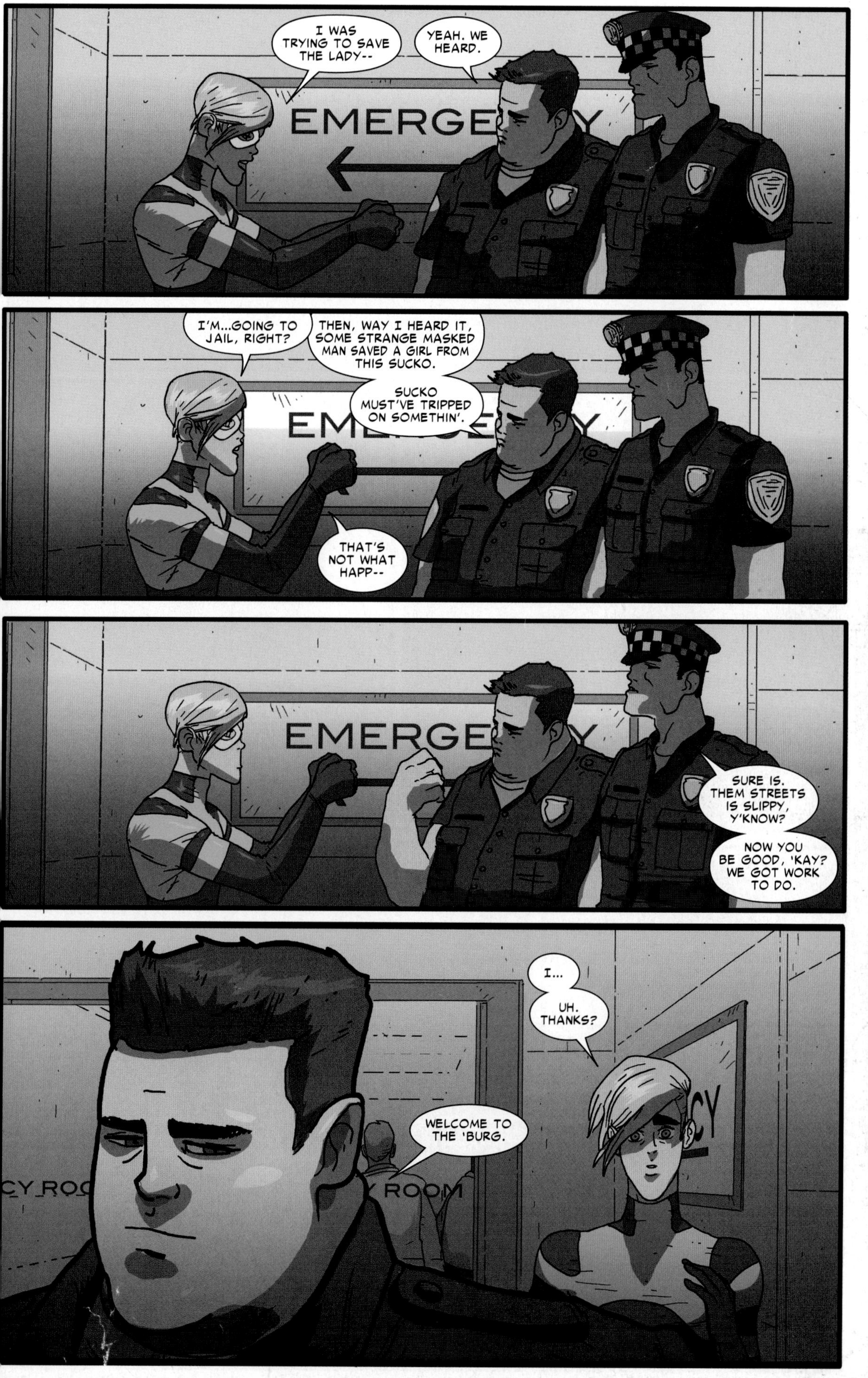
I WAS TRYING TO SAVE THE LADY--
YEAH. WE HEARD.
EMERGE
I'M...GOING TO JAIL, RIGHT?
THEN, WAY I HEARD IT, SOME STRANGE MASKED MAN SAVED A GIRL FROM THIS SUCKO.
SUCKO MUST'VE TRIPPED ON SOMETHIN'.
THAT'S NOT WHAT HAPP--
EMERGE
SURE IS. THEM STREETS IS SLIPPY, Y'KNOW?
NOW YOU BE GOOD, 'KAY? WE GOT WORK TO DO.
I...
UH. THANKS?
WELCOME TO THE 'BURG.

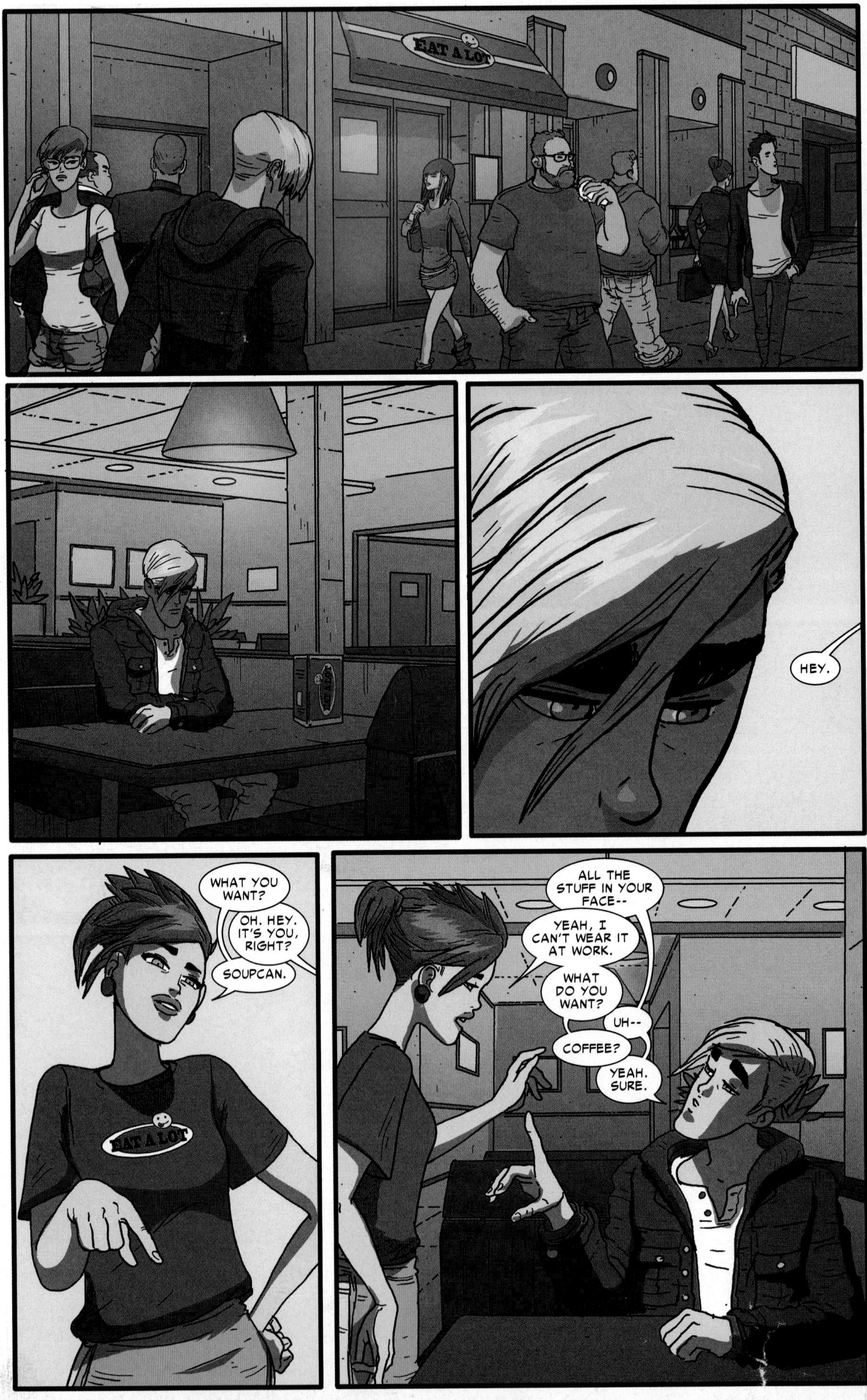
EAT A LOT
HEY.
WHAT YOU WANT?
OH. HEY. IT'S YOU, RIGHT?
SOUPCAN.
EAT A LOT
ALL THE STUFF IN YOUR FACE--
YEAH, I CAN'T WEAR IT AT WORK.
WHAT DO YOU WANT?
UH--
COFFEE?
YEAH. SURE.

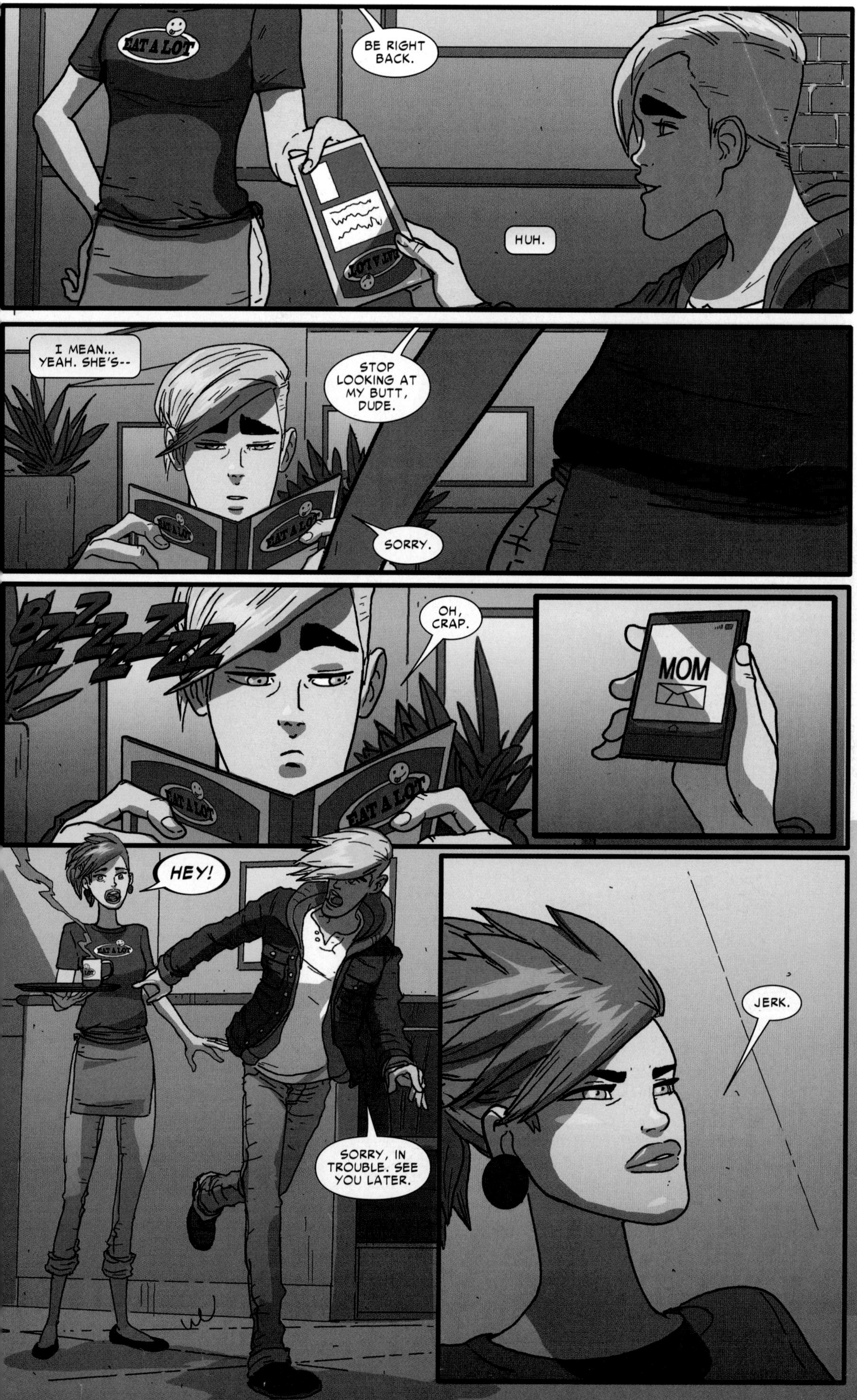
BE RIGHT BACK.
HUH.
I MEAN... YEAH. SHE'S--
STOP LOOKING AT MY BUTT, DUDE.
SORRY.
BZZZZZZ
OH, CRAP.
MOM
HEY!
SORRY, IN TROUBLE. SEE YOU LATER.
JERK.

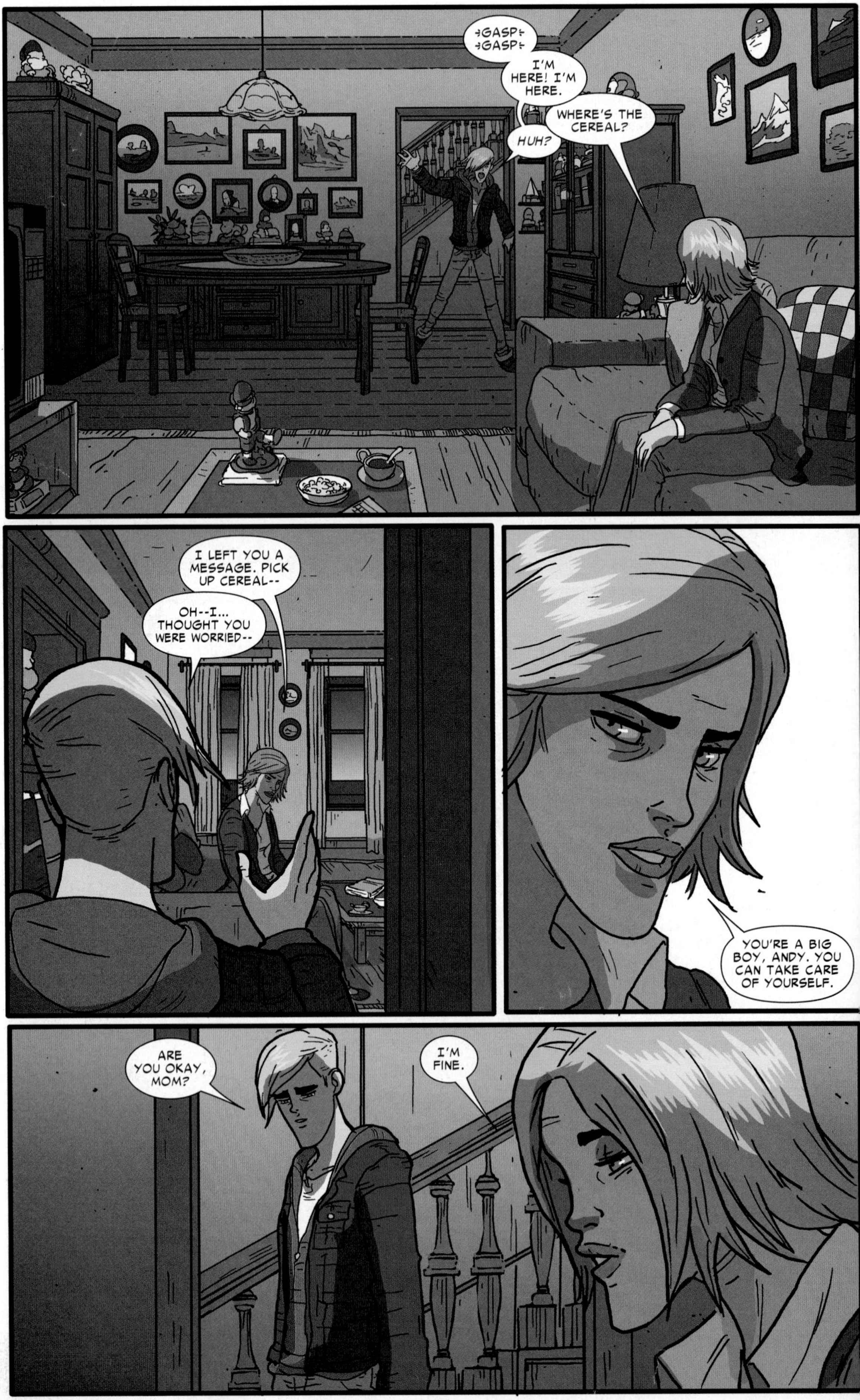

GASP GASP
I'M HERE! I'M HERE.
WHERE'S THE CEREAL?
HUH?
I LEFT YOU A MESSAGE. PICK UP CEREAL--
OH--I... THOUGHT YOU WERE WORRIED--
YOU'RE A BIG BOY, ANDY. YOU CAN TAKE CARE OF YOURSELF.
ARE YOU OKAY, MOM?
I'M FINE.

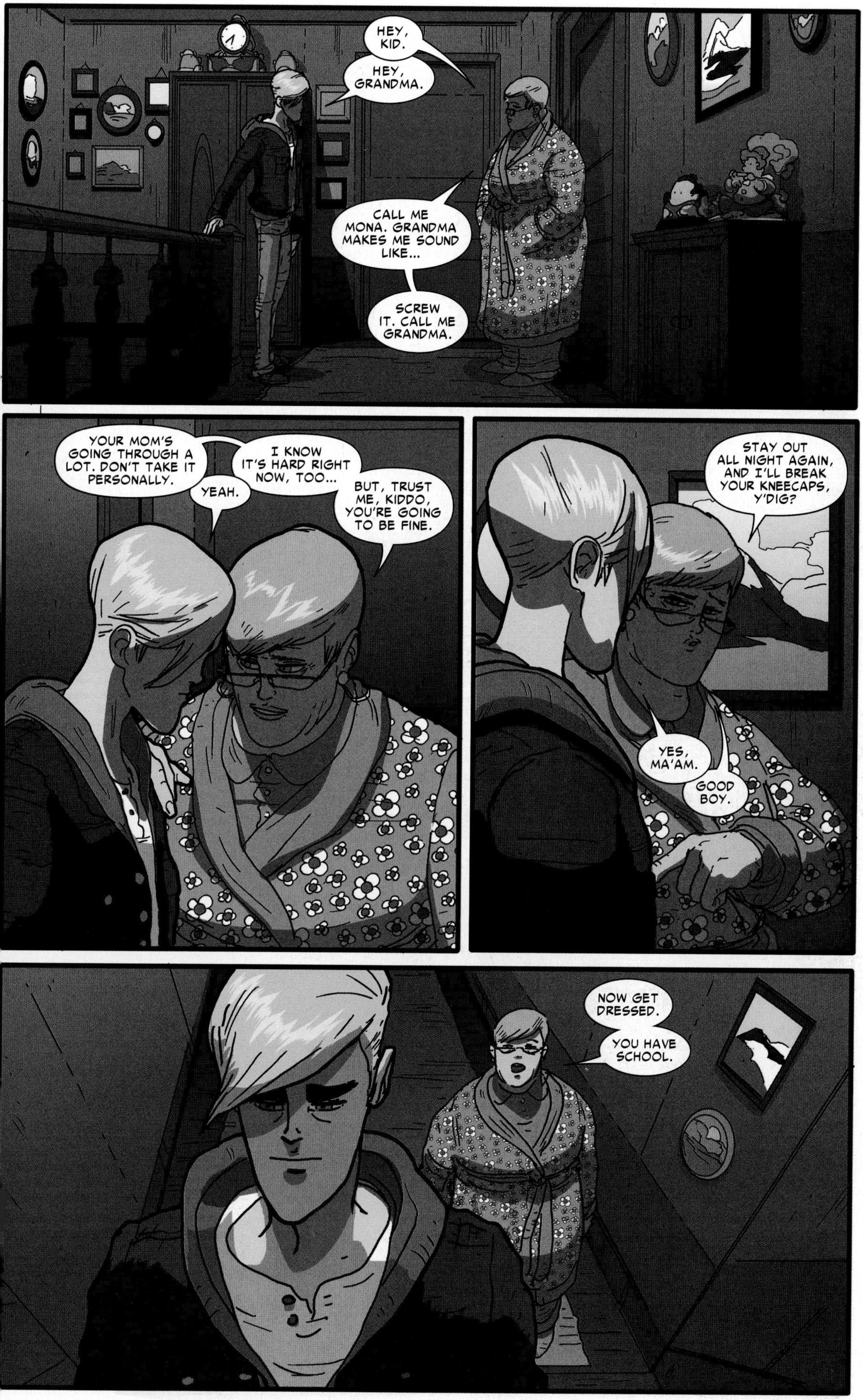
HEY, KID.
HEY, GRANDMA.
CALL ME MONA. GRANDMA MAKES ME SOUND LIKE...
SCREW IT. CALL ME GRANDMA.
YOUR MOM'S GOING THROUGH A LOT. DON'T TAKE IT PERSONALLY.
YEAH.
I KNOW IT'S HARD RIGHT NOW, TOO...
BUT, TRUST ME, KIDDO, YOU'RE GOING TO BE FINE.
STAY OUT ALL NIGHT AGAIN, AND I'LL BREAK YOUR KNEECAPS, Y'DIG?
YES, MA'AM.
GOOD BOY.
NOW GET DRESSED.
YOU HAVE SCHOOL.

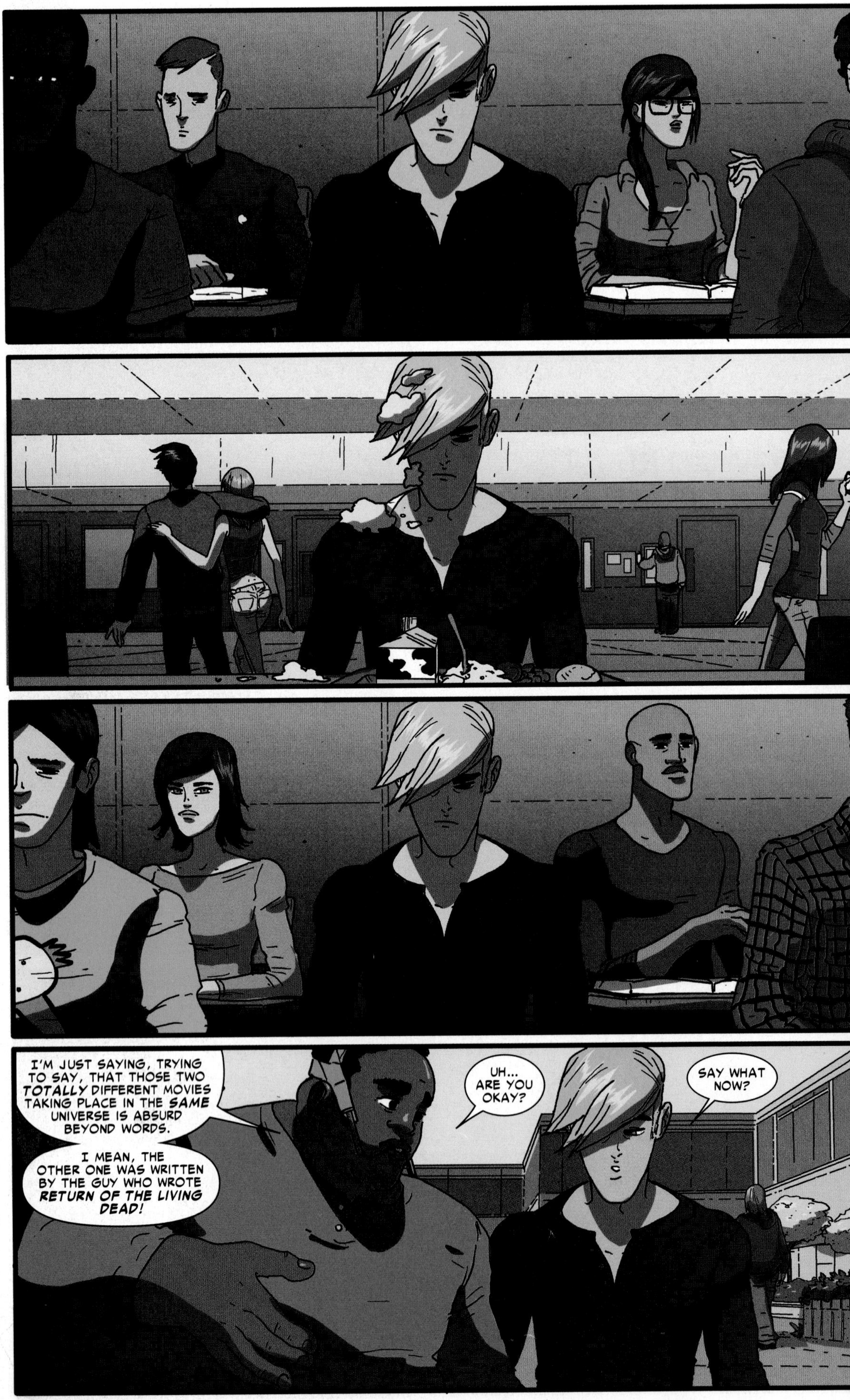
I'M JUST SAYING, TRYING TO SAY, THAT THOSE TWO TOTALLY DIFFERENT MOVIES TAKING PLACE IN THE SAME UNIVERSE IS ABSURD BEYOND WORDS.
I MEAN, THE OTHER ONE WAS WRITTEN BY THE GUY WHO WROTE RETURN OF THE LIVING DEAD!
UH... ARE YOU OKAY?
SAY WHAT NOW?

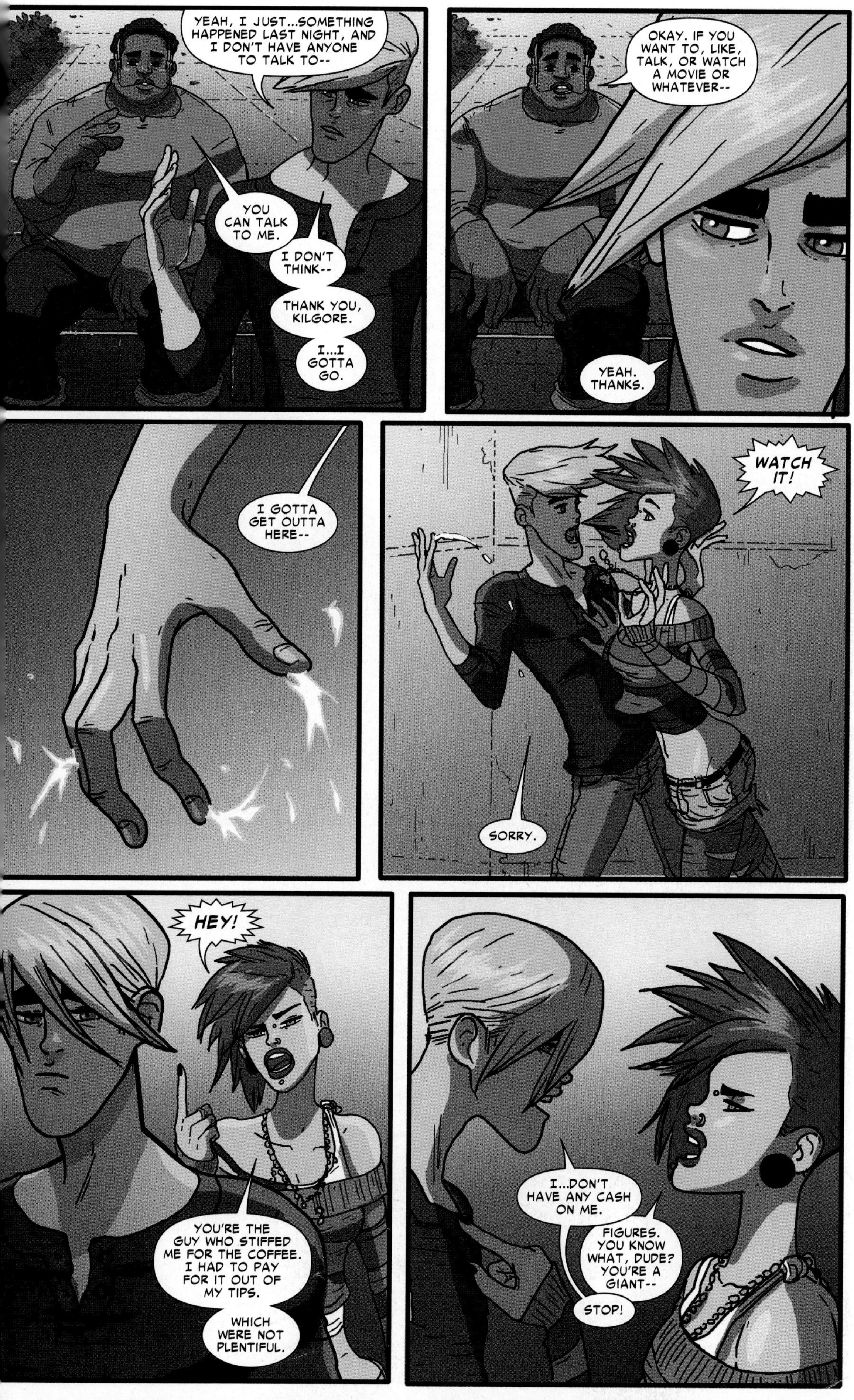
YEAH, I JUST...SOMETHING HAPPENED LAST NIGHT, AND I DON'T HAVE ANYONE TO TALK TO--
YOU CAN TALK TO ME.
I DON'T THINK--
THANK YOU, KILGORE.
I...I GOTTA GO.
OKAY. IF YOU WANT TO, LIKE, TALK, OR WATCH A MOVIE OR WHATEVER--
YEAH. THANKS.
I GOTTA GET OUTTA HERE--
WATCH IT!
SORRY.
HEY!
YOU'RE THE GUY WHO STIFFED ME FOR THE COFFEE. I HAD TO PAY FOR IT OUT OF MY TIPS.
WHICH WERE NOT PLENTIFUL.
I...DON'T HAVE ANY CASH ON ME.
FIGURES. YOU KNOW WHAT, DUDE? YOU'RE A GIANT--
STOP!

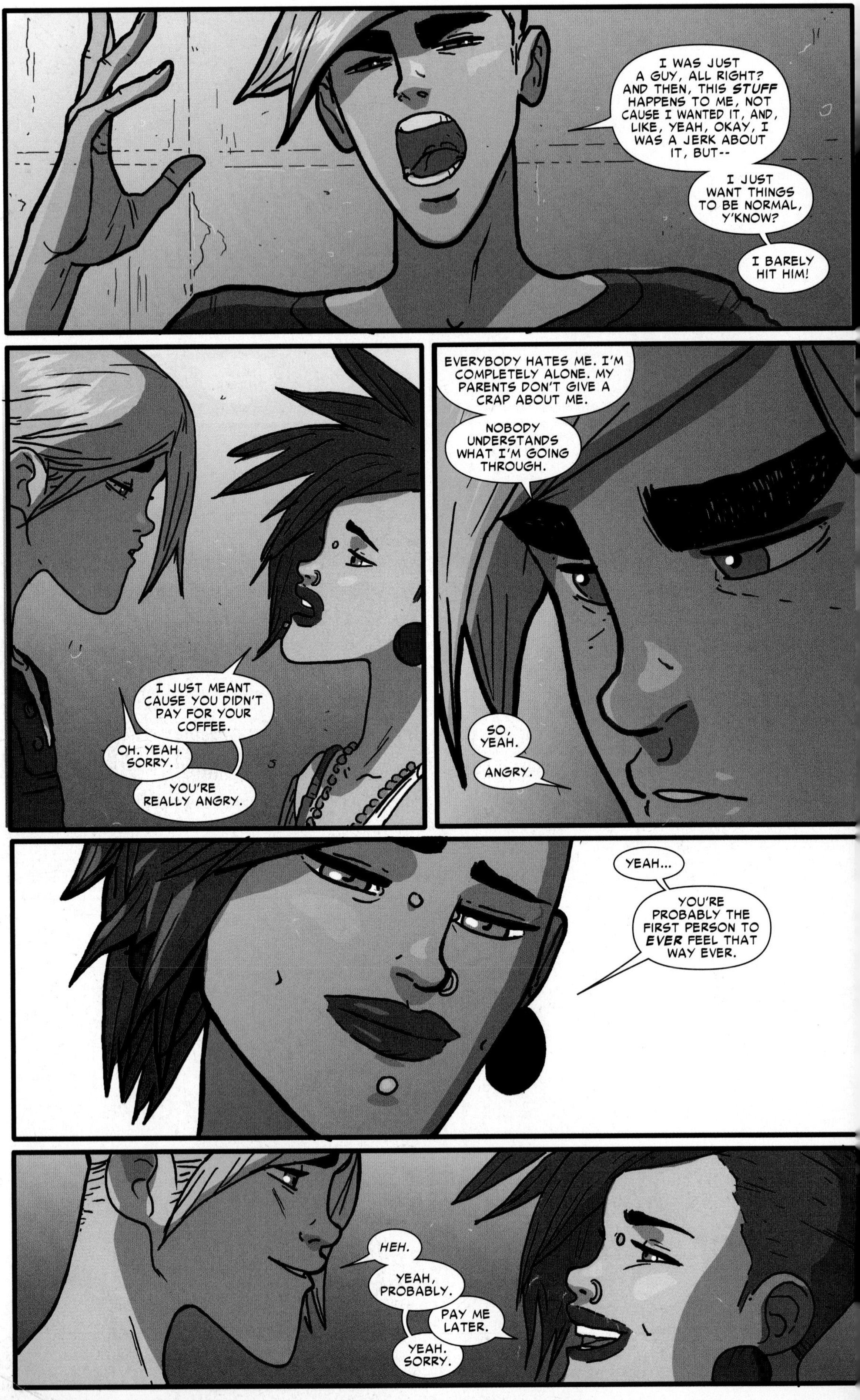
I WAS JUST A GUY, ALL RIGHT? AND THEN, THIS STUFF HAPPENS TO ME, NOT CAUSE I WANTED IT, AND, LIKE, YEAH, OKAY, I WAS A JERK ABOUT IT, BUT--
I JUST WANT THINGS TO BE NORMAL, Y'KNOW?
I BARELY HIT HIM!
I JUST MEANT CAUSE YOU DIDN'T PAY FOR YOUR COFFEE.
OH. YEAH. SORRY.
YOU'RE REALLY ANGRY.
EVERYBODY HATES ME. I'M COMPLETELY ALONE. MY PARENTS DON'T GIVE A CRAP ABOUT ME.
NOBODY UNDERSTANDS WHAT I'M GOING THROUGH.
SO, YEAH.
ANGRY.
YEAH...
YOU'RE PROBABLY THE FIRST PERSON TO EVER FEEL THAT WAY EVER.
HEH.
YEAH, PROBABLY.
PAY ME LATER.
YEAH. SORRY.

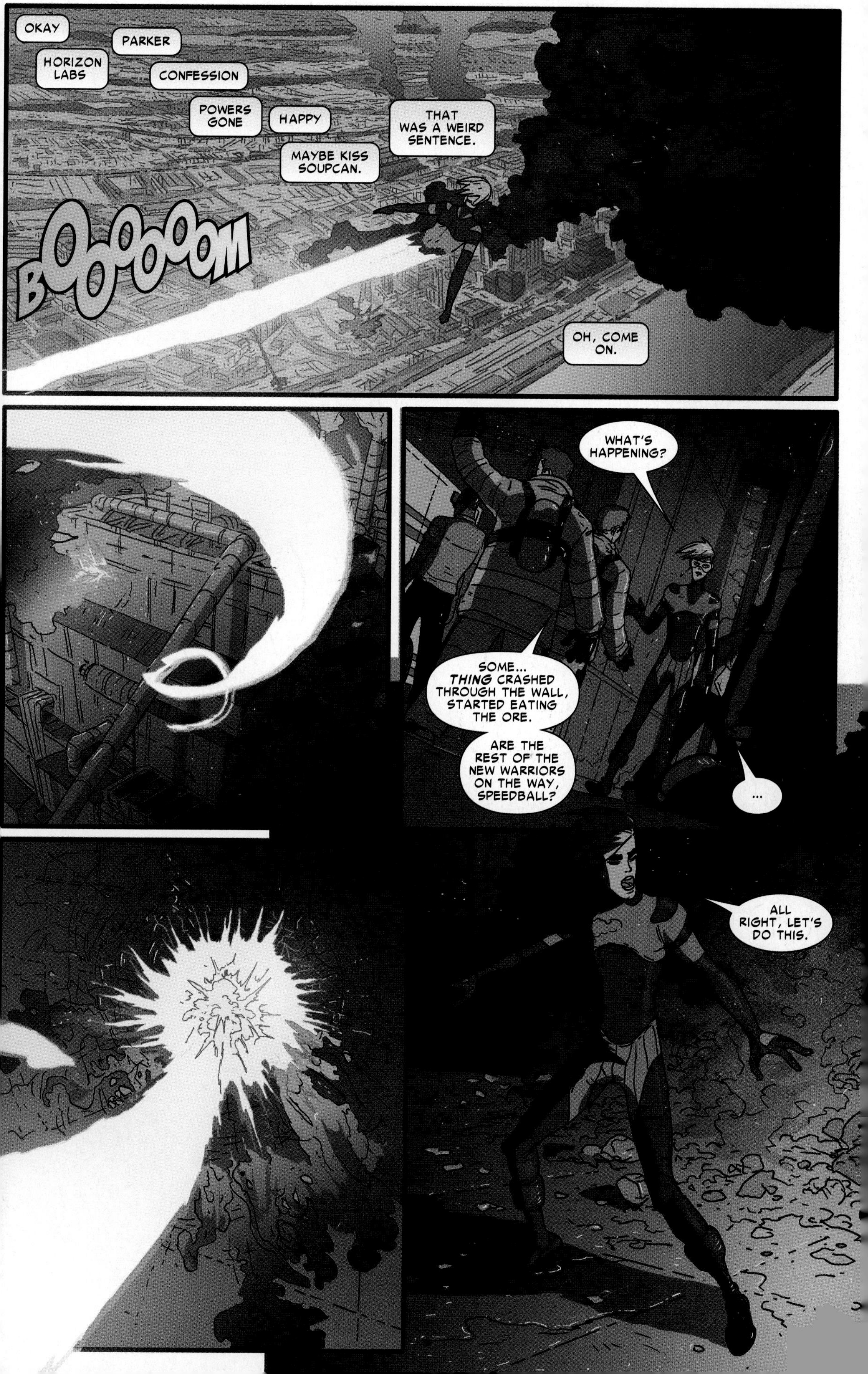

OKAY
PARKER
HORIZON LABS
CONFESSION
POWERS GONE
HAPPY
MAYBE KISS SOUPCAN.
THAT WAS A WEIRD SENTENCE.
BOOOOOOM
OH, COME ON.
WHAT'S HAPPENING?
SOME... *THING* CRASHED THROUGH THE WALL, STARTED EATING THE ORE.
ARE THE REST OF THE NEW WARRIORS ON THE WAY, SPEEDBALL?
...
ALL RIGHT, LET'S DO THIS.

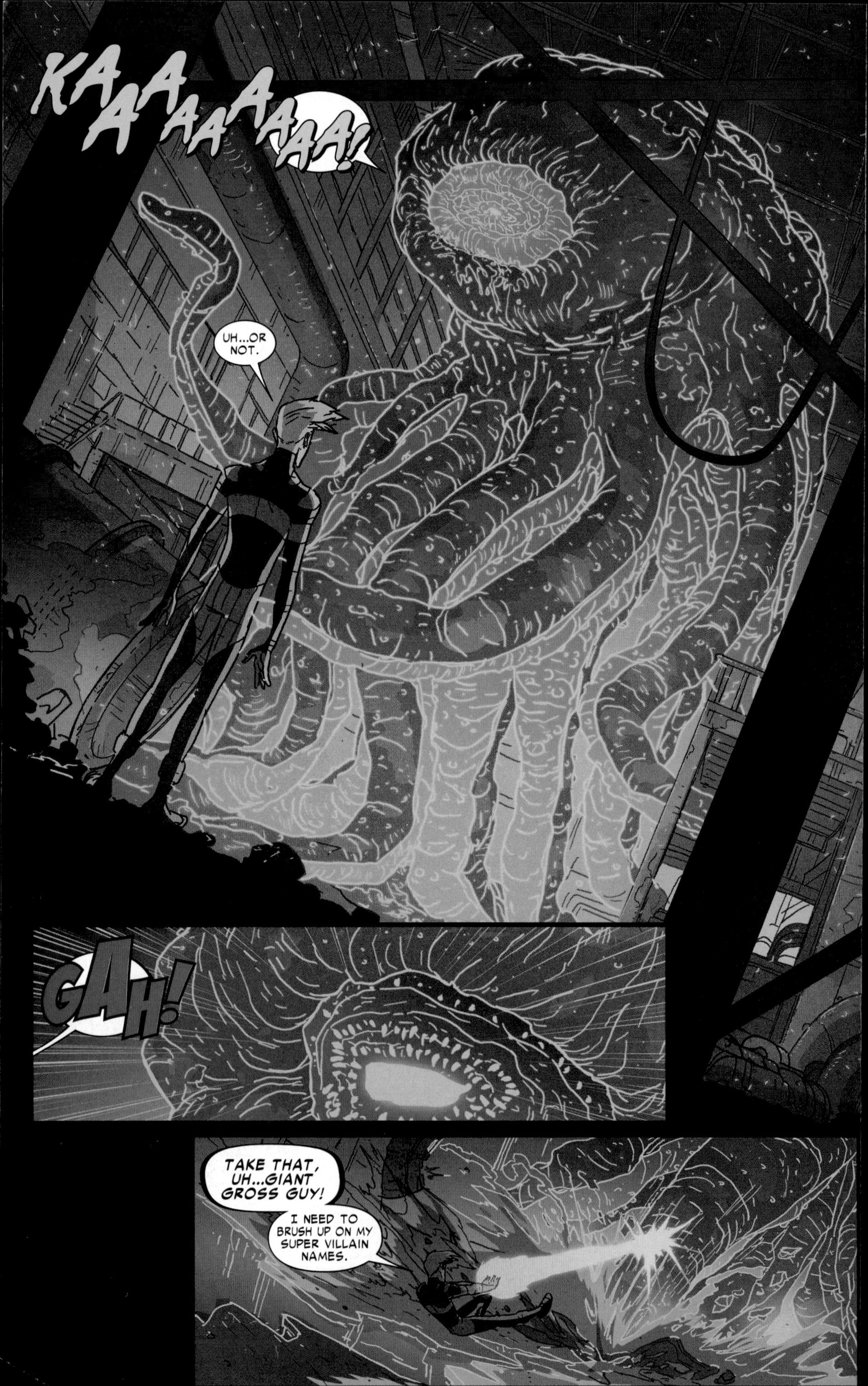
KAAAAAAAAAAA!
UH...OR NOT.
GAH!
TAKE THAT, UH...GIANT GROSS GUY!
I NEED TO BRUSH UP ON MY SUPER VILLAIN NAMES.

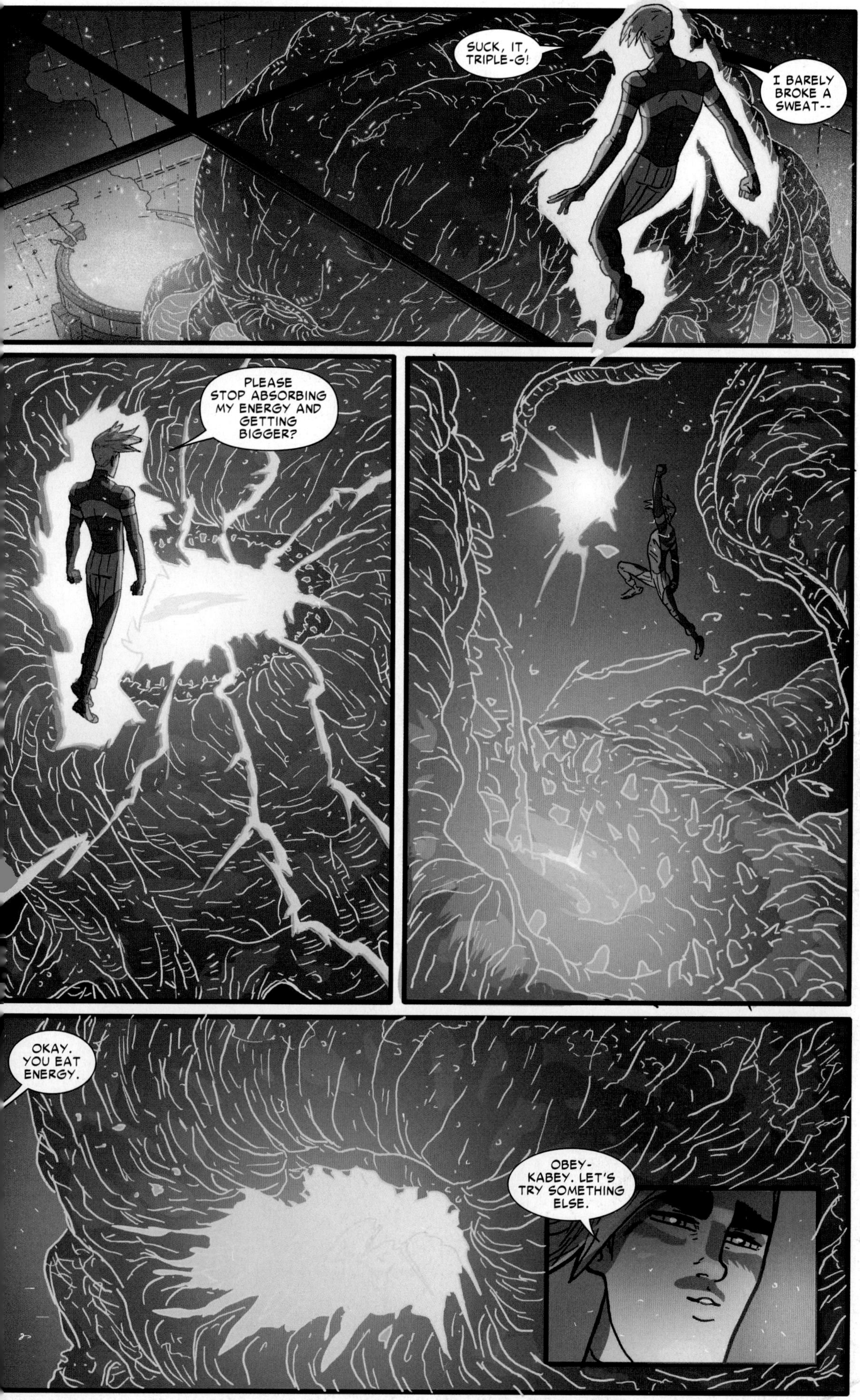
SUCK, IT, TRIPLE-G!
I BARELY BROKE A SWEAT--
PLEASE STOP ABSORBING MY ENERGY AND GETTING BIGGER?
OKAY. YOU EAT ENERGY.
OBEY-KABEY. LET'S TRY SOMETHING ELSE.

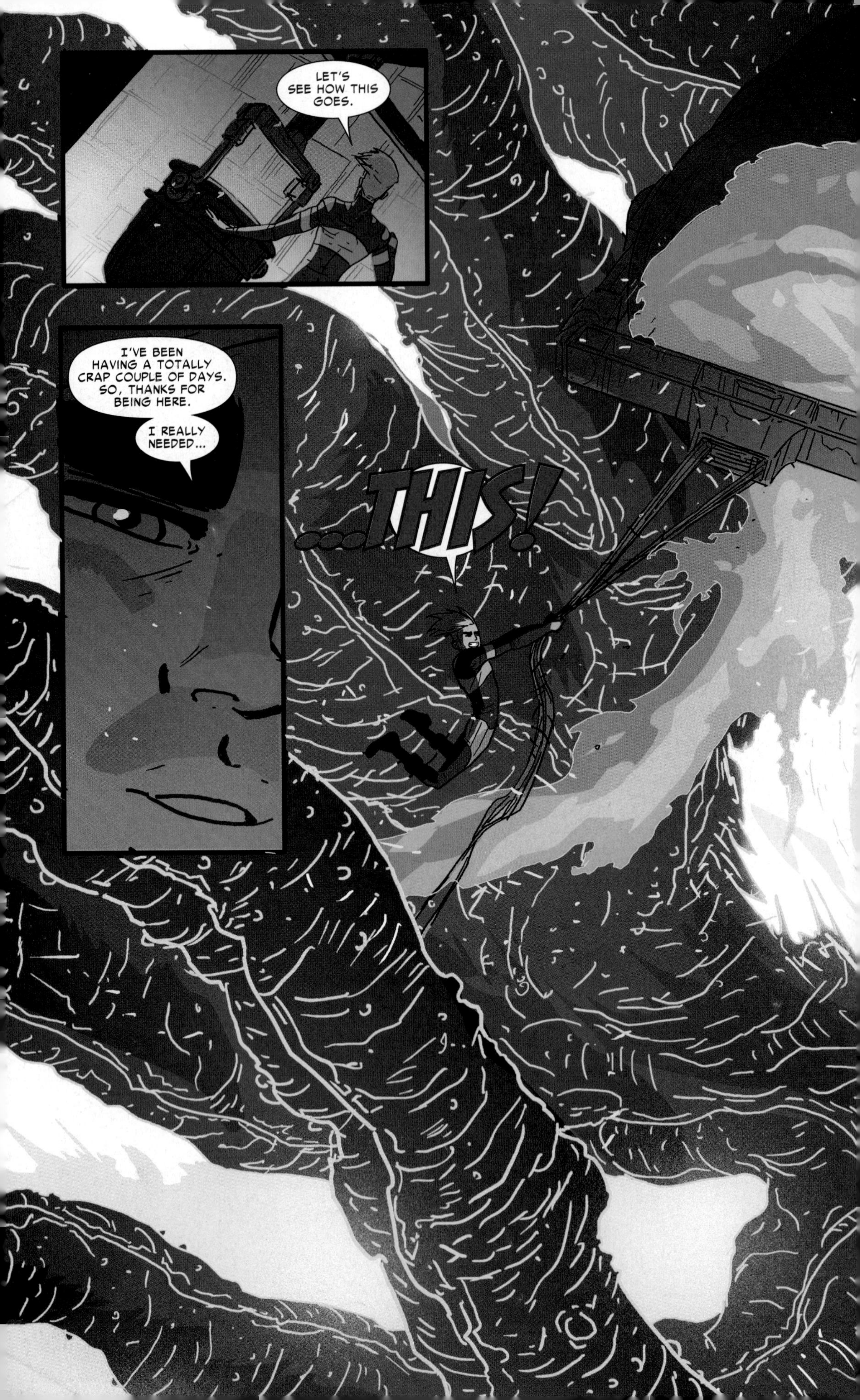
LET'S SEE HOW THIS GOES.
I'VE BEEN HAVING A TOTALLY CRAP COUPLE OF DAYS. SO, THANKS FOR BEING HERE.
I REALLY NEEDED...
...THIS!

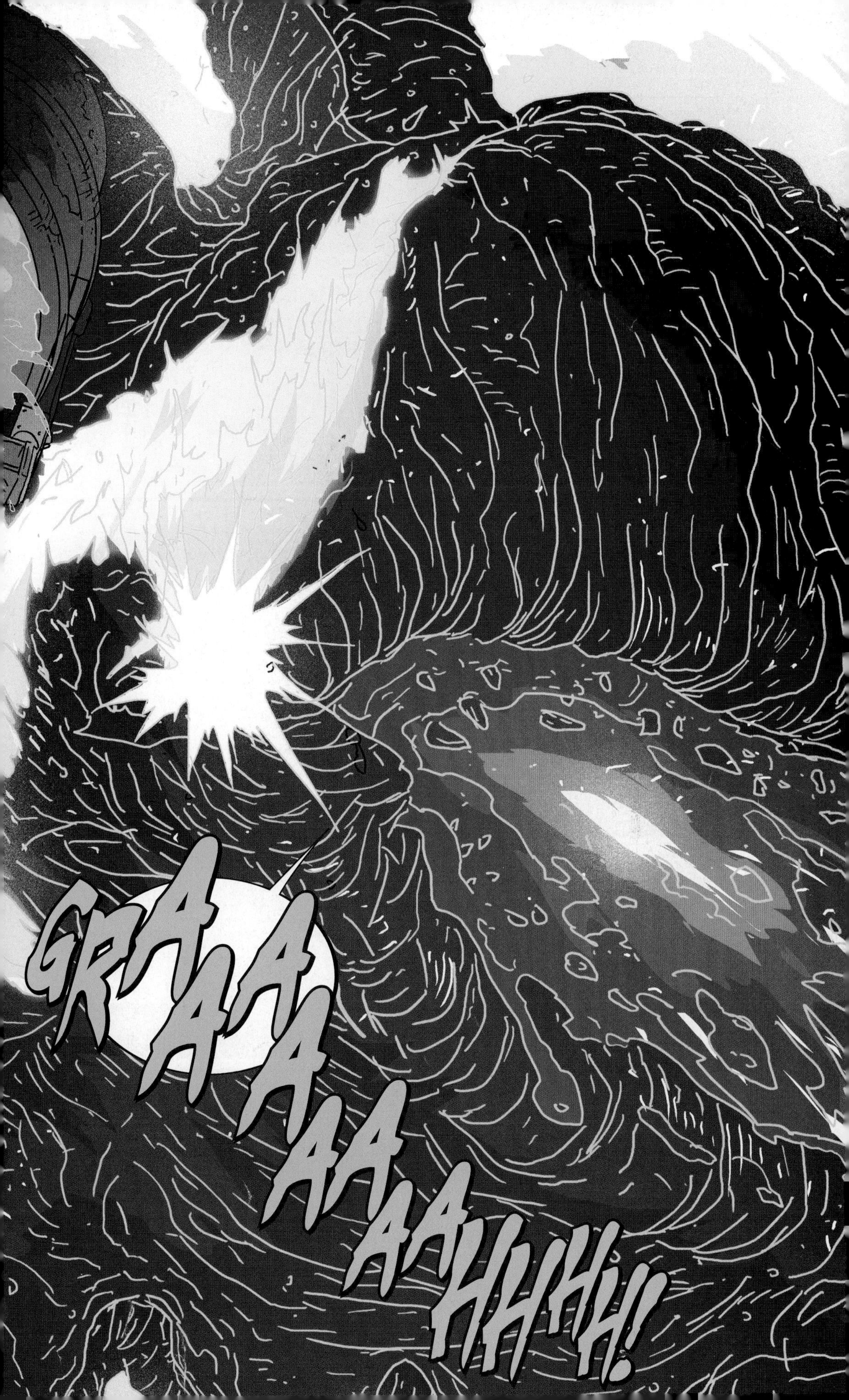
GRAAAAAAAAAHHHH!

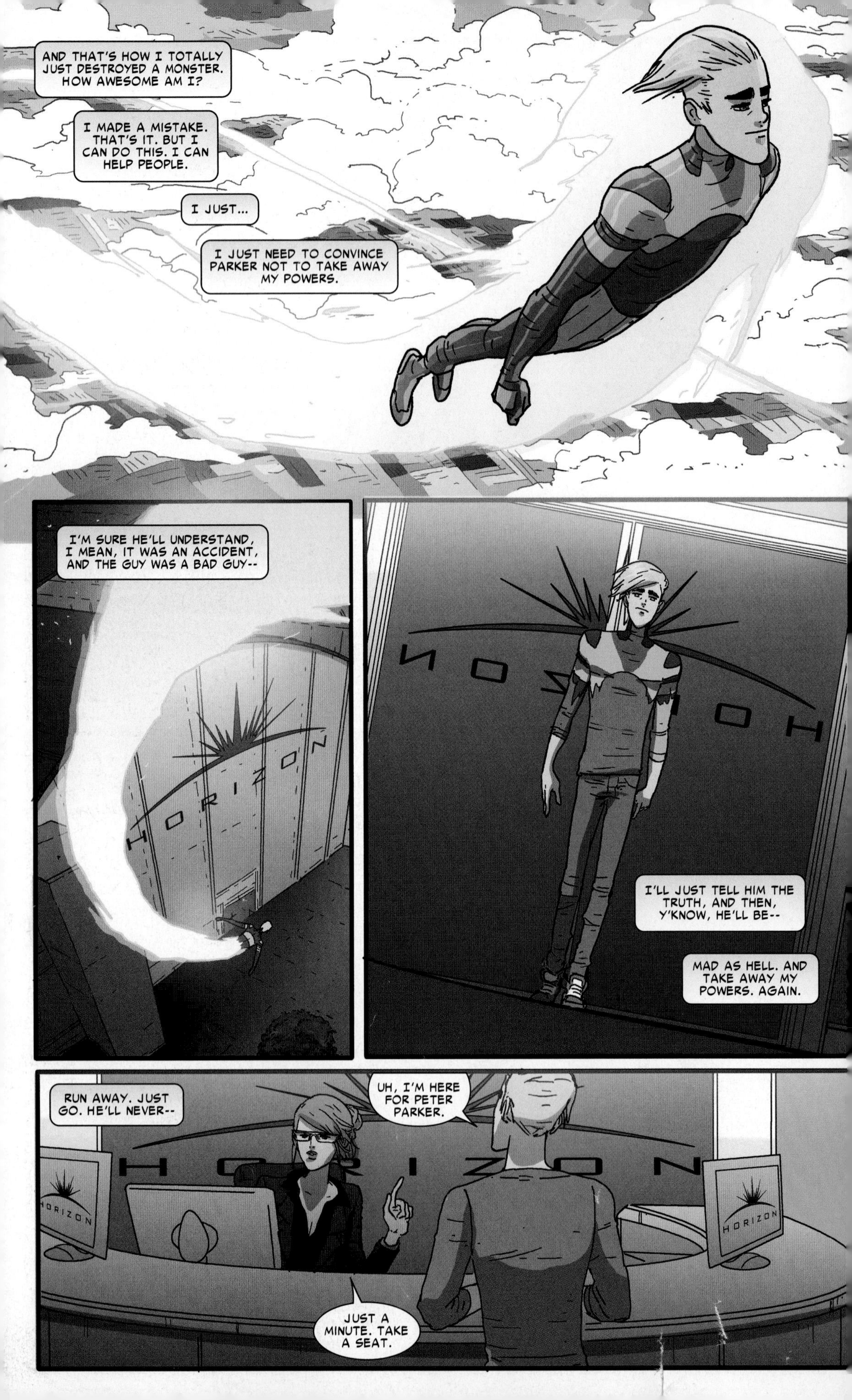
AND THAT'S HOW I TOTALLY JUST DESTROYED A MONSTER. HOW AWESOME AM I?
I MADE A MISTAKE. THAT'S IT. BUT I CAN DO THIS. I CAN HELP PEOPLE.
I JUST...
I JUST NEED TO CONVINCE PARKER NOT TO TAKE AWAY MY POWERS.
I'M SURE HE'LL UNDERSTAND, I MEAN, IT WAS AN ACCIDENT, AND THE GUY WAS A BAD GUY--
HORIZON
I'LL JUST TELL HIM THE TRUTH, AND THEN, Y'KNOW, HE'LL BE--
MAD AS HELL. AND TAKE AWAY MY POWERS. AGAIN.
RUN AWAY. JUST GO. HE'LL NEVER--
UH, I'M HERE FOR PETER PARKER.
HORIZON
JUST A MINUTE. TAKE A SEAT.

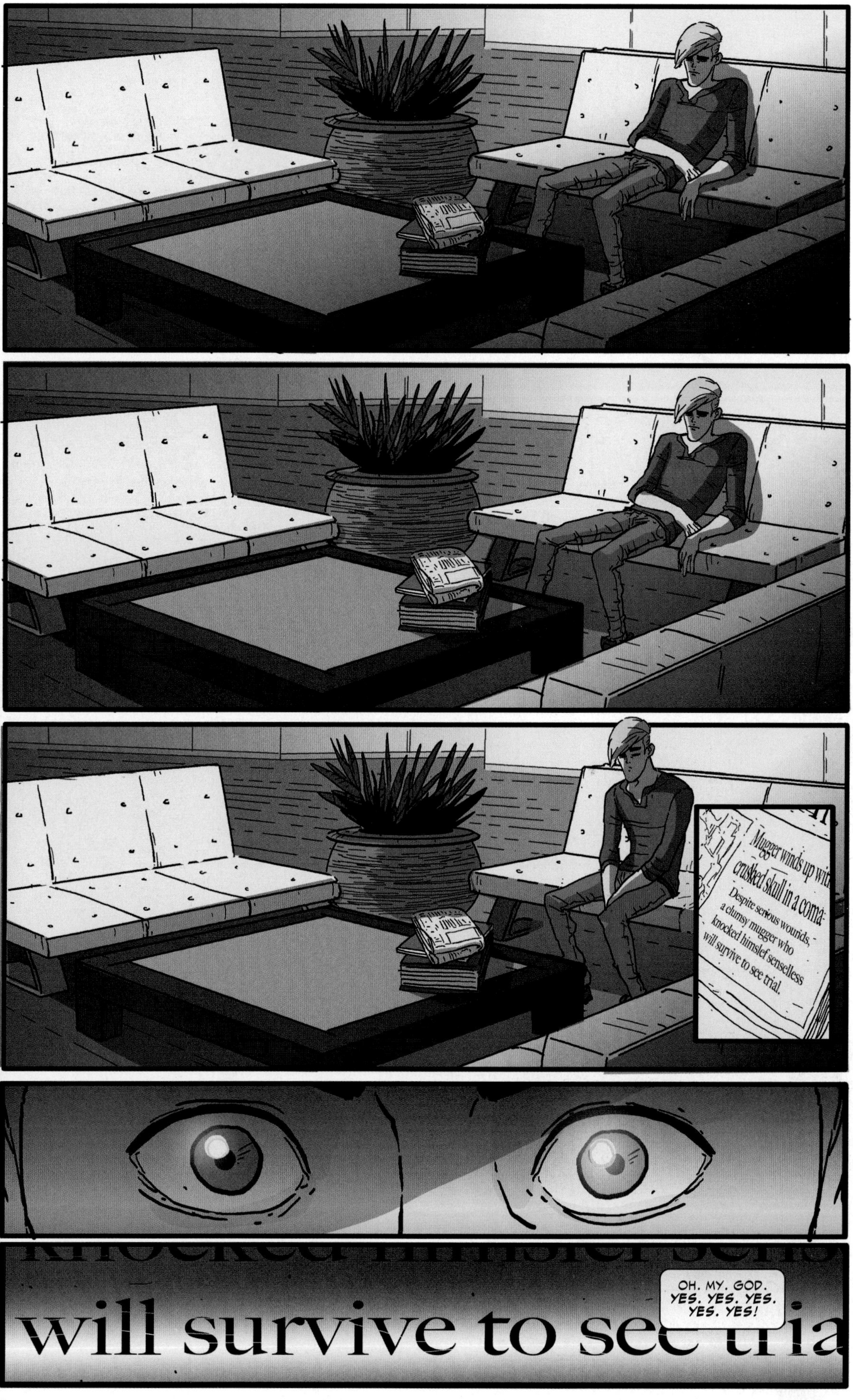
Mugger winds up wit
crushed skull in a coma:
Despite serious wounds, a clumsy mugger who knocked himslef senseless will survive to see trial.
will survive to see tria
OH. MY. GOD. YES. YES. YES. YES. YES!

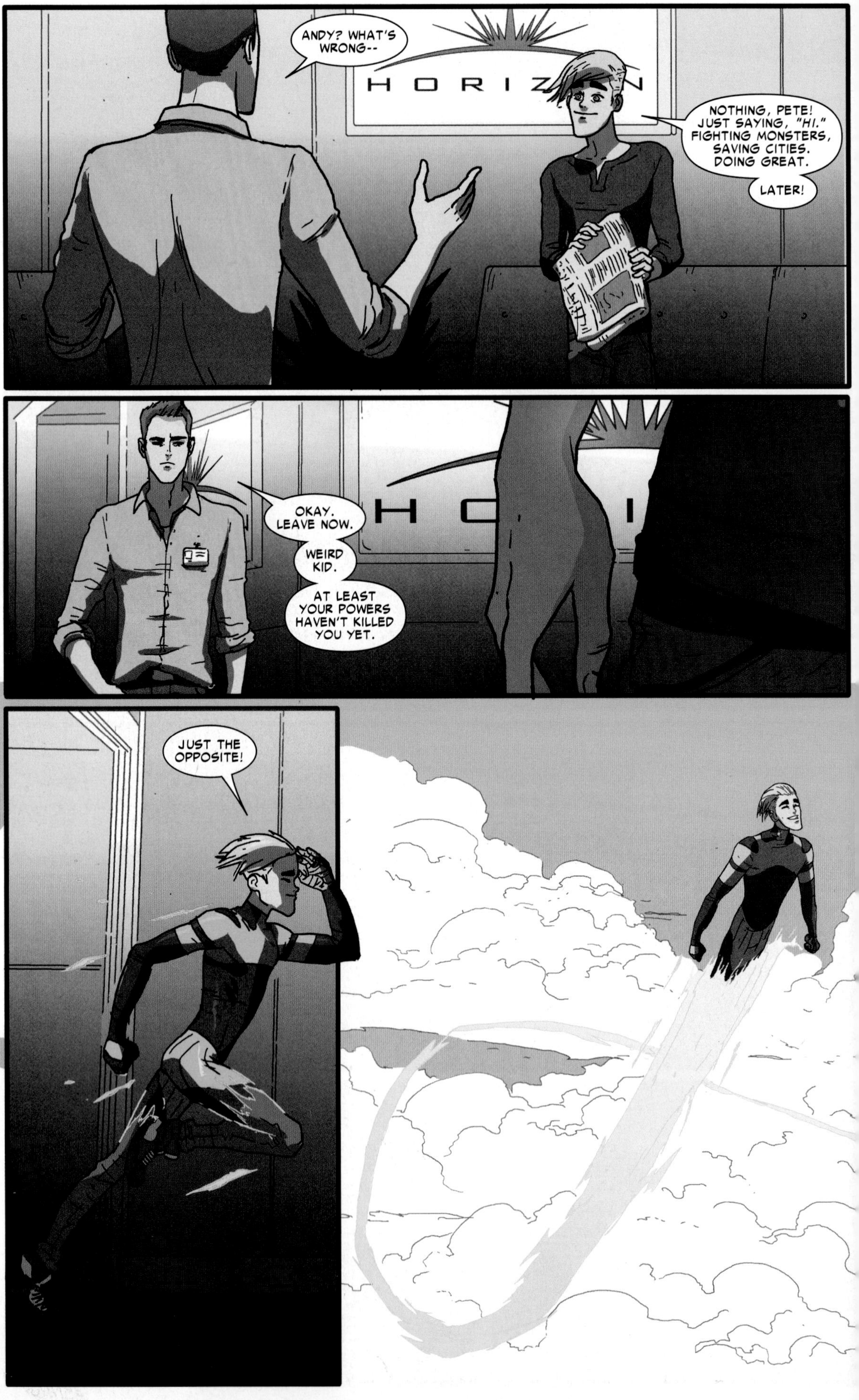
ANDY? WHAT'S WRONG--
HORIZ N
NOTHING, PETE! JUST SAYING, "HI." FIGHTING MONSTERS, SAVING CITIES. DOING GREAT.
LATER!
OKAY. LEAVE NOW.
WEIRD KID.
AT LEAST YOUR POWERS HAVEN'T KILLED YOU YET.
JUST THE OPPOSITE!

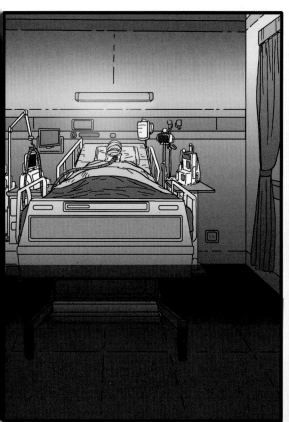

DUDE.

I'M THE GUY WHO, LIKE, UH, STOPPED YOUR MUGGER-ING.

I'M...SO SORRY. I DIDN'T MEAN TO, LIKE, DO...THIS.

I JUST...LIKE, I'VE BEEN GOING THROUGH A LOT, Y'KNOW? I MEAN, AFTER I PUNCHED YOU, I... WELL, I THOUGHT I KILLED YOU.

AND I WAS GOING TO GET RID OF MY POWERS, BUT, YOU'RE NOT DEAD, AND I THINK--

YOU WERE TOTALLY IN THE WRONG, Y'KNOW?

HERE'S THE THING, DUDE, I DIDN'T ASK FOR THIS GIG, Y'KNOW? I WAS PERFECTLY HAPPY SITTING IN THE BACK OF CLASS AND GETTING IGNORED AND BEING WICKED GOOD AT HALO.

BUT, Y'KNOW, STUFF HAPPENED, AND, YOU WERE THE BAD GUY AND NEEDED TAKEN CARE OF, SO I JUST DID WHAT I HAD TO DO, AND I REALLY JUST DON'T WANT TO GO TO JAIL.

I'M GLAD YOU'RE ALIVE, AND I'M NOT GOING TO GET IN TROU--

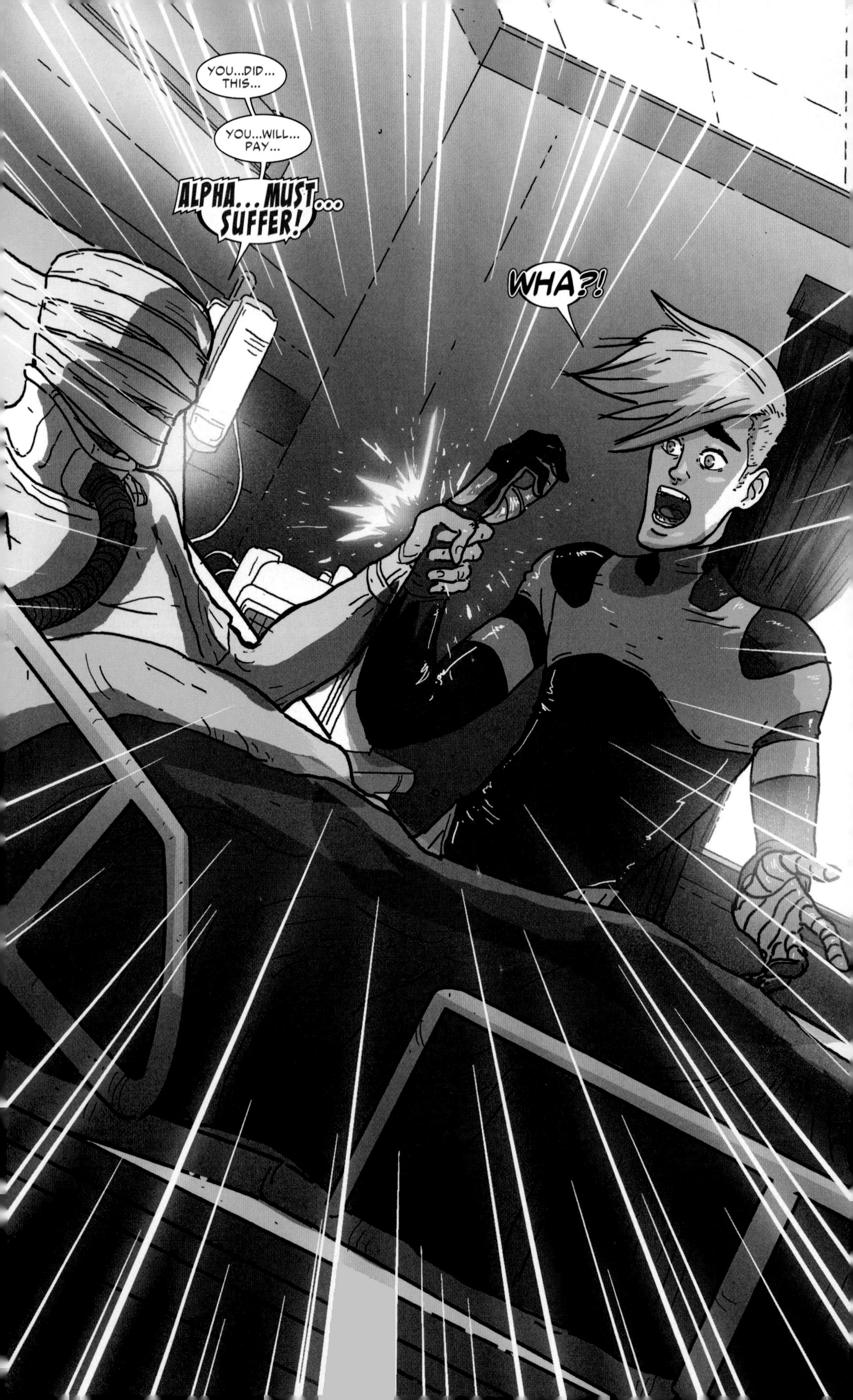
YOU...DID... THIS...
YOU...WILL... PAY...
ALPHA... MUST... SUFFER!
WHA?!

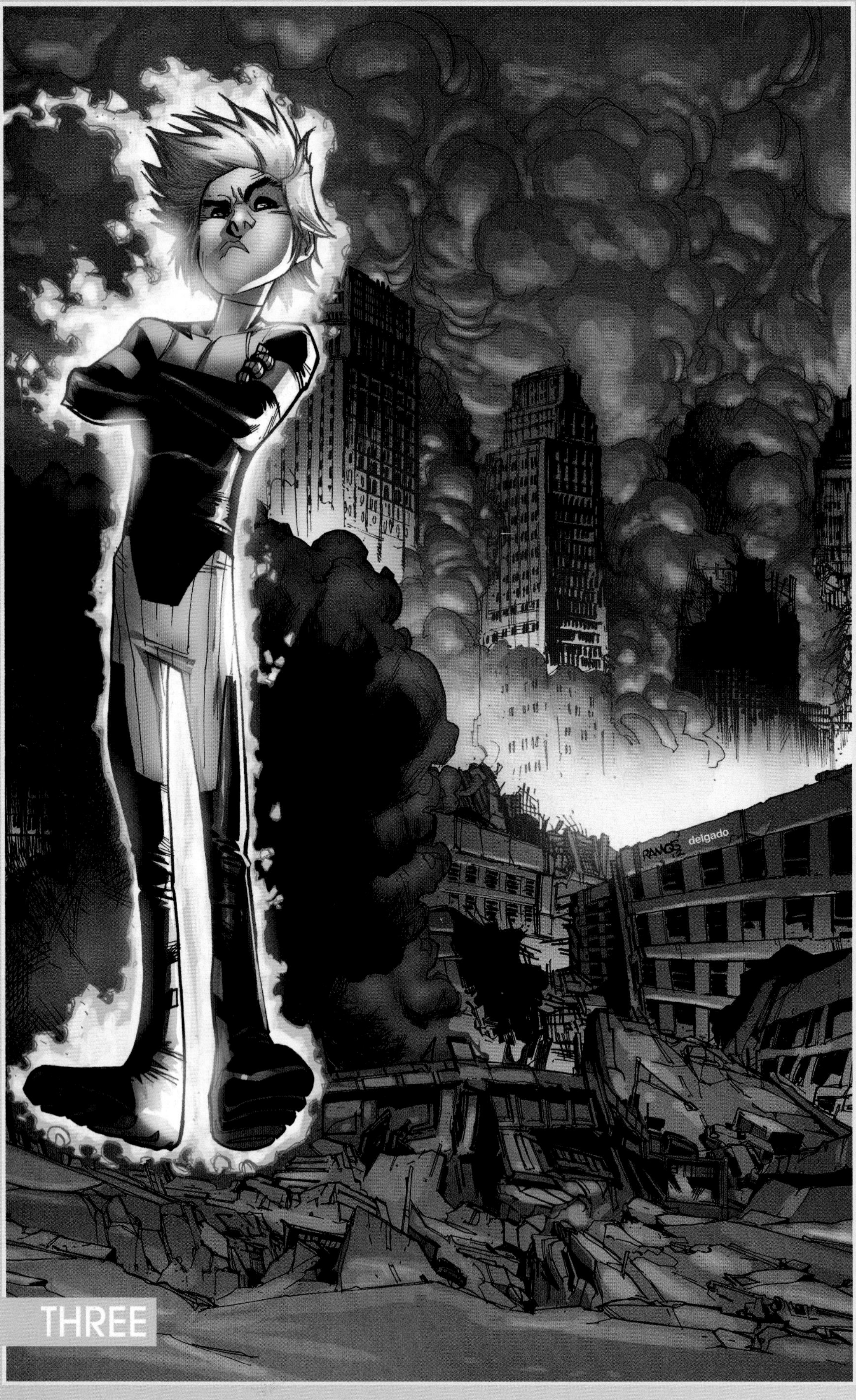
RAMOS
delgado

THREE

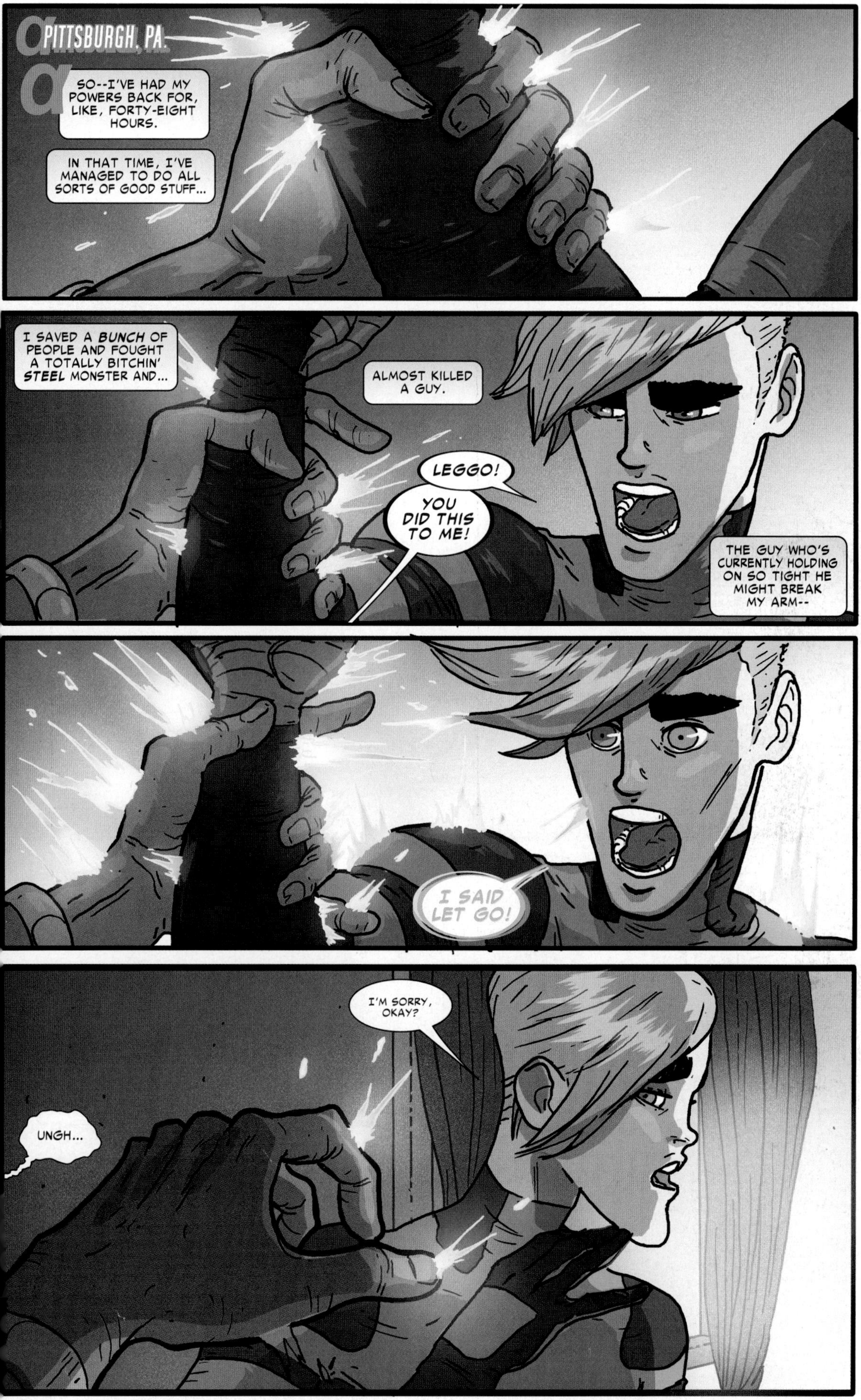
PITTSBURGH, PA.
SO--I'VE HAD MY POWERS BACK FOR, LIKE, FORTY-EIGHT HOURS.
IN THAT TIME, I'VE MANAGED TO DO ALL SORTS OF GOOD STUFF...
I SAVED A *BUNCH* OF PEOPLE AND FOUGHT A TOTALLY BITCHIN' *STEEL* MONSTER AND...
ALMOST KILLED A GUY.
LEGGO!
YOU DID THIS TO ME!
THE GUY WHO'S CURRENTLY HOLDING ON SO TIGHT HE MIGHT BREAK MY ARM--
I SAID LET GO!
I'M SORRY, OKAY?
UNGH...

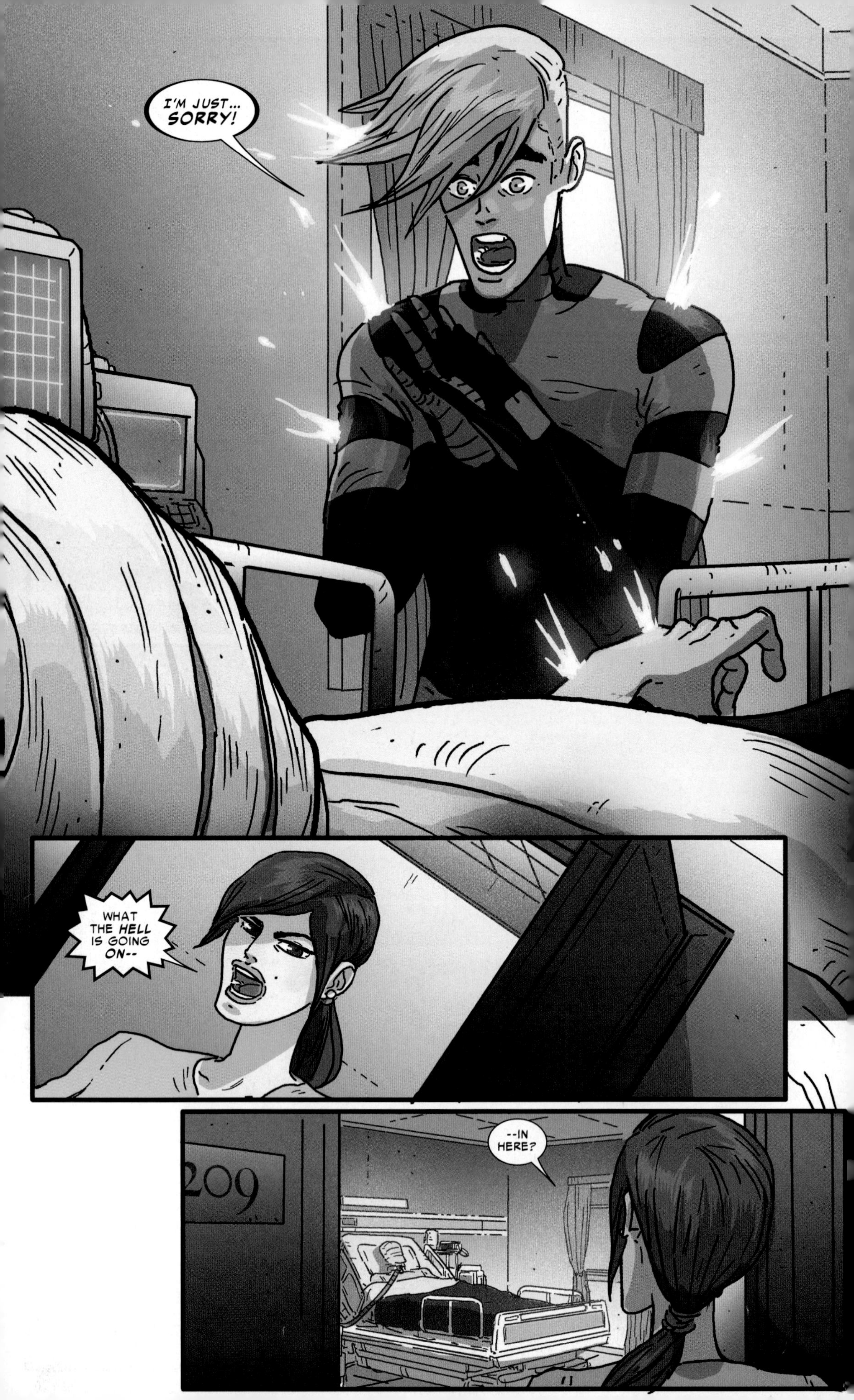
I'M JUST... SORRY!
WHAT THE HELL IS GOING ON--
209
--IN HERE?

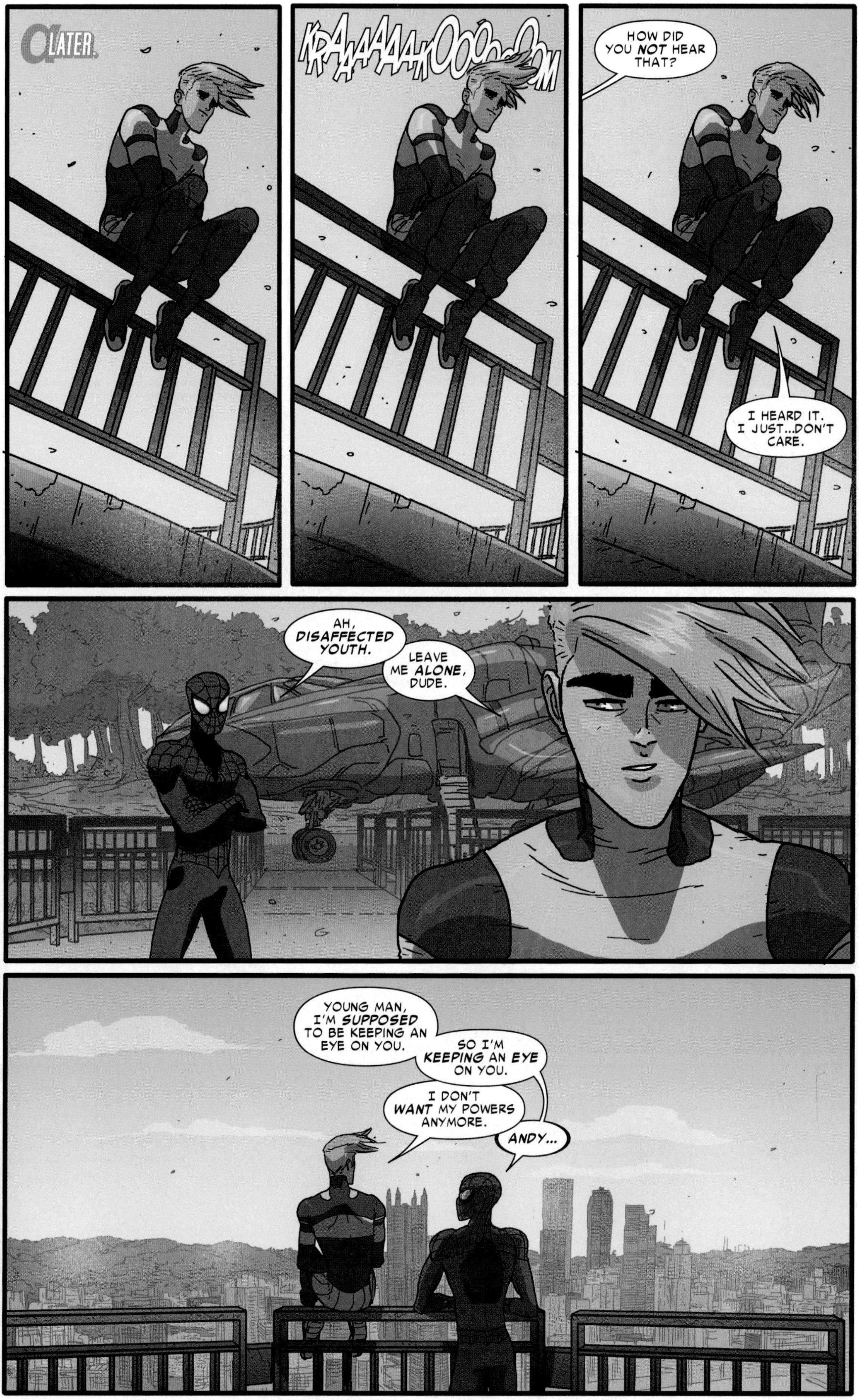
LATER.
KRAAAAAKOOOOOOM
HOW DID YOU NOT HEAR THAT?
I HEARD IT. I JUST...DON'T CARE.
AH, DISAFFECTED YOUTH.
LEAVE ME ALONE, DUDE.
YOUNG MAN, I'M SUPPOSED TO BE KEEPING AN EYE ON YOU.
SO I'M KEEPING AN EYE ON YOU.
I DON'T WANT MY POWERS ANYMORE.
ANDY...

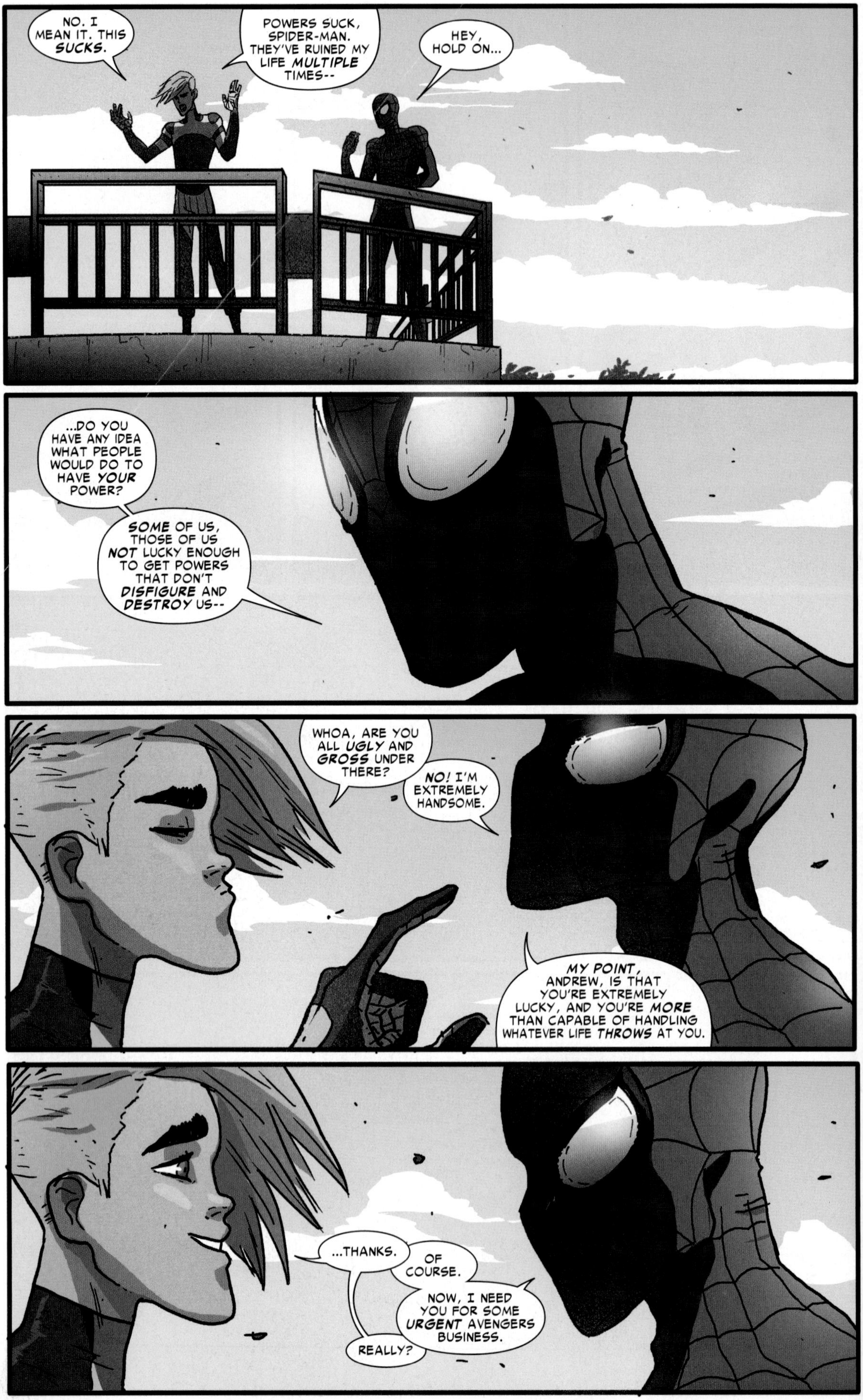

NO. I MEAN IT. THIS SUCKS.
POWERS SUCK, SPIDER-MAN. THEY'VE RUINED MY LIFE MULTIPLE TIMES--
HEY, HOLD ON...
...DO YOU HAVE ANY IDEA WHAT PEOPLE WOULD DO TO HAVE YOUR POWER?
SOME OF US, THOSE OF US NOT LUCKY ENOUGH TO GET POWERS THAT DON'T DISFIGURE AND DESTROY US--
WHOA, ARE YOU ALL UGLY AND GROSS UNDER THERE?
NO! I'M EXTREMELY HANDSOME.
MY POINT, ANDREW, IS THAT YOU'RE EXTREMELY LUCKY, AND YOU'RE MORE THAN CAPABLE OF HANDLING WHATEVER LIFE THROWS AT YOU.
...THANKS.
OF COURSE.
NOW, I NEED YOU FOR SOME URGENT AVENGERS BUSINESS.
REALLY?

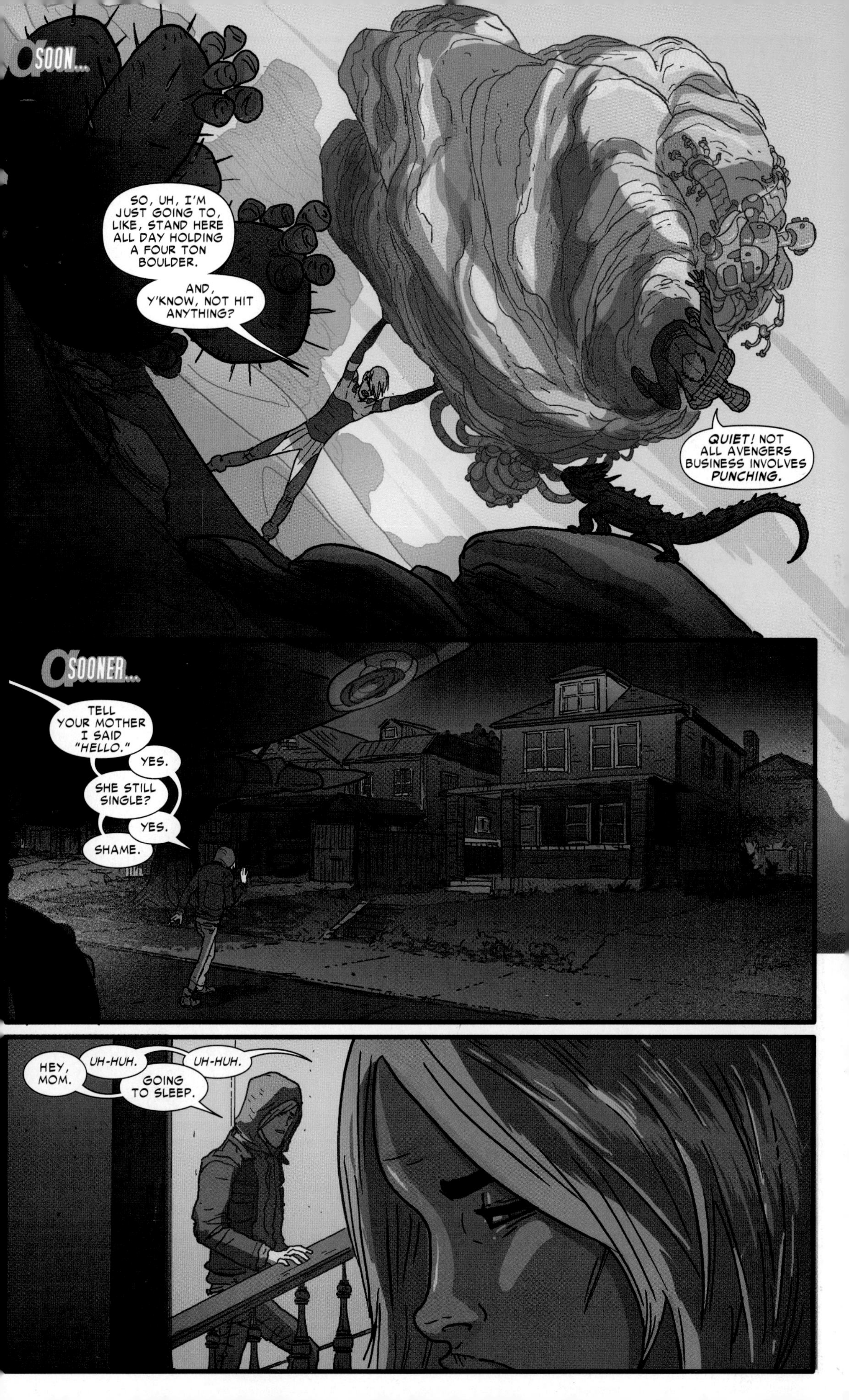

SOON...
SO, UH, I'M JUST GOING TO, LIKE, STAND HERE ALL DAY HOLDING A FOUR TON BOULDER.
AND, Y'KNOW, NOT HIT ANYTHING?
QUIET! NOT ALL AVENGERS BUSINESS INVOLVES PUNCHING.
SOONER...
TELL YOUR MOTHER I SAID "HELLO."
YES.
SHE STILL SINGLE?
YES.
SHAME.
HEY, MOM.
UH-HUH.
GOING TO SLEEP.
UH-HUH.

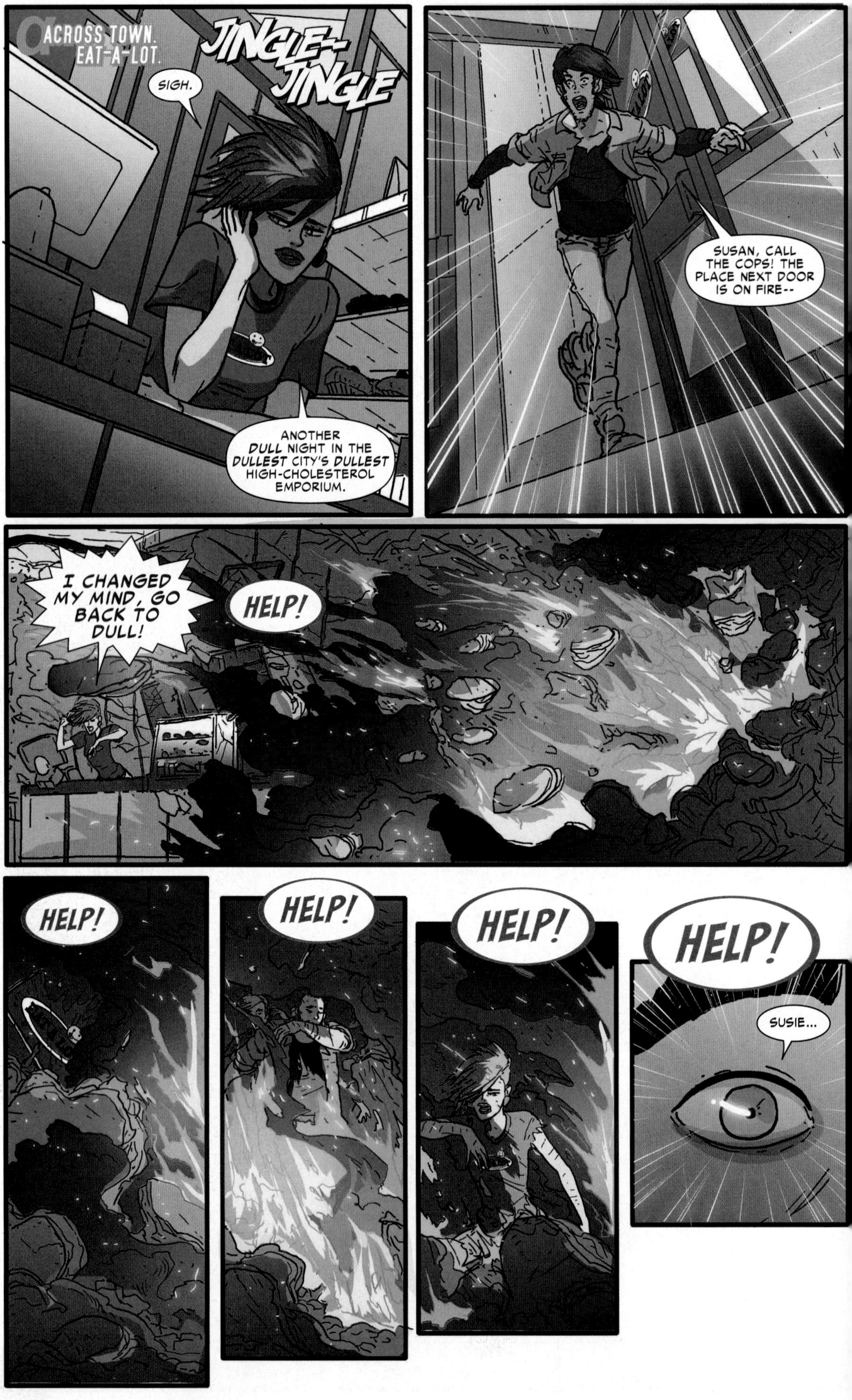
ACROSS TOWN. EAT-A-LOT.
JINGLE-JINGLE
SIGH.
ANOTHER DULL NIGHT IN THE DULLEST CITY'S DULLEST HIGH-CHOLESTEROL EMPORIUM.
SUSAN, CALL THE COPS! THE PLACE NEXT DOOR IS ON FIRE--
I CHANGED MY MIND, GO BACK TO DULL!
HELP!
HELP!
HELP!
HELP!
HELP!
SUSIE...

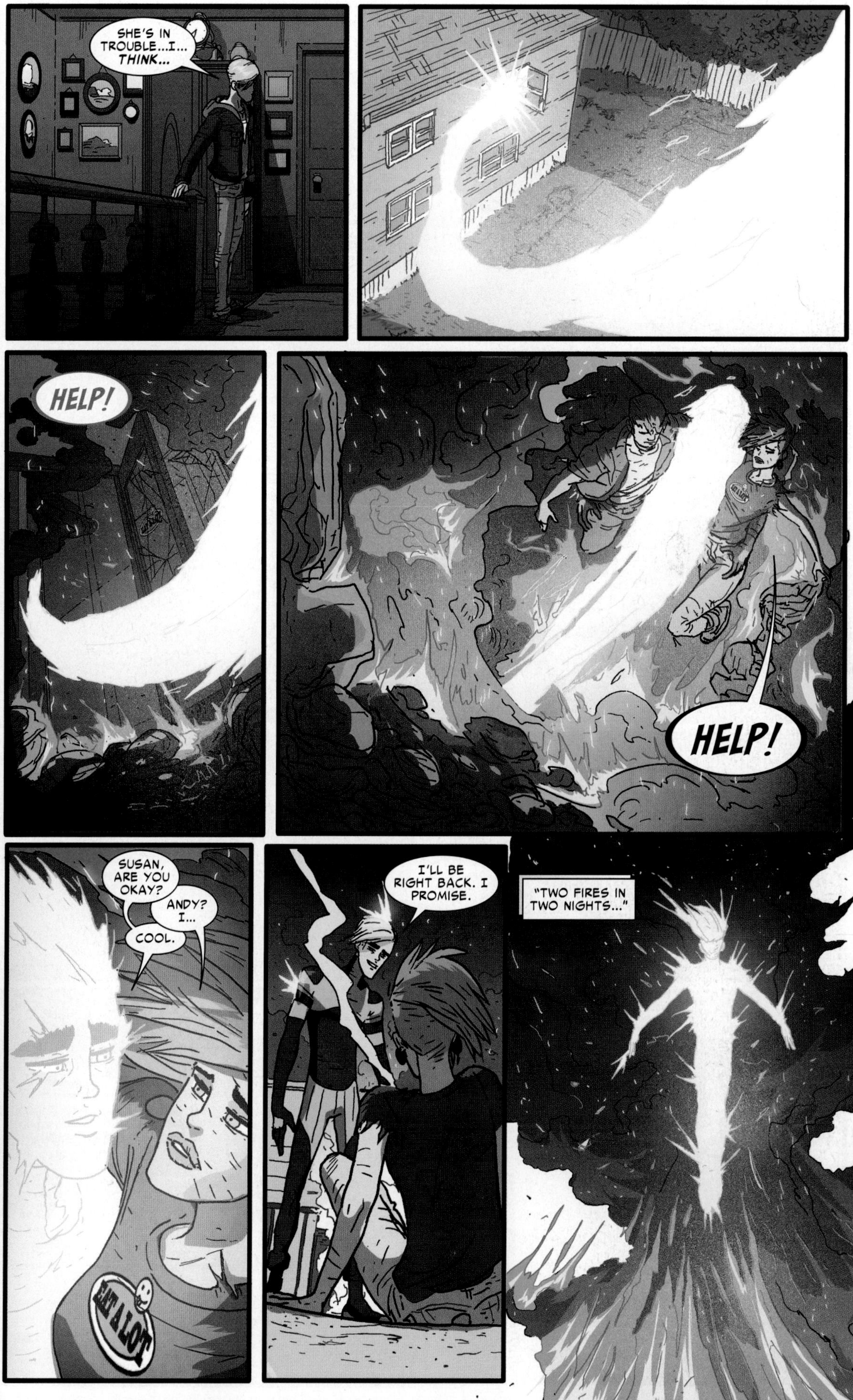
SHE'S IN TROUBLE...I... *THINK*...
HELP!
HELP!
SUSAN, ARE YOU OKAY?
ANDY? I...
COOL.
EAT A LOT
I'LL BE RIGHT BACK. I PROMISE.
"TWO FIRES IN TWO NIGHTS..."

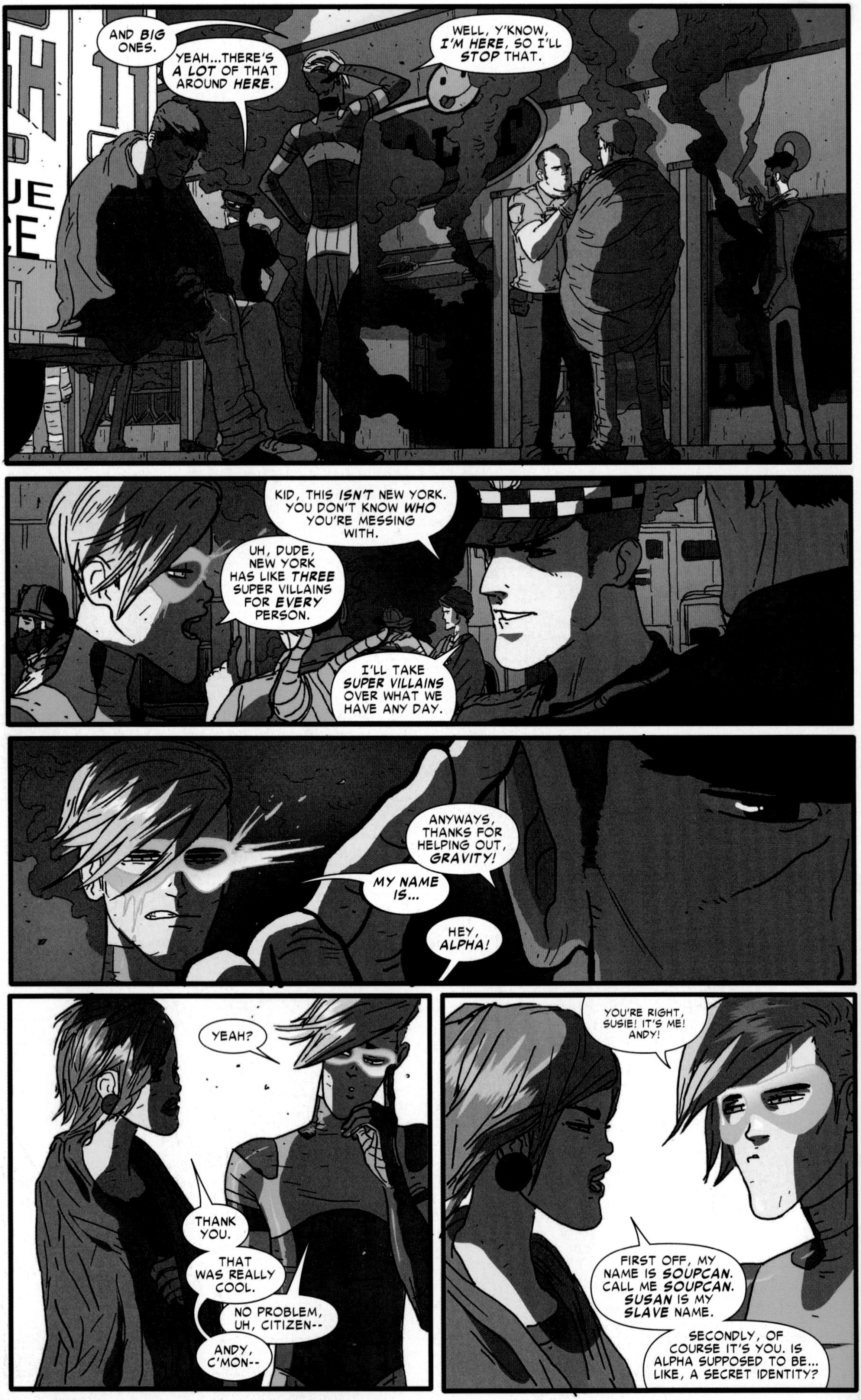

AND BIG ONES.
YEAH...THERE'S A LOT OF THAT AROUND HERE.
WELL, Y'KNOW, I'M HERE, SO I'LL STOP THAT.
KID, THIS ISN'T NEW YORK. YOU DON'T KNOW WHO YOU'RE MESSING WITH.
UH, DUDE, NEW YORK HAS LIKE THREE SUPER VILLAINS FOR EVERY PERSON.
I'LL TAKE SUPER VILLAINS OVER WHAT WE HAVE ANY DAY.
ANYWAYS, THANKS FOR HELPING OUT, GRAVITY!
MY NAME IS...
HEY, ALPHA!
YEAH?
THANK YOU.
THAT WAS REALLY COOL.
NO PROBLEM, UH, CITIZEN--
ANDY, C'MON--
YOU'RE RIGHT, SUSIE! IT'S ME! ANDY!
FIRST OFF, MY NAME IS SOUPCAN. CALL ME SOUPCAN. SUSAN IS MY SLAVE NAME.
SECONDLY, OF COURSE IT'S YOU. IS ALPHA SUPPOSED TO BE... LIKE, A SECRET IDENTITY?

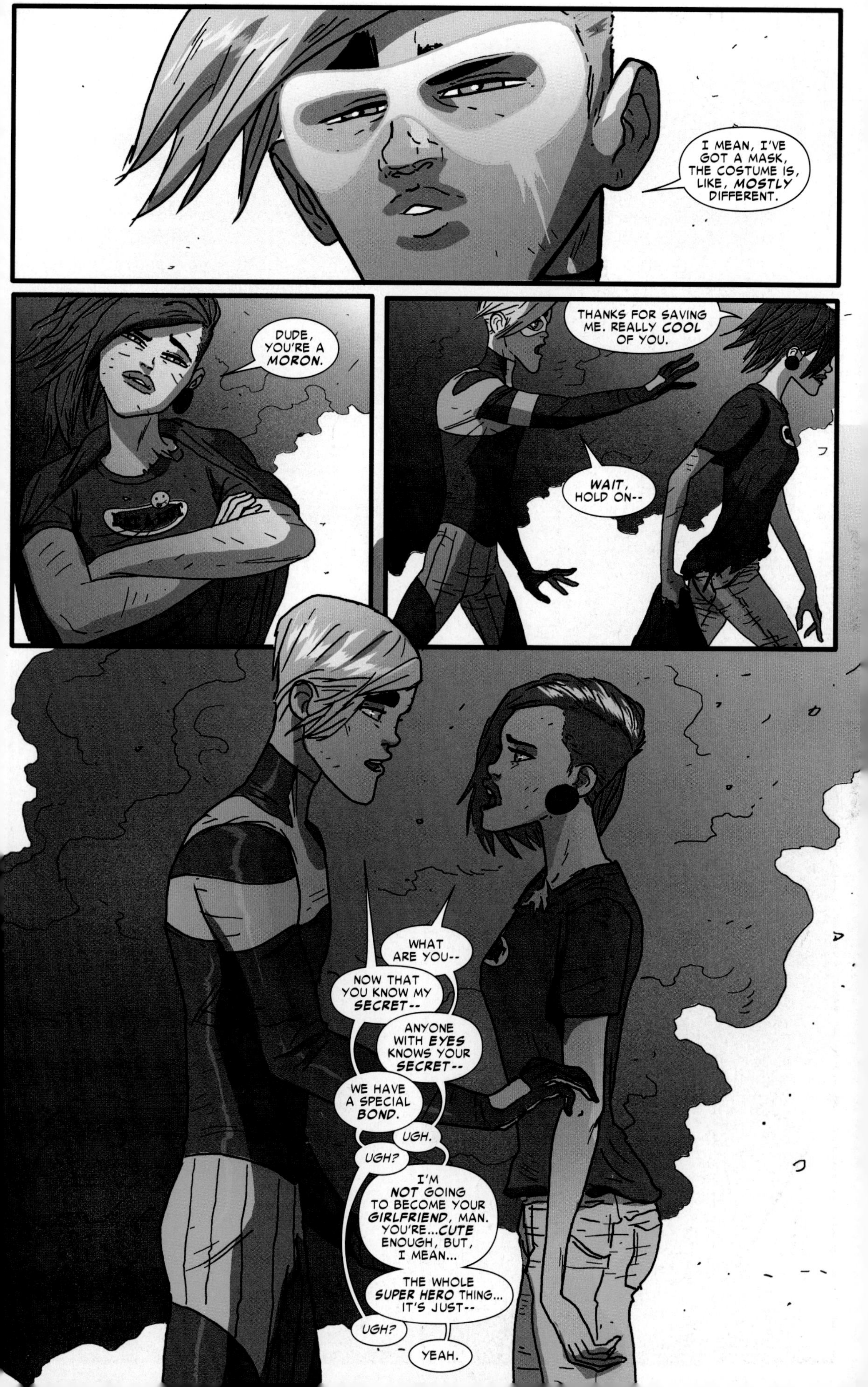
I MEAN, I'VE GOT A MASK, THE COSTUME IS, LIKE, MOSTLY DIFFERENT.
DUDE, YOU'RE A MORON.
THANKS FOR SAVING ME. REALLY COOL OF YOU.
WAIT, HOLD ON--
WHAT ARE YOU--
NOW THAT YOU KNOW MY SECRET--
ANYONE WITH EYES KNOWS YOUR SECRET--
WE HAVE A SPECIAL BOND.
UGH.
UGH?
I'M NOT GOING TO BECOME YOUR GIRLFRIEND, MAN. YOU'RE...CUTE ENOUGH, BUT, I MEAN...
THE WHOLE SUPER HERO THING... IT'S JUST--
UGH?
YEAH.

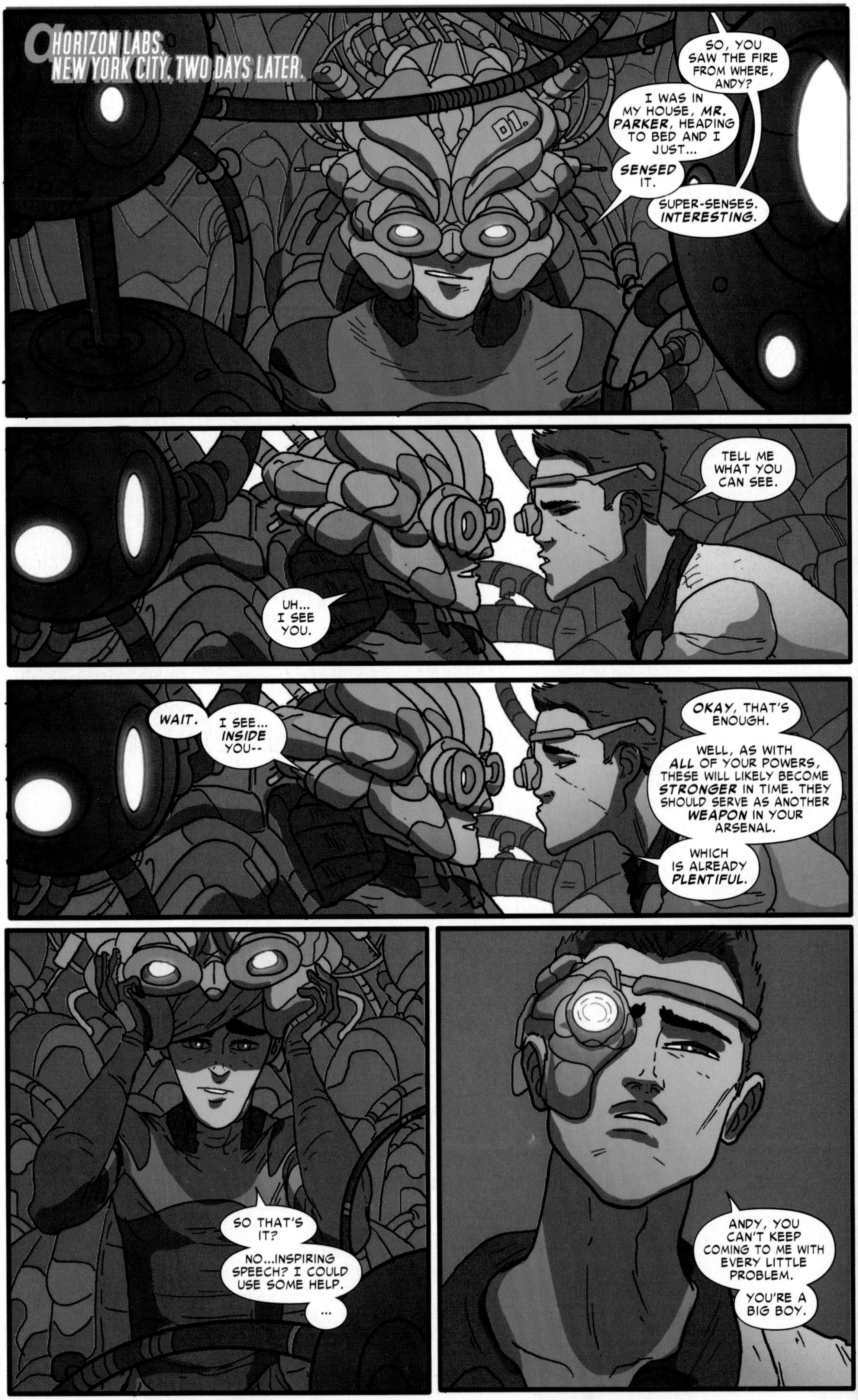
HORIZON LABS. NEW YORK CITY, TWO DAYS LATER.
SO, YOU SAW THE FIRE FROM WHERE, ANDY?
I WAS IN MY HOUSE, MR. PARKER, HEADING TO BED AND I JUST...
SENSED IT.
SUPER-SENSES. INTERESTING.
D1.
TELL ME WHAT YOU CAN SEE.
UH... I SEE YOU.
WAIT.
I SEE... INSIDE YOU--
OKAY, THAT'S ENOUGH.
WELL, AS WITH ALL OF YOUR POWERS, THESE WILL LIKELY BECOME STRONGER IN TIME. THEY SHOULD SERVE AS ANOTHER WEAPON IN YOUR ARSENAL.
WHICH IS ALREADY PLENTIFUL.
SO THAT'S IT?
NO...INSPIRING SPEECH? I COULD USE SOME HELP.
...
ANDY, YOU CAN'T KEEP COMING TO ME WITH EVERY LITTLE PROBLEM.
YOU'RE A BIG BOY.

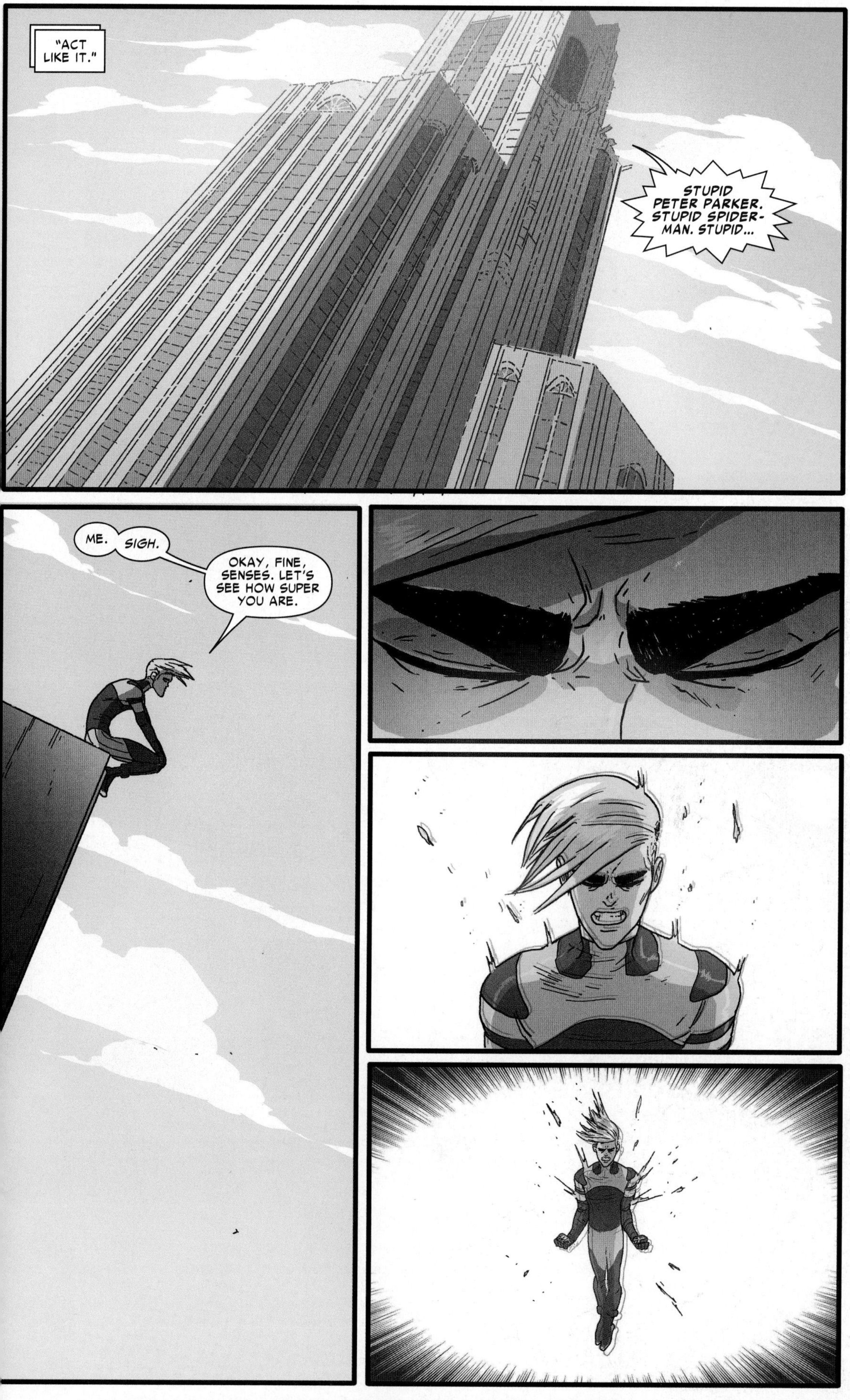
"ACT LIKE IT."
STUPID PETER PARKER. STUPID SPIDER-MAN. STUPID...
ME.
SIGH.
OKAY, FINE, SENSES. LET'S SEE HOW SUPER YOU ARE.

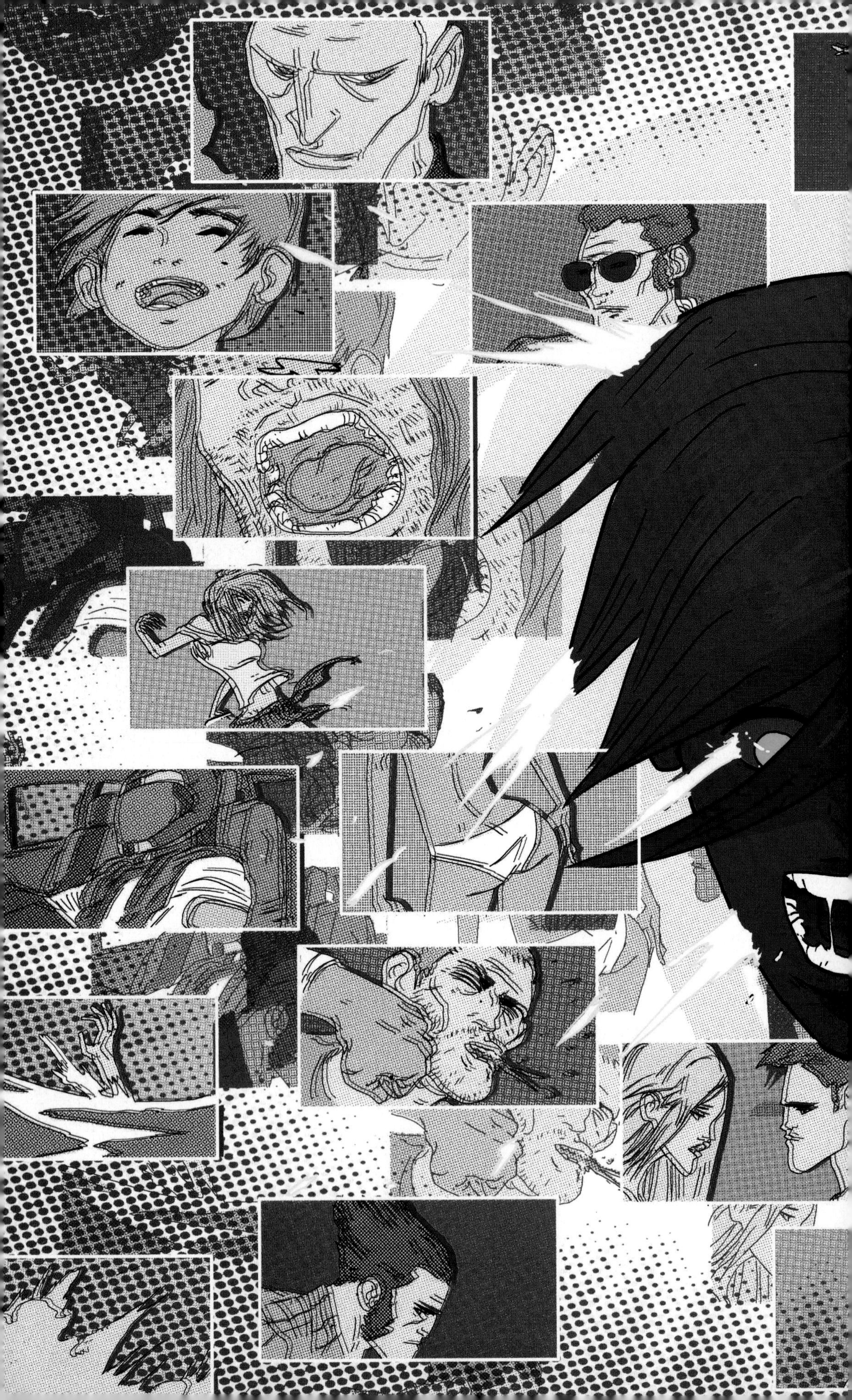

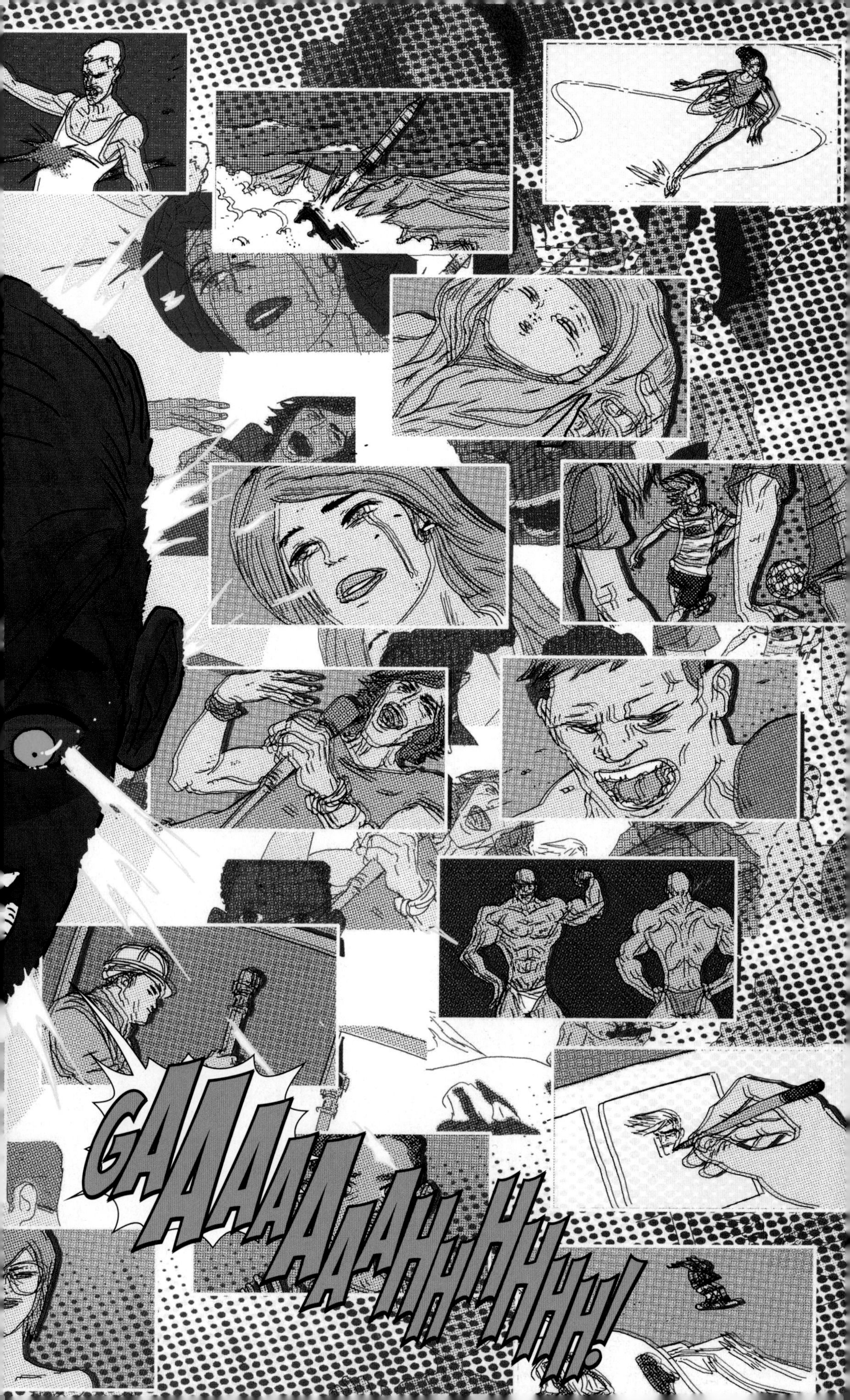
GAAAAAAAHHHHH!

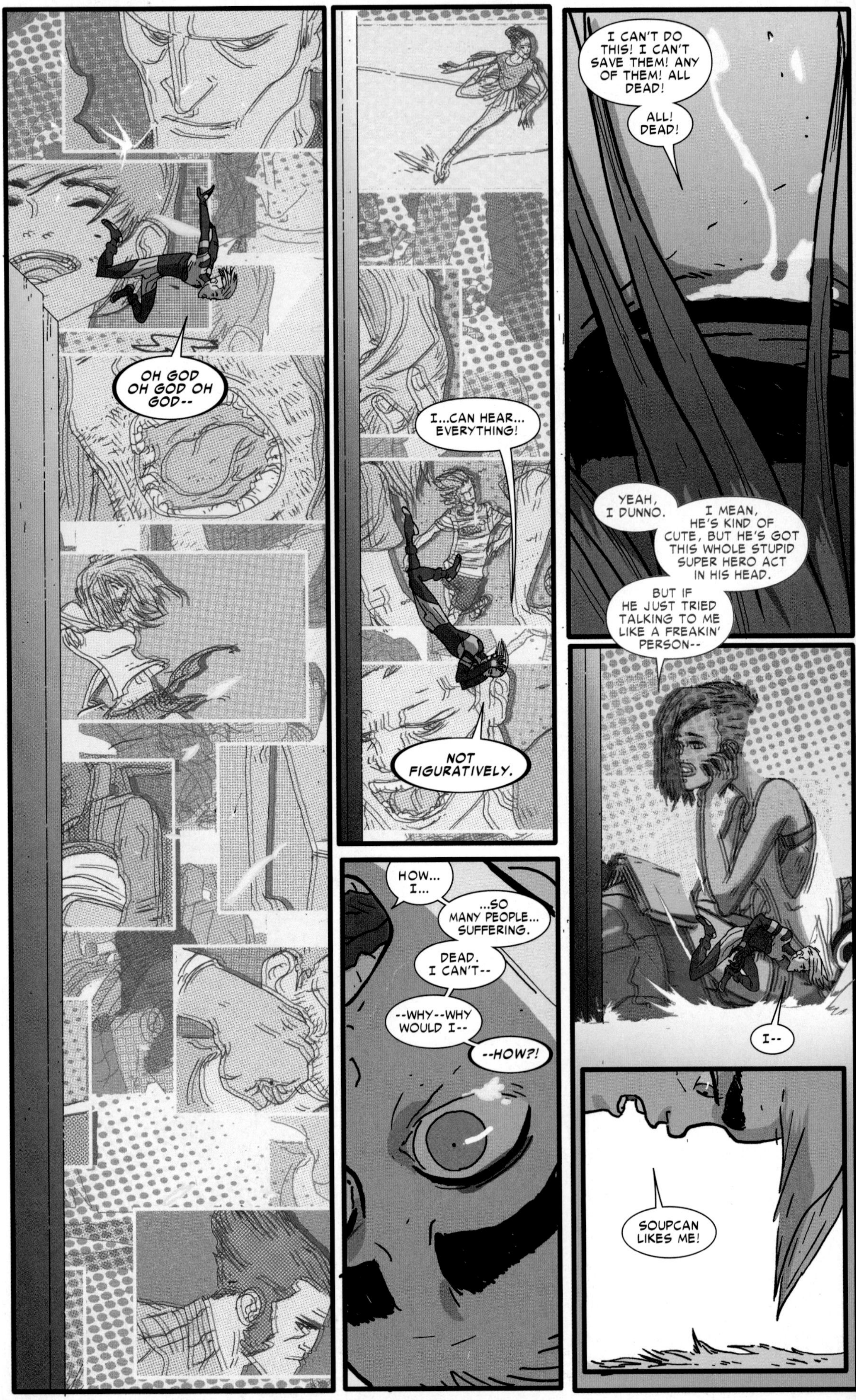
OH GOD OH GOD OH GOD--
I...CAN HEAR... EVERYTHING!
NOT FIGURATIVELY.
HOW... I...
...SO MANY PEOPLE... SUFFERING.
DEAD. I CAN'T--
--WHY--WHY WOULD I--
--HOW?!
I CAN'T DO THIS! I CAN'T SAVE THEM! ANY OF THEM! ALL DEAD!
ALL! DEAD!
YEAH, I DUNNO.
I MEAN, HE'S KIND OF CUTE, BUT HE'S GOT THIS WHOLE STUPID SUPER HERO ACT IN HIS HEAD.
BUT IF HE JUST TRIED TALKING TO ME LIKE A FREAKIN' PERSON--
I--
SOUPCAN LIKES ME!

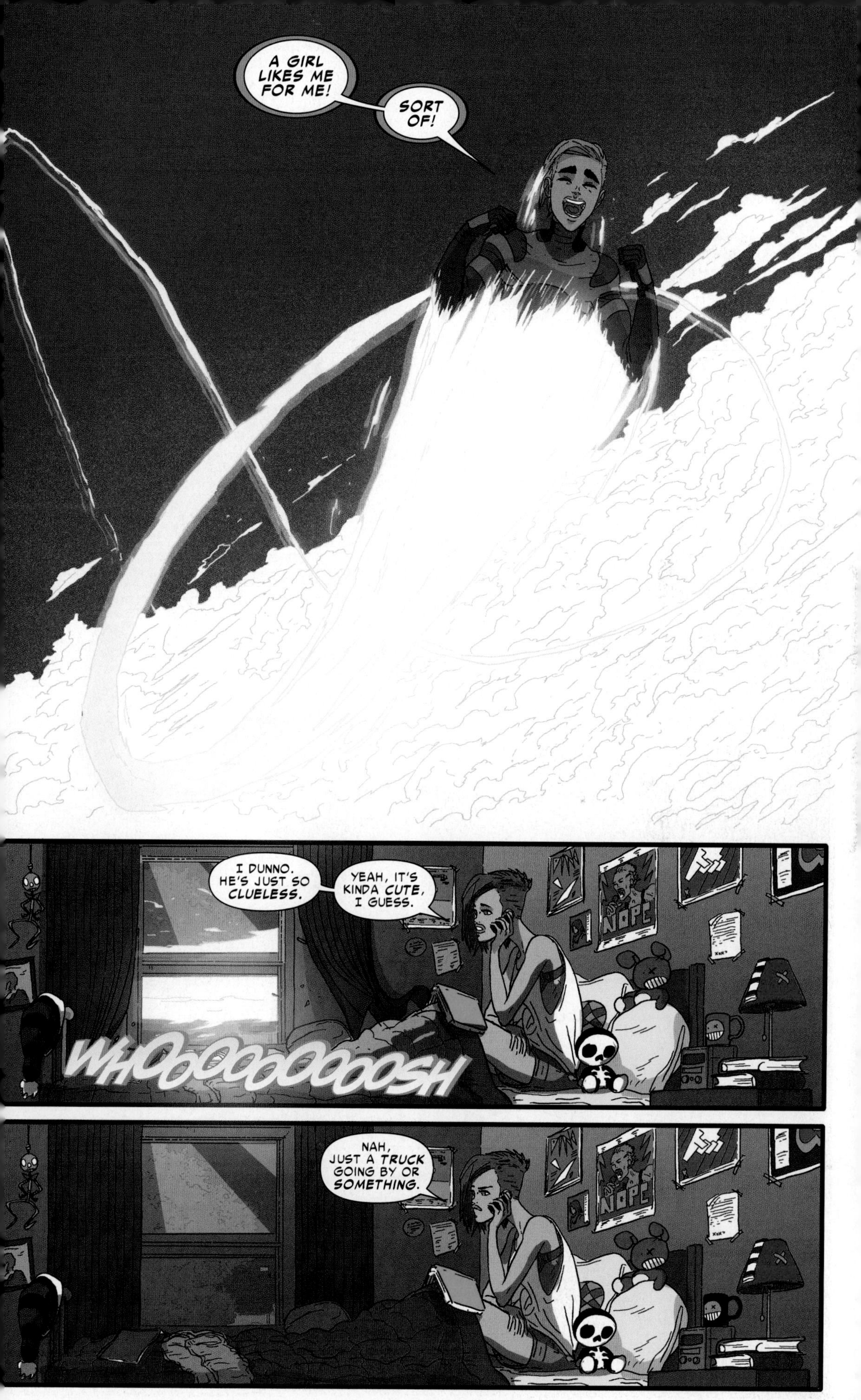
A GIRL LIKES ME FOR ME!
SORT OF!
I DUNNO. HE'S JUST SO CLUELESS.
YEAH, IT'S KINDA CUTE, I GUESS.
WHOOOOOOOOOOSH
NOPE
NAH, JUST A TRUCK GOING BY OR SOMETHING.
NOPE

"I CAN'T BELIEVE I THOUGHT THIS WAS A *BAD* THING!"

"I MEAN, I'M LIKE *SUPER-AWESOME*, GOT AN *ALMOST SUPER-AWESOME* GIRLFRIEND, AND TOTALLY *DIDN'T* KILL ANYBODY!"

OR, Y'KNOW, *YOU*. HOW YOU DOING ANYWAYS?

ANY MORE *WEIRD* VOCAL OUTBURSTS ABOUT *REVENGE*?

NO?

WELL, LOOK MAN, IT LOOKS LIKE YOU'RE DOING *BETTER*.

AND *I'M* COMPLETELY ACES, SO, COOL ON *US*!

SEE YOU TOMORROW.

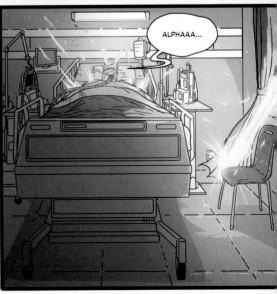

ALPHAAA...

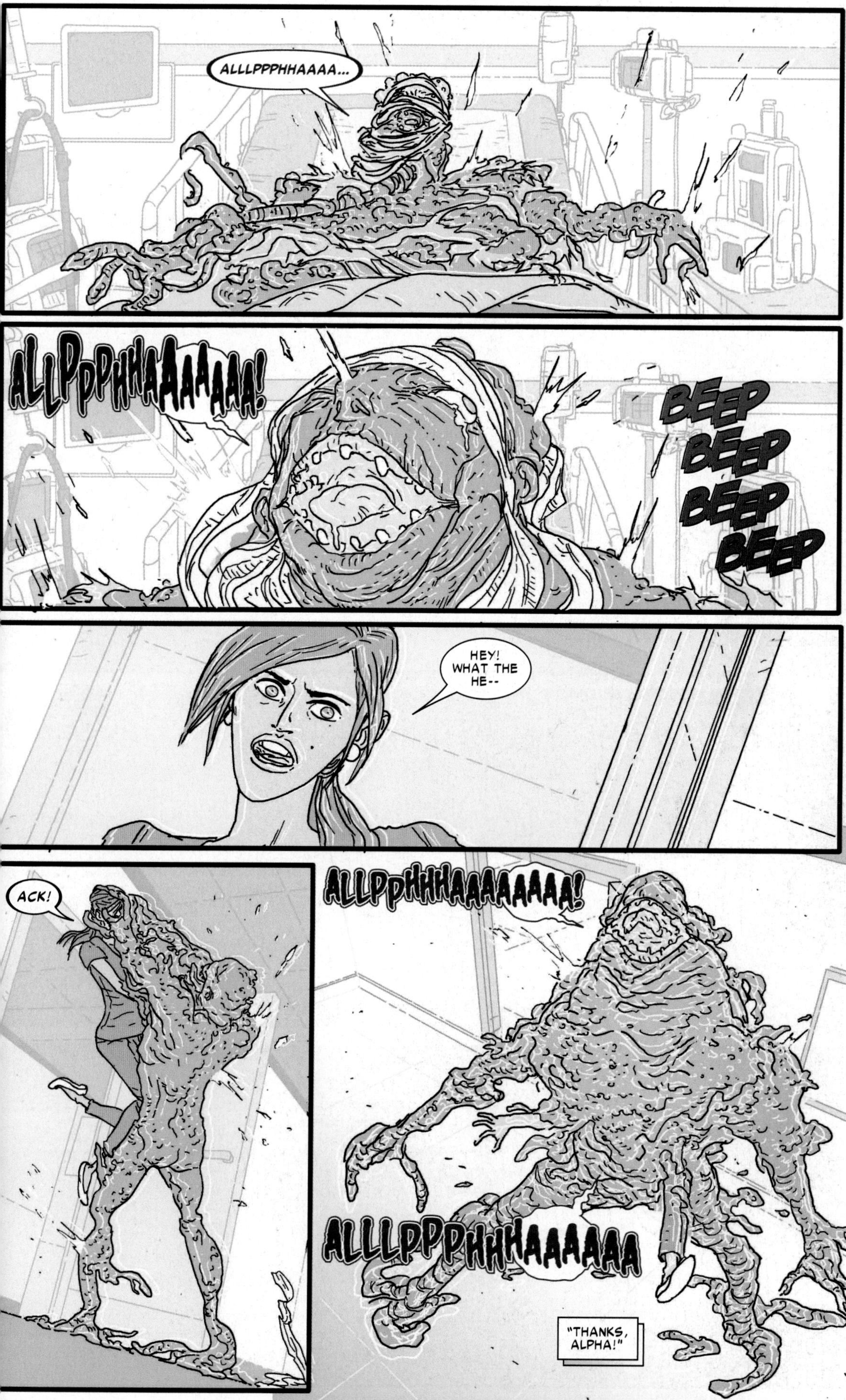
ALLLPPPHHAAAA...
ALLPPPHHAAAAAAA!
BEEP
BEEP
BEEP
BEEP
HEY! WHAT THE HE--
ACK!
ALLPPHHHAAAAAAAA!
ALLLPPPHHAAAAAA
"THANKS, ALPHA!"

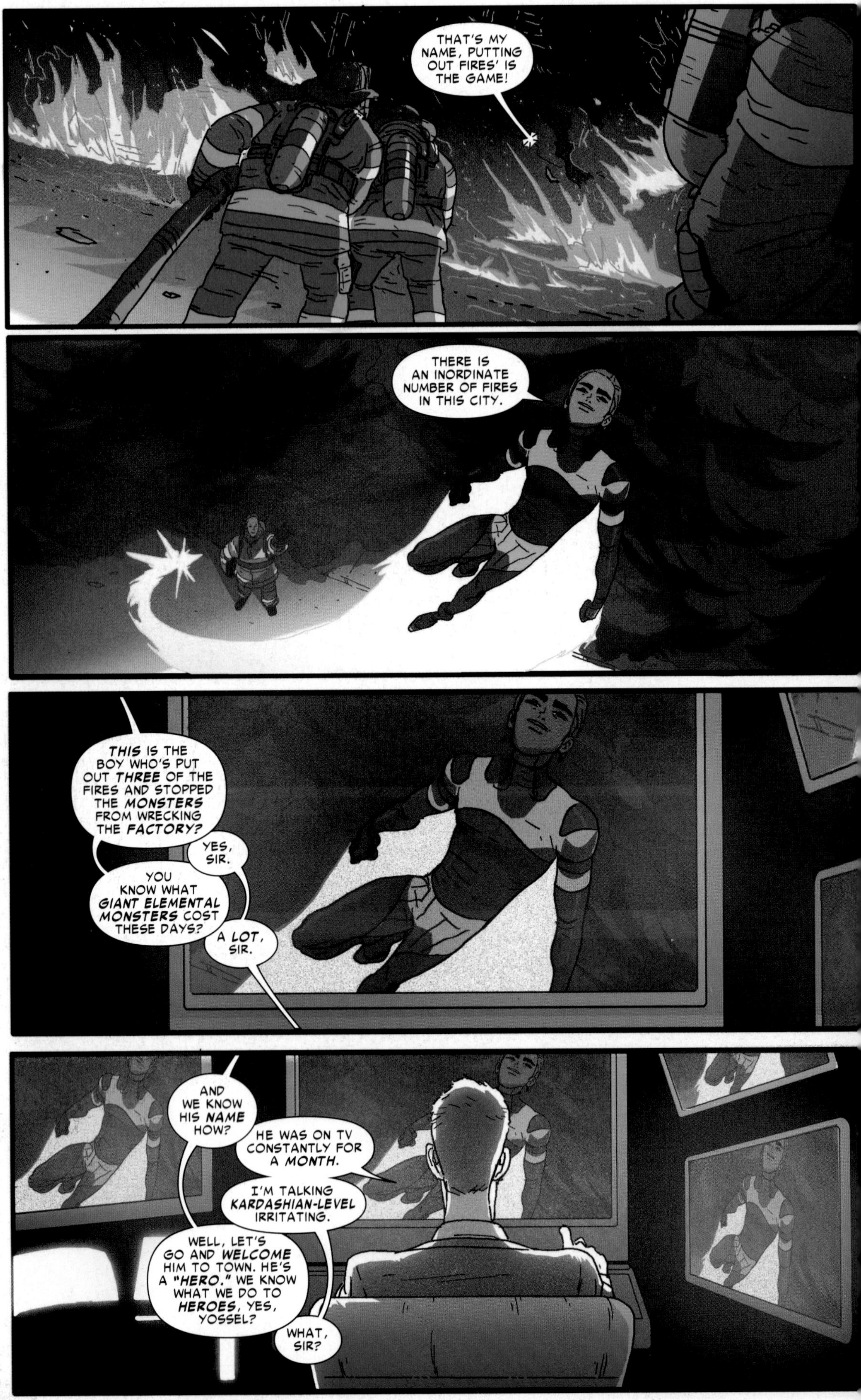
THAT'S MY NAME, PUTTING OUT FIRES' IS THE GAME!
THERE IS AN INORDINATE NUMBER OF FIRES IN THIS CITY.
THIS IS THE BOY WHO'S PUT OUT THREE OF THE FIRES AND STOPPED THE MONSTERS FROM WRECKING THE FACTORY?
YES, SIR.
YOU KNOW WHAT GIANT ELEMENTAL MONSTERS COST THESE DAYS?
A LOT, SIR.
AND WE KNOW HIS NAME HOW?
HE WAS ON TV CONSTANTLY FOR A MONTH.
I'M TALKING KARDASHIAN-LEVEL IRRITATING.
WELL, LET'S GO AND WELCOME HIM TO TOWN. HE'S A "HERO." WE KNOW WHAT WE DO TO HEROES, YES, YOSSEL?
WHAT, SIR?

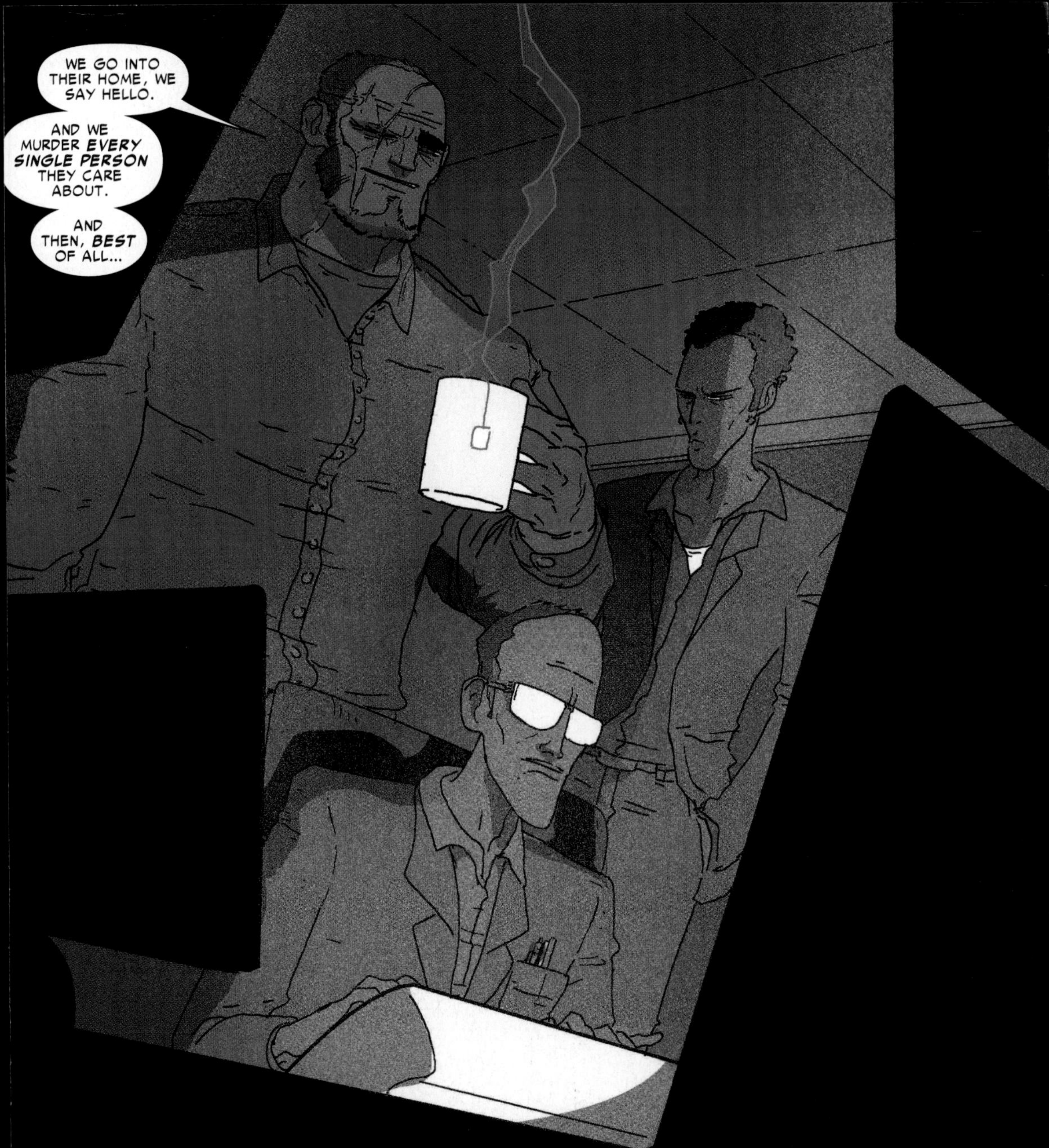
WE GO INTO THEIR HOME, WE SAY HELLO.
AND WE MURDER *EVERY SINGLE PERSON* THEY CARE ABOUT.
AND THEN, *BEST* OF ALL...

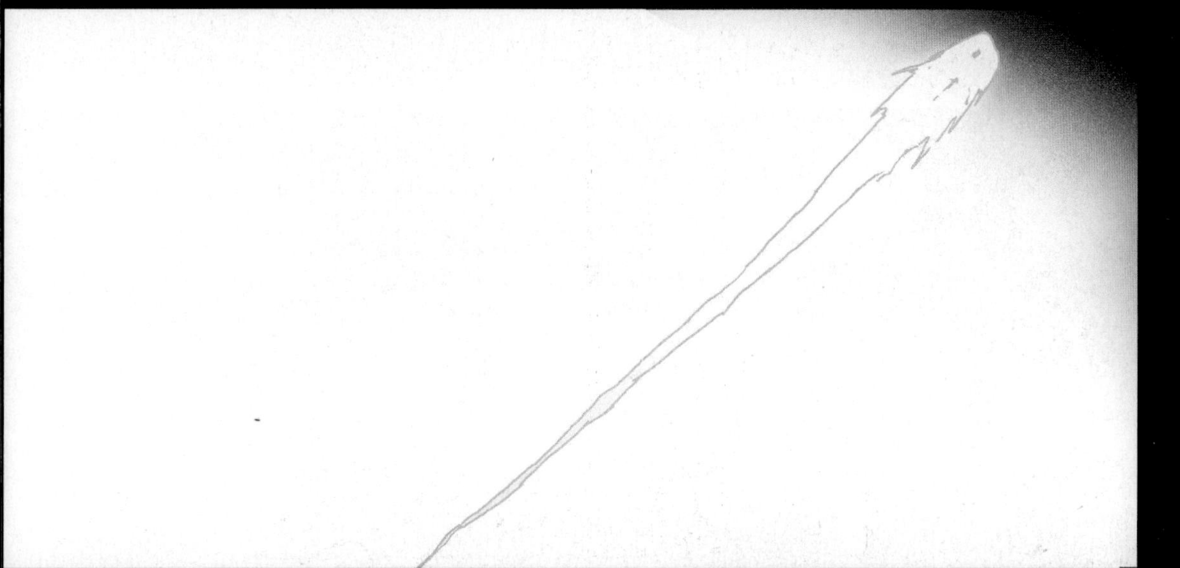

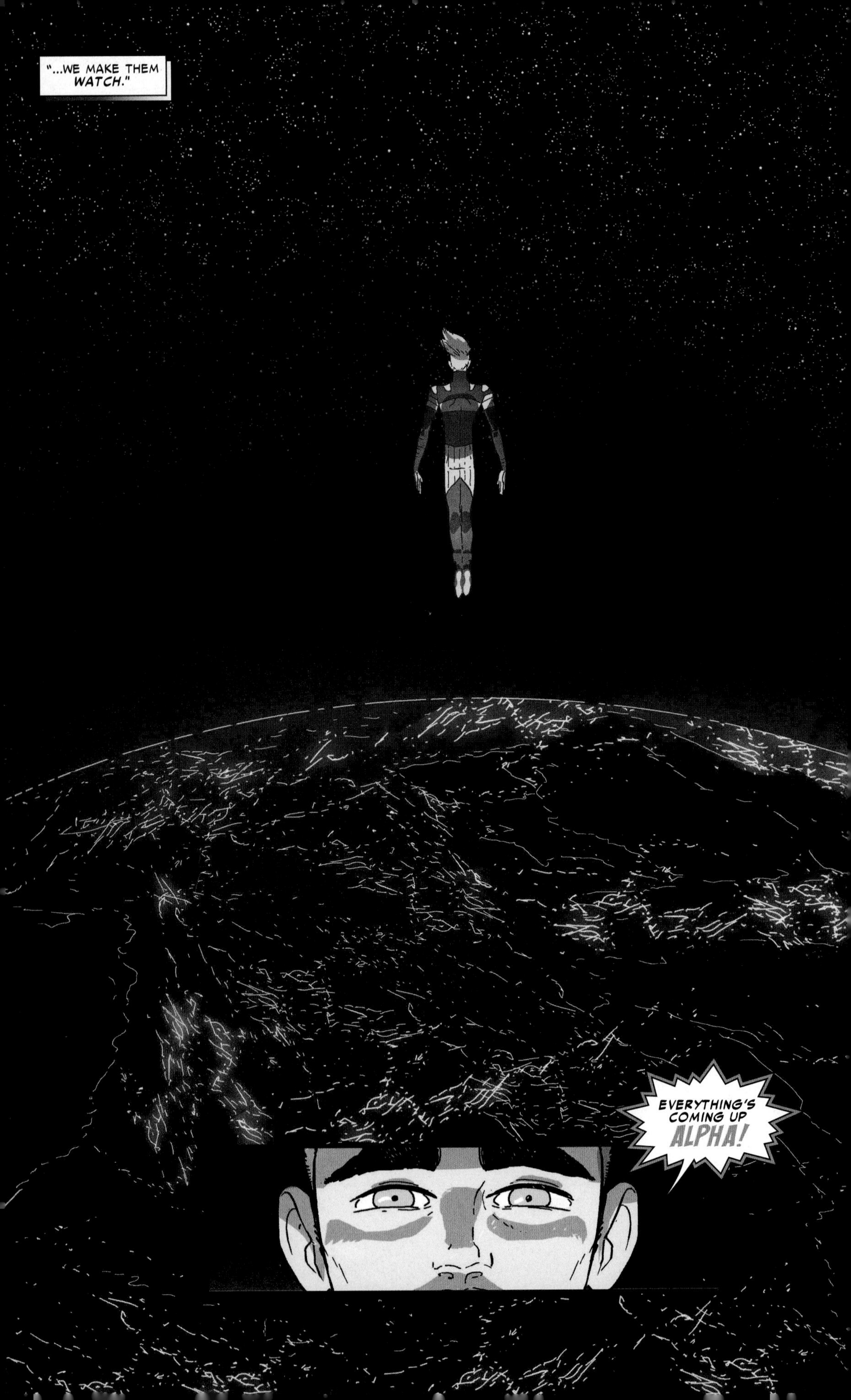
"...WE MAKE THEM WATCH."
EVERYTHING'S COMING UP ALPHA!

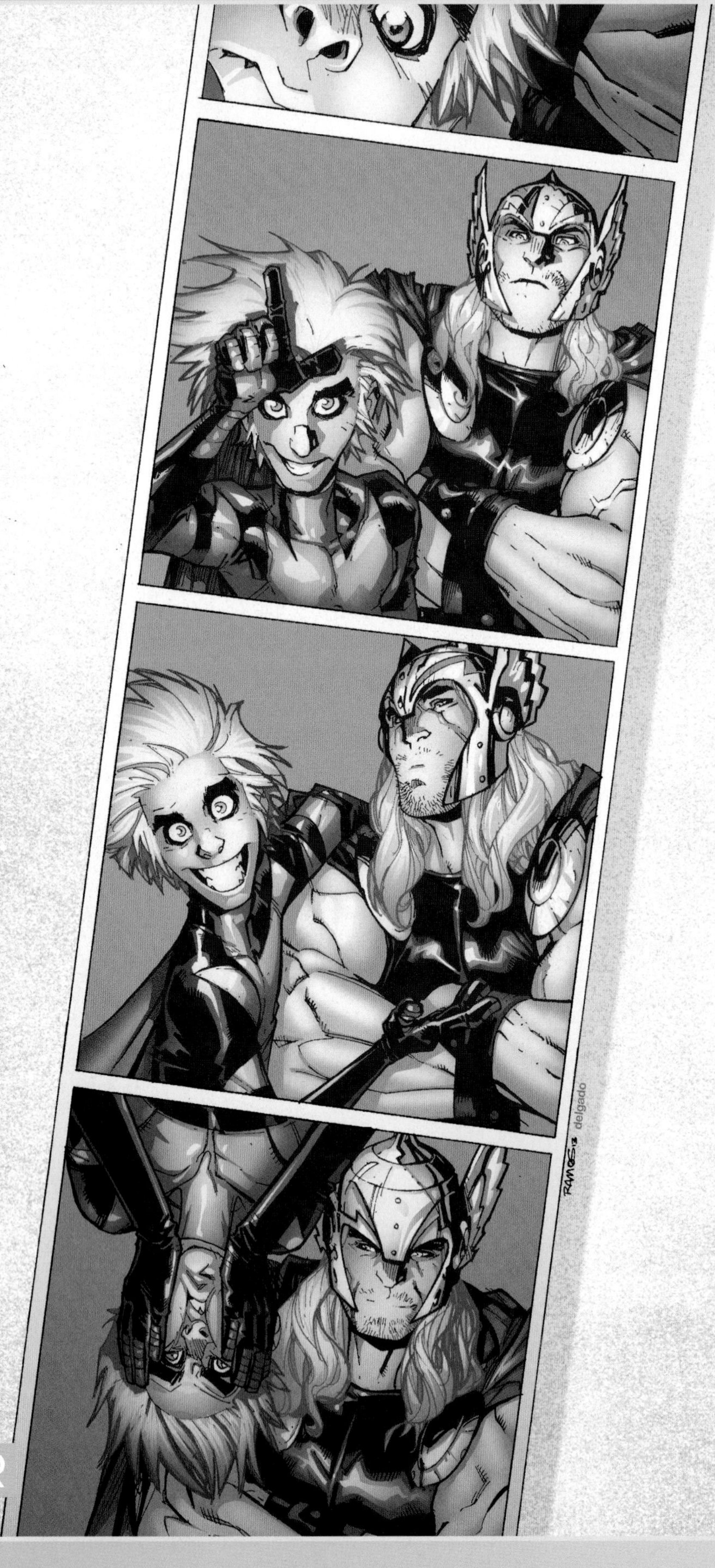
delgado

FOUR

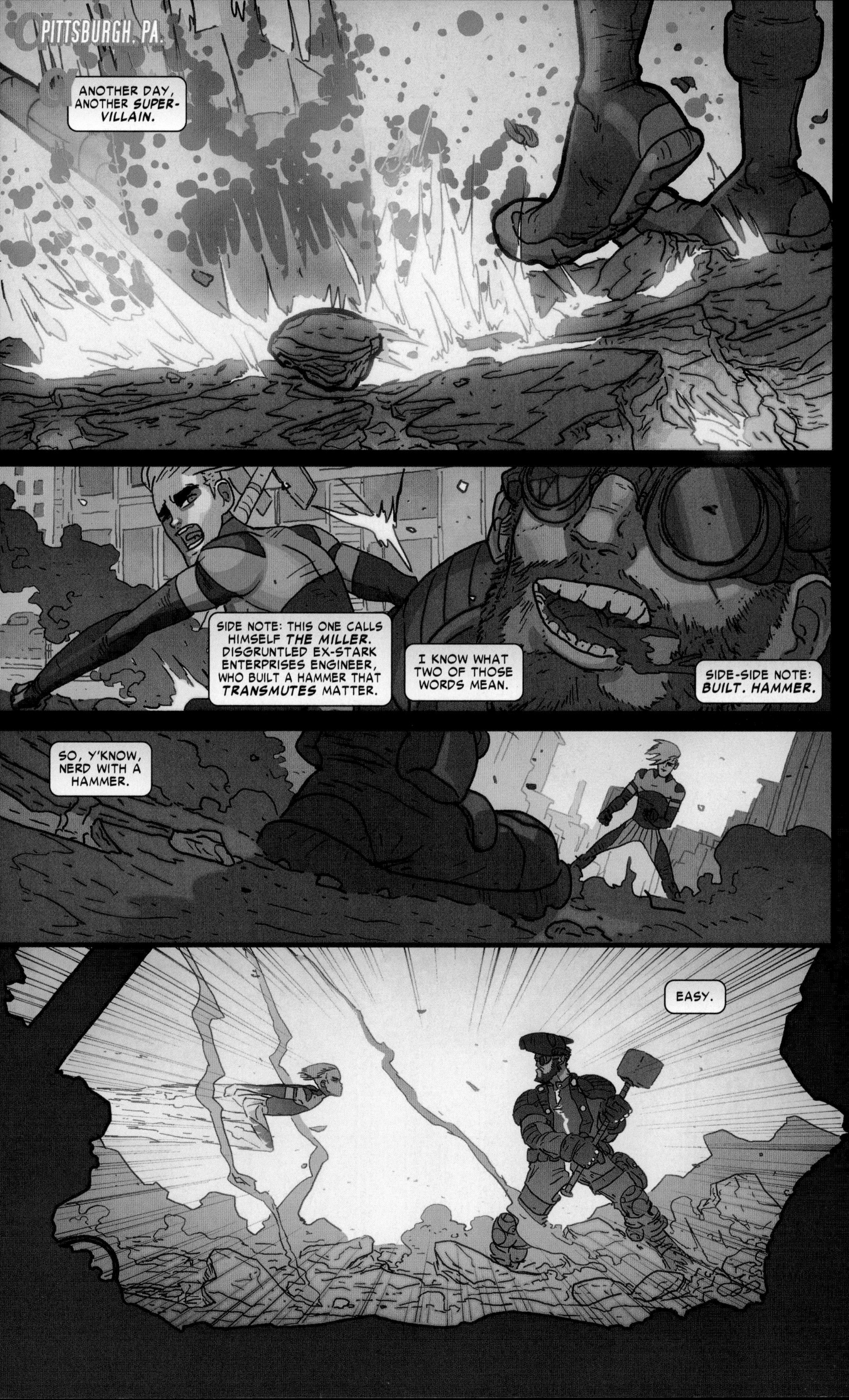
PITTSBURGH, PA.
ANOTHER DAY, ANOTHER SUPER-VILLAIN.
SIDE NOTE: THIS ONE CALLS HIMSELF THE MILLER. DISGRUNTLED EX-STARK ENTERPRISES ENGINEER, WHO BUILT A HAMMER THAT TRANSMUTES MATTER.
I KNOW WHAT TWO OF THOSE WORDS MEAN.
SIDE-SIDE NOTE: BUILT. HAMMER.
SO, Y'KNOW, NERD WITH A HAMMER.
EASY.

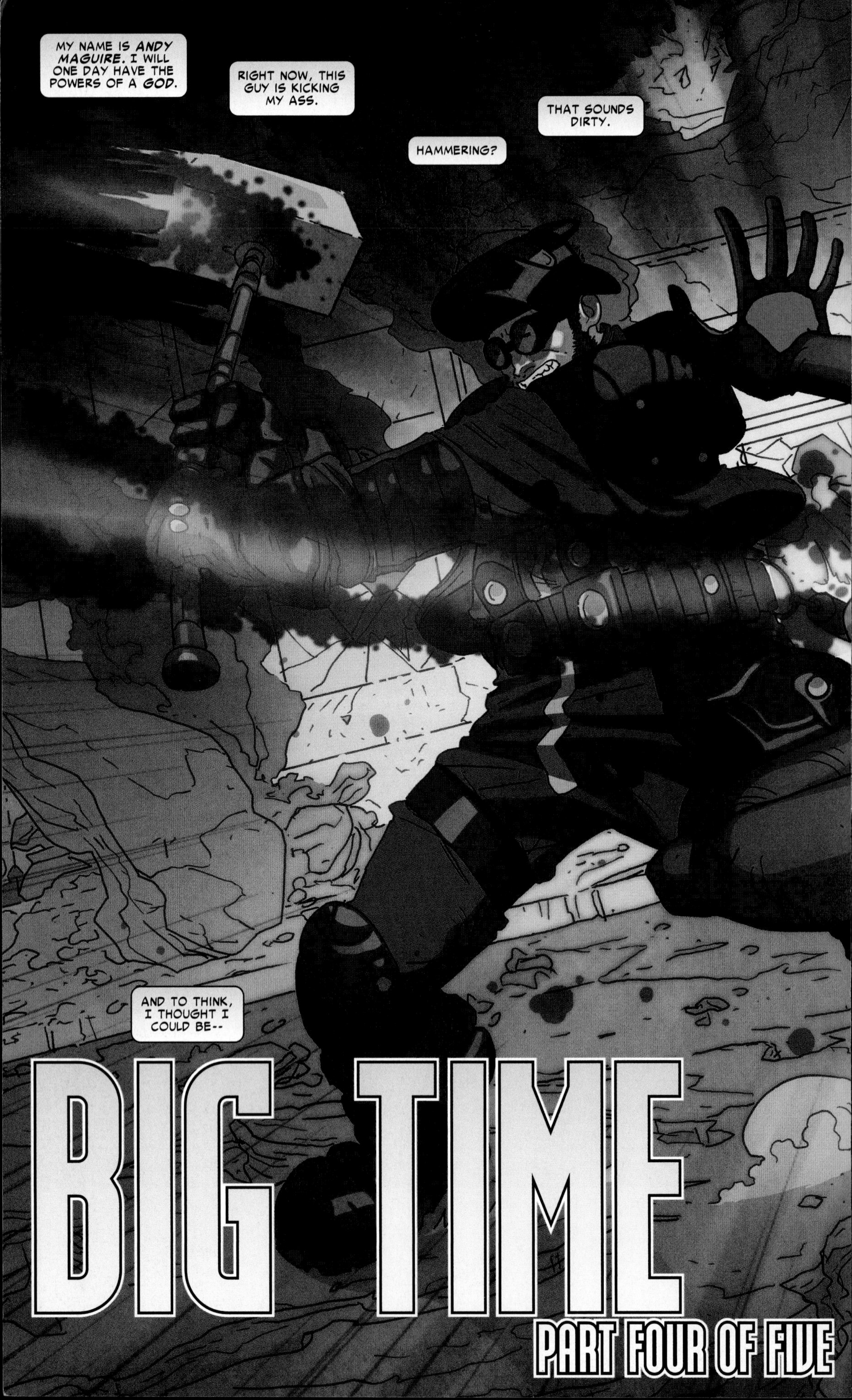
MY NAME IS ANDY MAGUIRE. I WILL ONE DAY HAVE THE POWERS OF A GOD.
RIGHT NOW, THIS GUY IS KICKING MY ASS.
HAMMERING?
THAT SOUNDS DIRTY.
AND TO THINK, I THOUGHT I COULD BE--
BIG TIME
PART FOUR OF FIVE

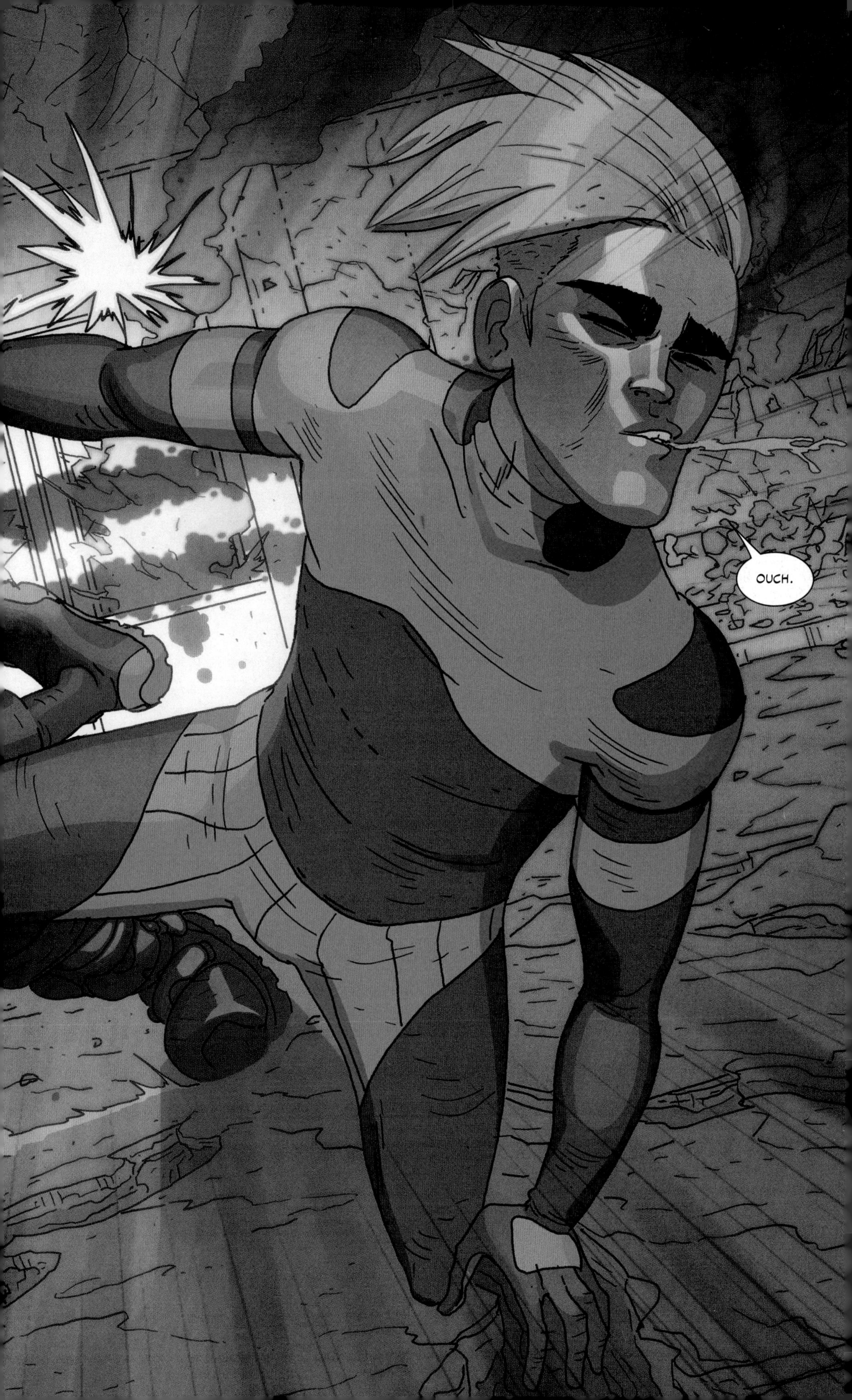
OUCH.

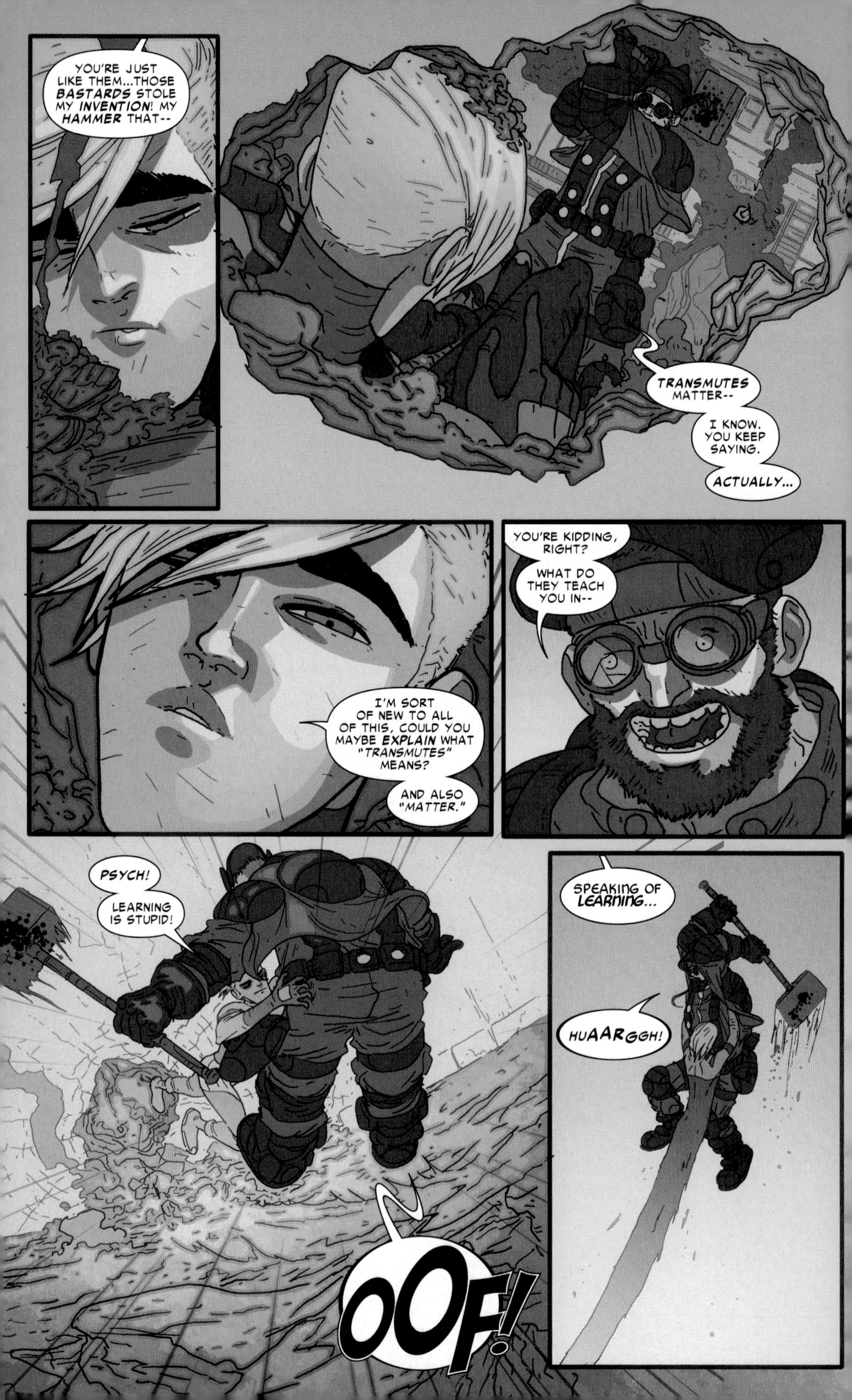
YOU'RE JUST LIKE THEM...THOSE BASTARDS STOLE MY INVENTION! MY HAMMER THAT--
TRANSMUTES MATTER--
I KNOW. YOU KEEP SAYING.
ACTUALLY...
YOU'RE KIDDING, RIGHT?
WHAT DO THEY TEACH YOU IN--
I'M SORT OF NEW TO ALL OF THIS, COULD YOU MAYBE EXPLAIN WHAT "TRANSMUTES" MEANS?
AND ALSO "MATTER."
PSYCH!
LEARNING IS STUPID!
OOF!
SPEAKING OF LEARNING...
HUAARGGH!

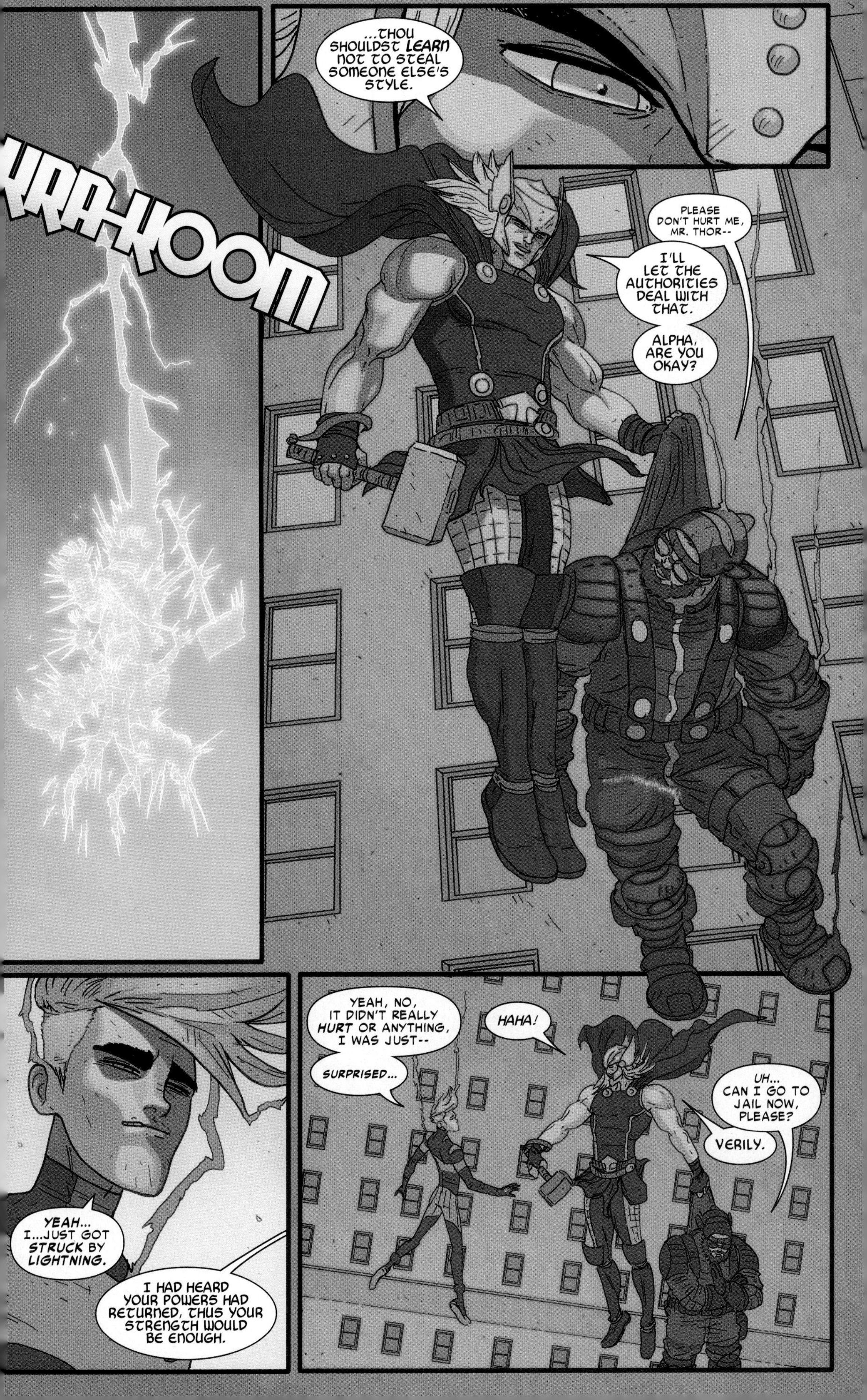

KRA-KOOM
...THOU SHOULDST LEARN NOT TO STEAL SOMEONE ELSE'S STYLE.
PLEASE DON'T HURT ME, MR. THOR--
I'LL LET THE AUTHORITIES DEAL WITH THAT.
ALPHA, ARE YOU OKAY?
YEAH... I...JUST GOT STRUCK BY LIGHTNING.
I HAD HEARD YOUR POWERS HAD RETURNED, THUS YOUR STRENGTH WOULD BE ENOUGH.
YEAH, NO, IT DIDN'T REALLY HURT OR ANYTHING, I WAS JUST--
SURPRISED...
HAHA!
UH... CAN I GO TO JAIL NOW, PLEASE?
VERILY.

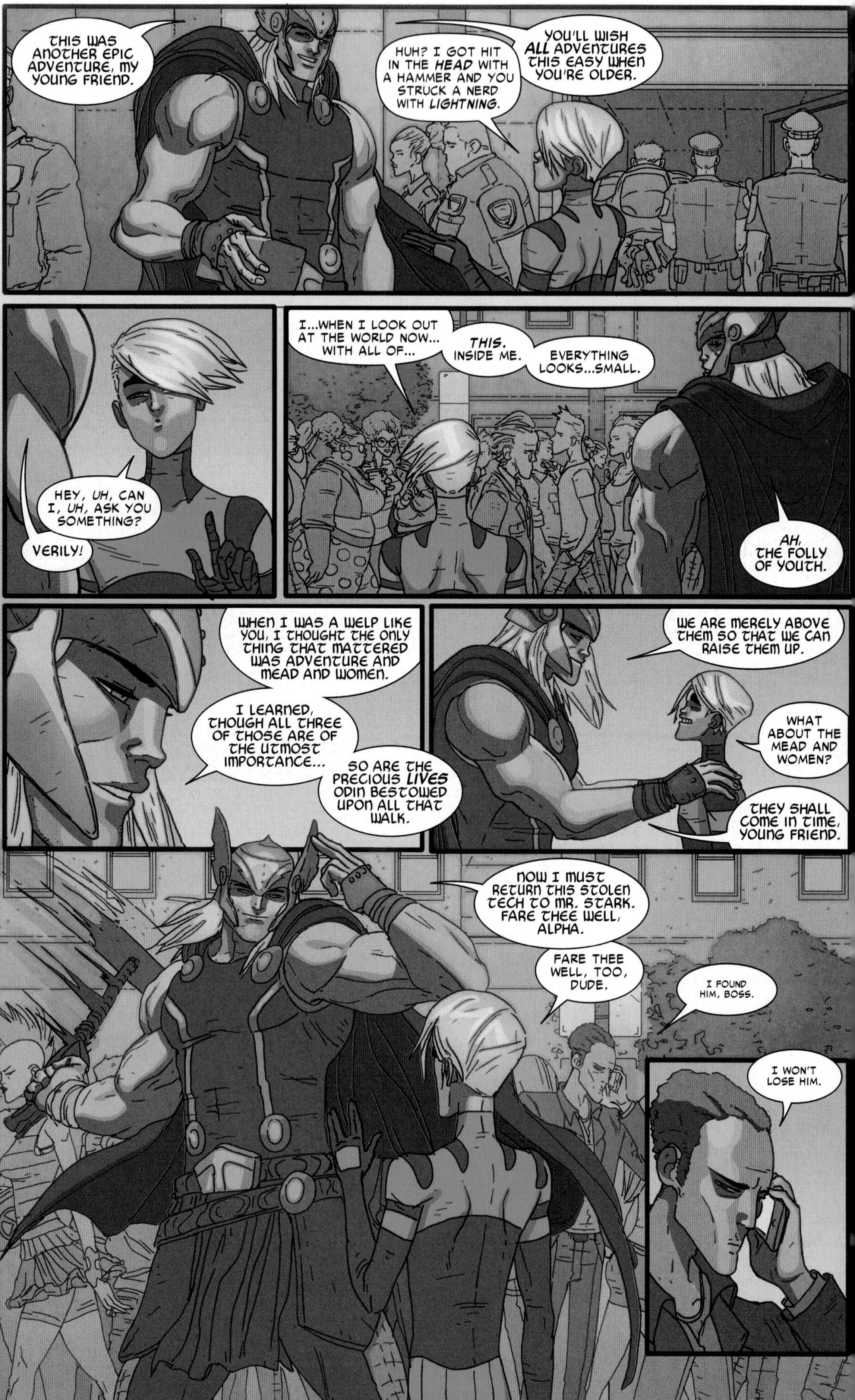
THIS WAS ANOTHER EPIC ADVENTURE, MY YOUNG FRIEND.
HUH? I GOT HIT IN THE HEAD WITH A HAMMER AND YOU STRUCK A NERD WITH LIGHTNING.
YOU'LL WISH ALL ADVENTURES THIS EASY WHEN YOU'RE OLDER.
HEY, UH, CAN I, UH, ASK YOU SOMETHING?
VERILY!
I...WHEN I LOOK OUT AT THE WORLD NOW... WITH ALL OF...
THIS. INSIDE ME.
EVERYTHING LOOKS...SMALL.
AH, THE FOLLY OF YOUTH.
WHEN I WAS A WELP LIKE YOU, I THOUGHT THE ONLY THING THAT MATTERED WAS ADVENTURE AND MEAD AND WOMEN.
I LEARNED, THOUGH ALL THREE OF THOSE ARE OF THE UTMOST IMPORTANCE...
SO ARE THE PRECIOUS LIVES ODIN BESTOWED UPON ALL THAT WALK.
WE ARE MERELY ABOVE THEM SO THAT WE CAN RAISE THEM UP.
WHAT ABOUT THE MEAD AND WOMEN?
THEY SHALL COME IN TIME, YOUNG FRIEND.
NOW I MUST RETURN THIS STOLEN TECH TO MR. STARK. FARE THEE WELL, ALPHA.
FARE THEE WELL, TOO, DUDE.
I FOUND HIM, BOSS.
I WON'T LOSE HIM.

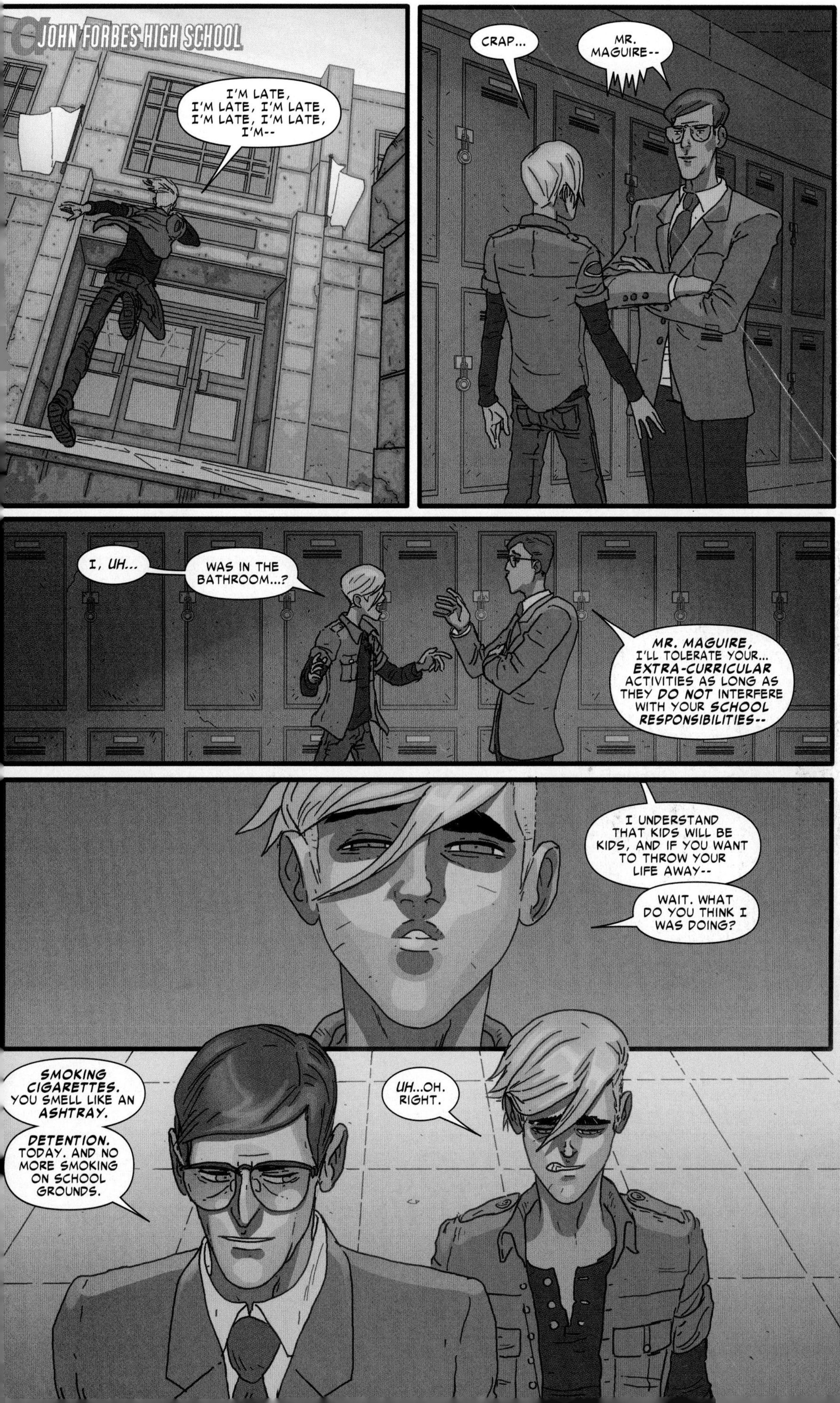
JOHN FORBES HIGH SCHOOL
I'M LATE, I'M LATE, I'M LATE, I'M LATE, I'M LATE, I'M--
CRAP...
MR. MAGUIRE--
I, UH...
WAS IN THE BATHROOM...?
MR. MAGUIRE, I'LL TOLERATE YOUR... EXTRA-CURRICULAR ACTIVITIES AS LONG AS THEY DO NOT INTERFERE WITH YOUR SCHOOL RESPONSIBILITIES--
I UNDERSTAND THAT KIDS WILL BE KIDS, AND IF YOU WANT TO THROW YOUR LIFE AWAY--
WAIT. WHAT DO YOU THINK I WAS DOING?
SMOKING CIGARETTES. YOU SMELL LIKE AN ASHTRAY.
DETENTION. TODAY. AND NO MORE SMOKING ON SCHOOL GROUNDS.
UH...OH. RIGHT.

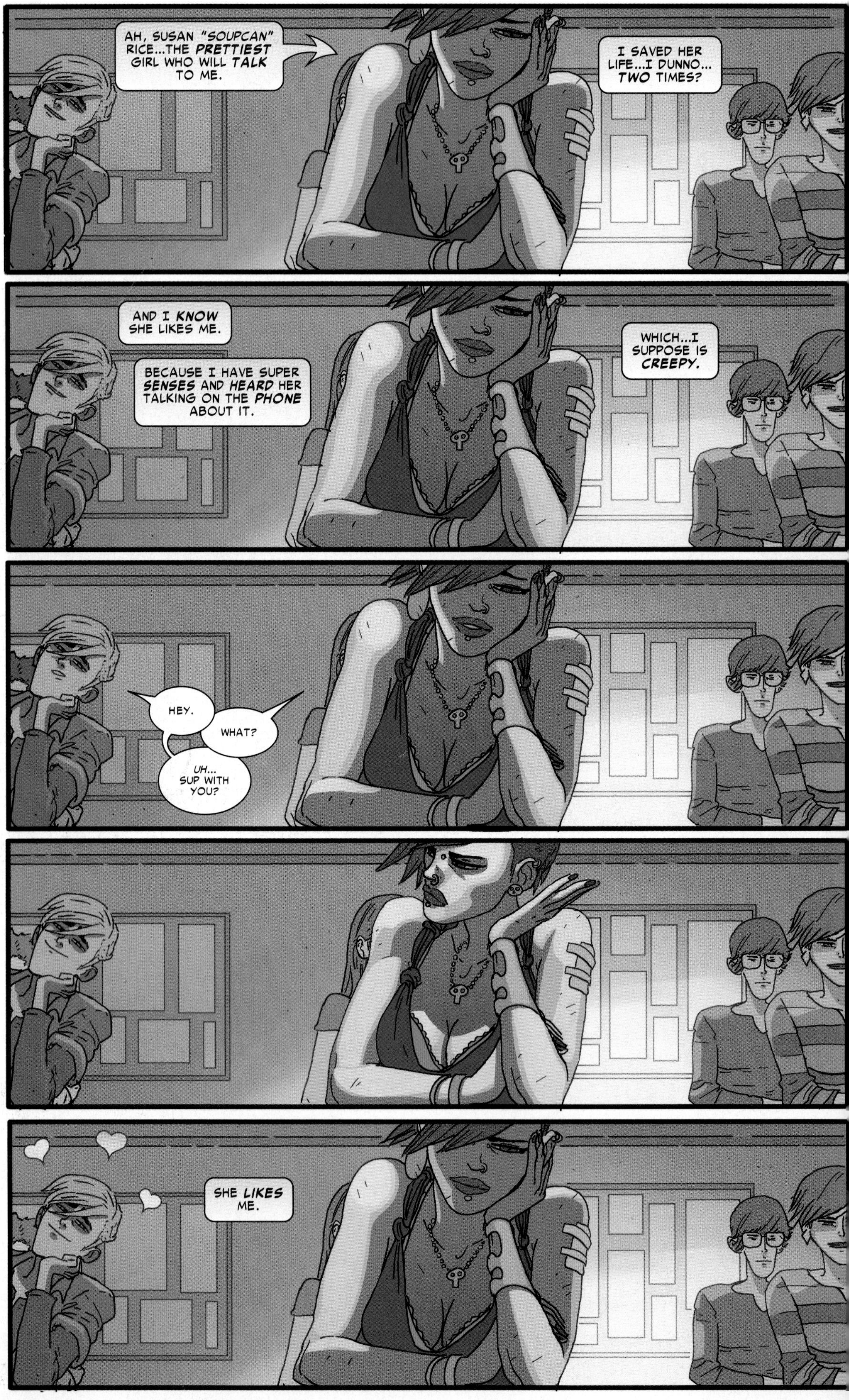
AH, SUSAN "SOUPCAN" RICE...THE PRETTIEST GIRL WHO WILL TALK TO ME.
I SAVED HER LIFE...I DUNNO... TWO TIMES?
AND I KNOW SHE LIKES ME.
BECAUSE I HAVE SUPER SENSES AND HEARD HER TALKING ON THE PHONE ABOUT IT.
WHICH...I SUPPOSE IS CREEPY.
HEY.
WHAT?
UH... SUP WITH YOU?
SHE LIKES ME.

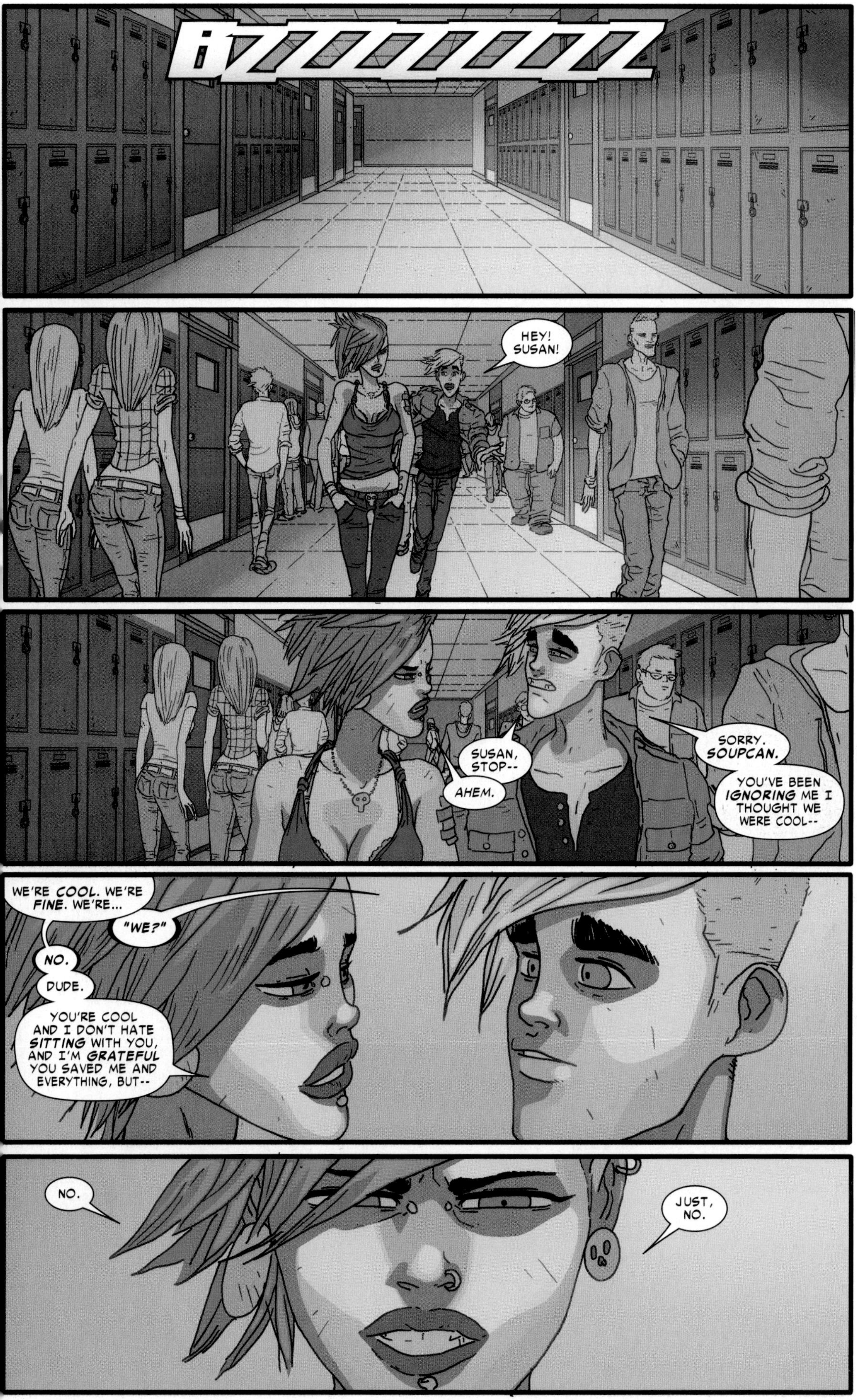
BZZZZZZZ
HEY! SUSAN!
SUSAN, STOP--
AHEM.
SORRY. SOUPCAN.
YOU'VE BEEN IGNORING ME I THOUGHT WE WERE COOL--
WE'RE COOL. WE'RE FINE. WE'RE...
"WE?"
NO.
DUDE.
YOU'RE COOL AND I DON'T HATE SITTING WITH YOU, AND I'M GRATEFUL YOU SAVED ME AND EVERYTHING, BUT--
NO.
JUST, NO.

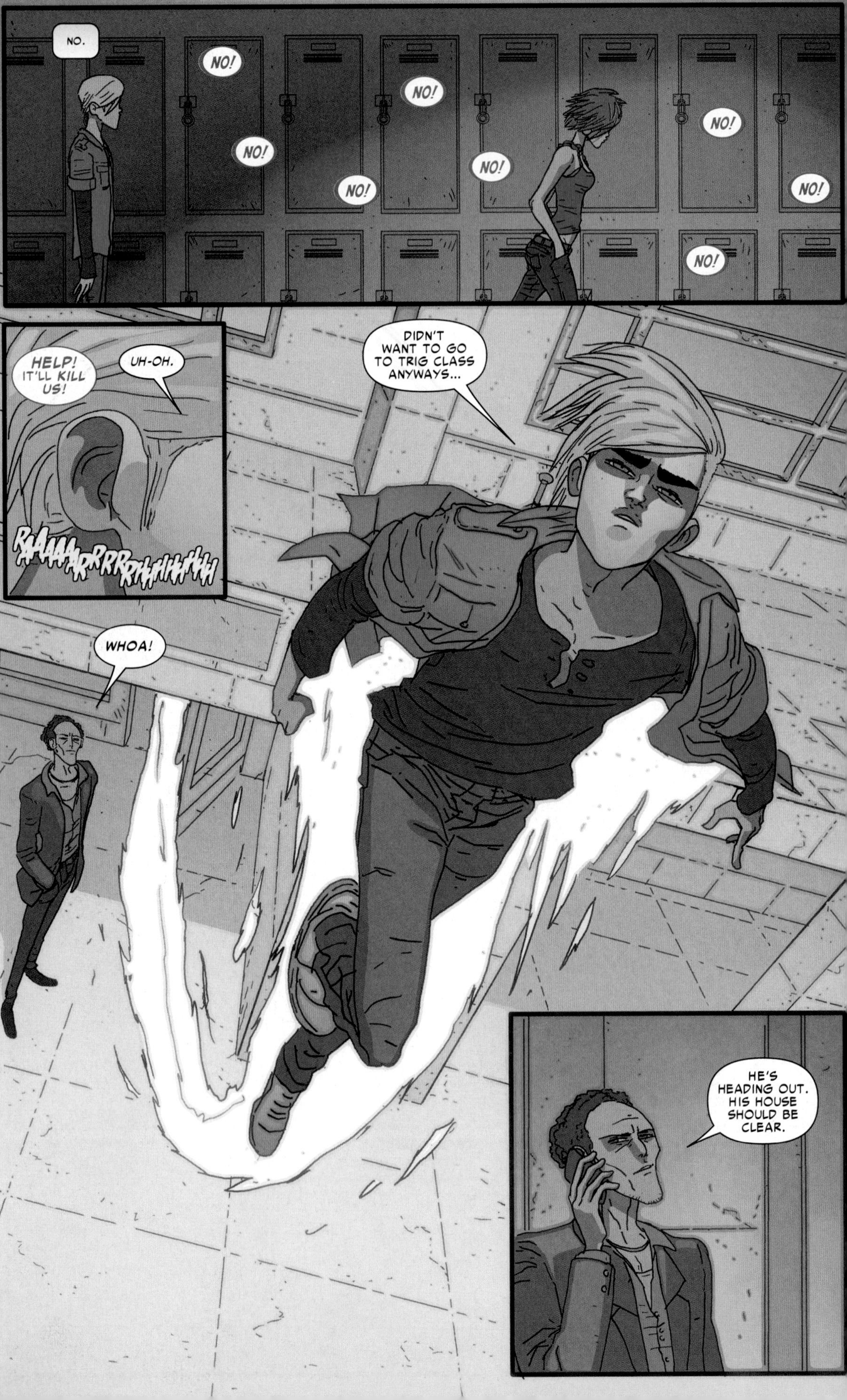
NO.
NO!
NO!
NO!
NO!
NO!
NO!
NO!
NO!
HELP! IT'LL KILL US!
UH-OH.
RAAAAARRRRHHHHHH
DIDN'T WANT TO GO TO TRIG CLASS ANYWAYS...
WHOA!
HE'S HEADING OUT. HIS HOUSE SHOULD BE CLEAR.

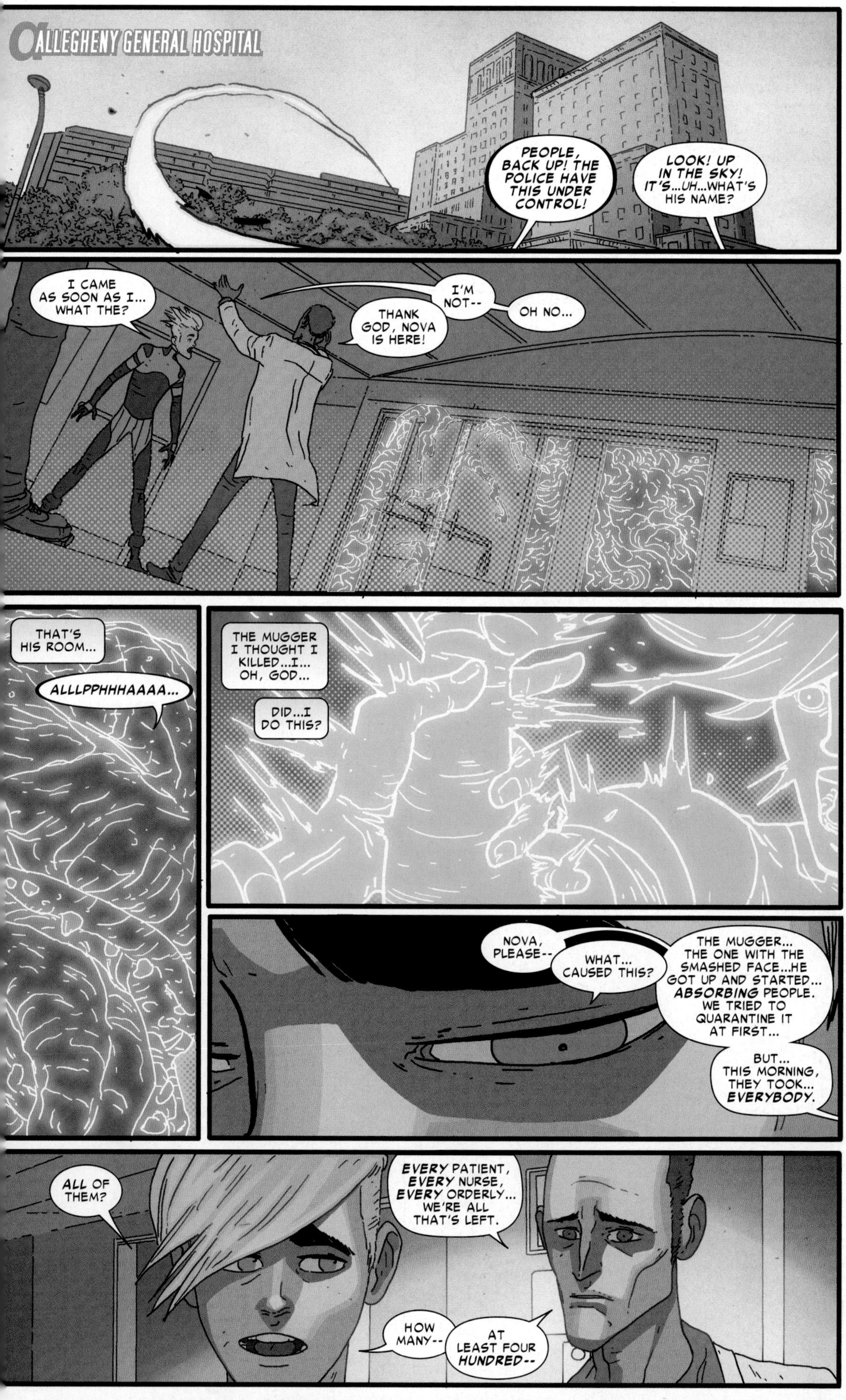
ALLEGHENY GENERAL HOSPITAL
PEOPLE, BACK UP! THE POLICE HAVE THIS UNDER CONTROL!
LOOK! UP IN THE SKY! IT'S...UH...WHAT'S HIS NAME?
I CAME AS SOON AS I... WHAT THE?
THANK GOD, NOVA IS HERE!
I'M NOT--
OH NO...
THAT'S HIS ROOM...
ALLLPPHHHAAAA...
THE MUGGER I THOUGHT I KILLED...I... OH, GOD...
DID...I DO THIS?
NOVA, PLEASE--
WHAT... CAUSED THIS?
THE MUGGER... THE ONE WITH THE SMASHED FACE...HE GOT UP AND STARTED... ABSORBING PEOPLE. WE TRIED TO QUARANTINE IT AT FIRST...
BUT... THIS MORNING, THEY TOOK... EVERYBODY.
ALL OF THEM?
EVERY PATIENT, EVERY NURSE, EVERY ORDERLY... WE'RE ALL THAT'S LEFT.
HOW MANY--
AT LEAST FOUR HUNDRED--

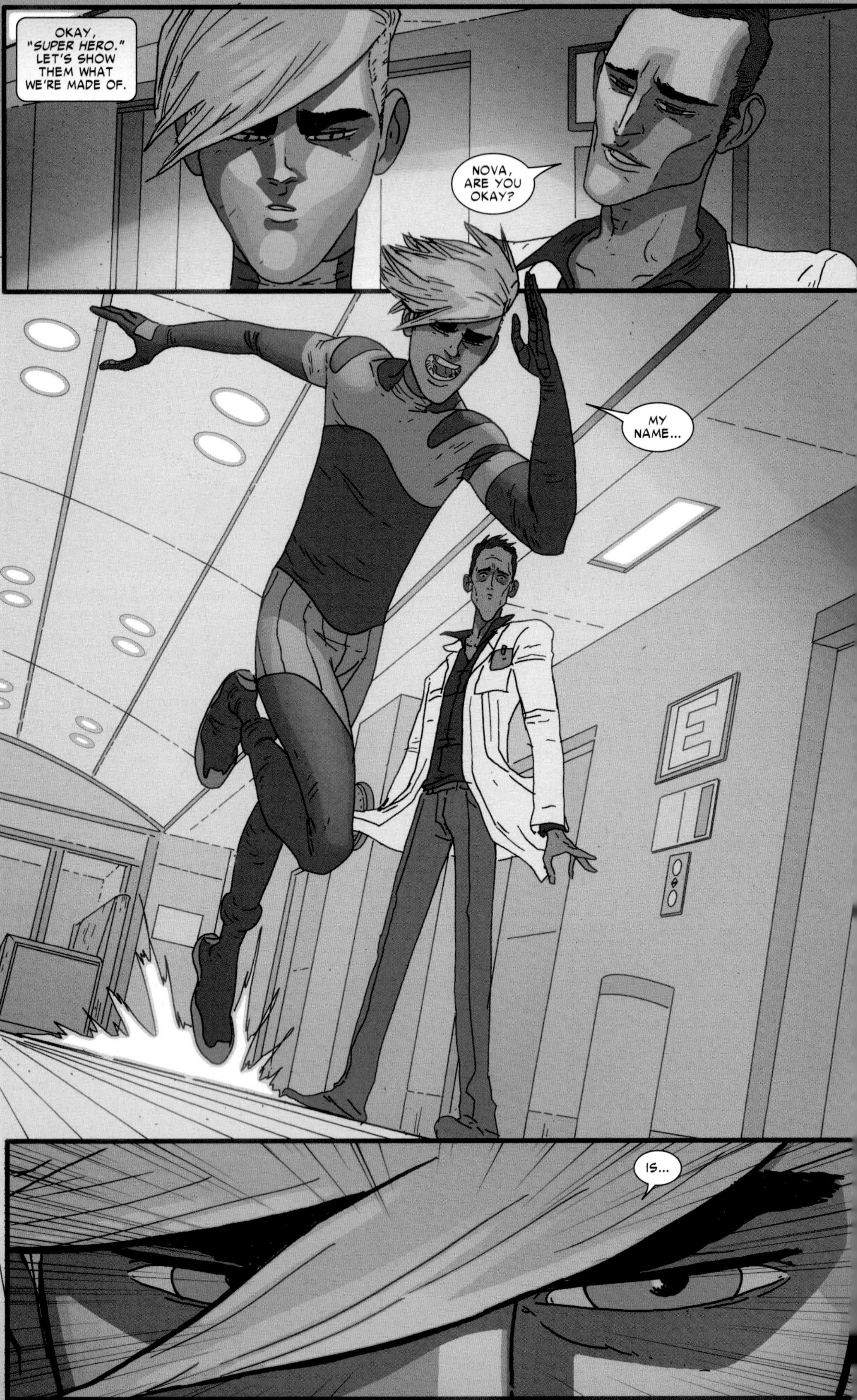
OKAY, "SUPER HERO." LET'S SHOW THEM WHAT WE'RE MADE OF.
NOVA, ARE YOU OKAY?
MY NAME...
IS...

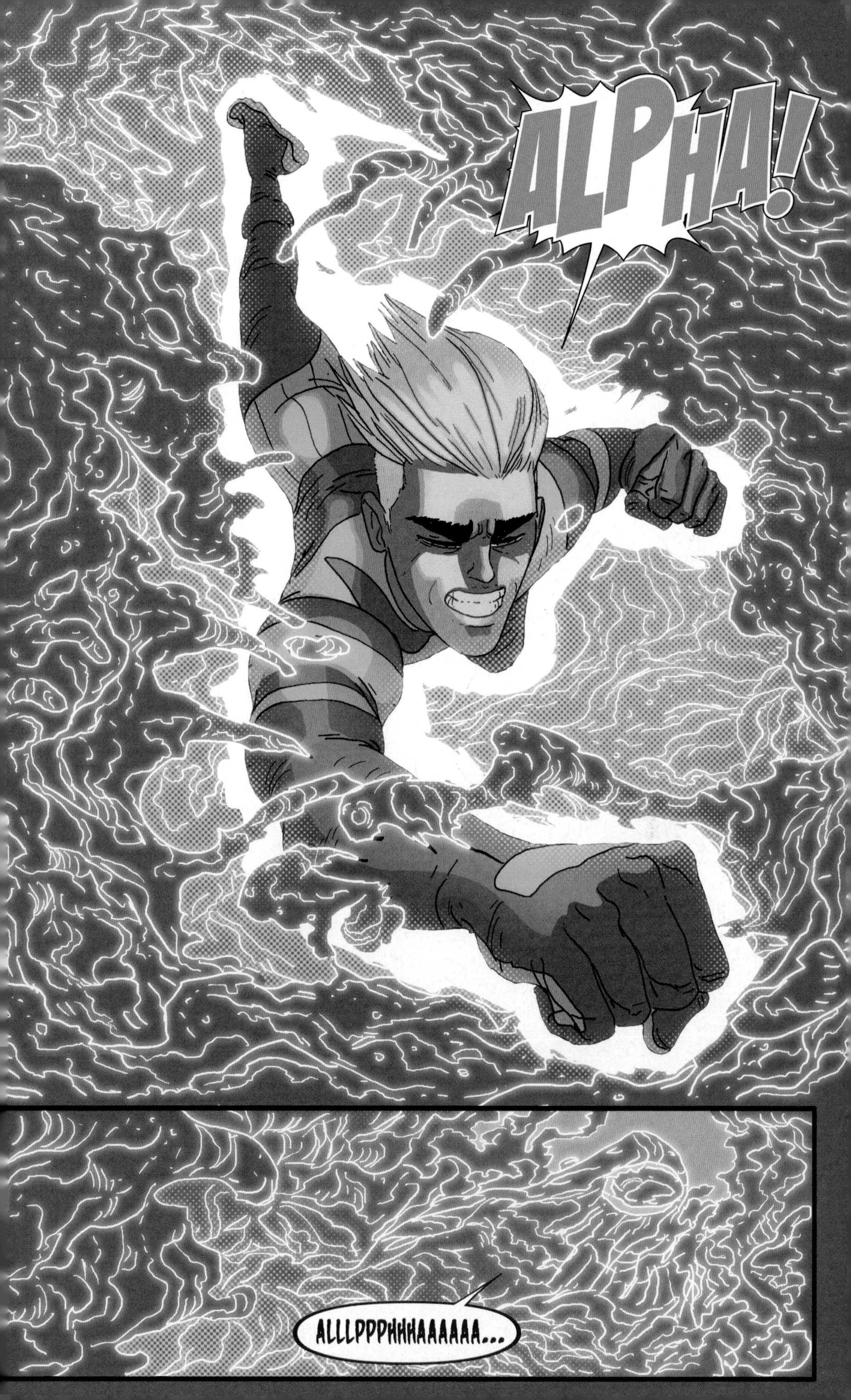
ALPHA!
ALLLPPPHHHAAAAAA...

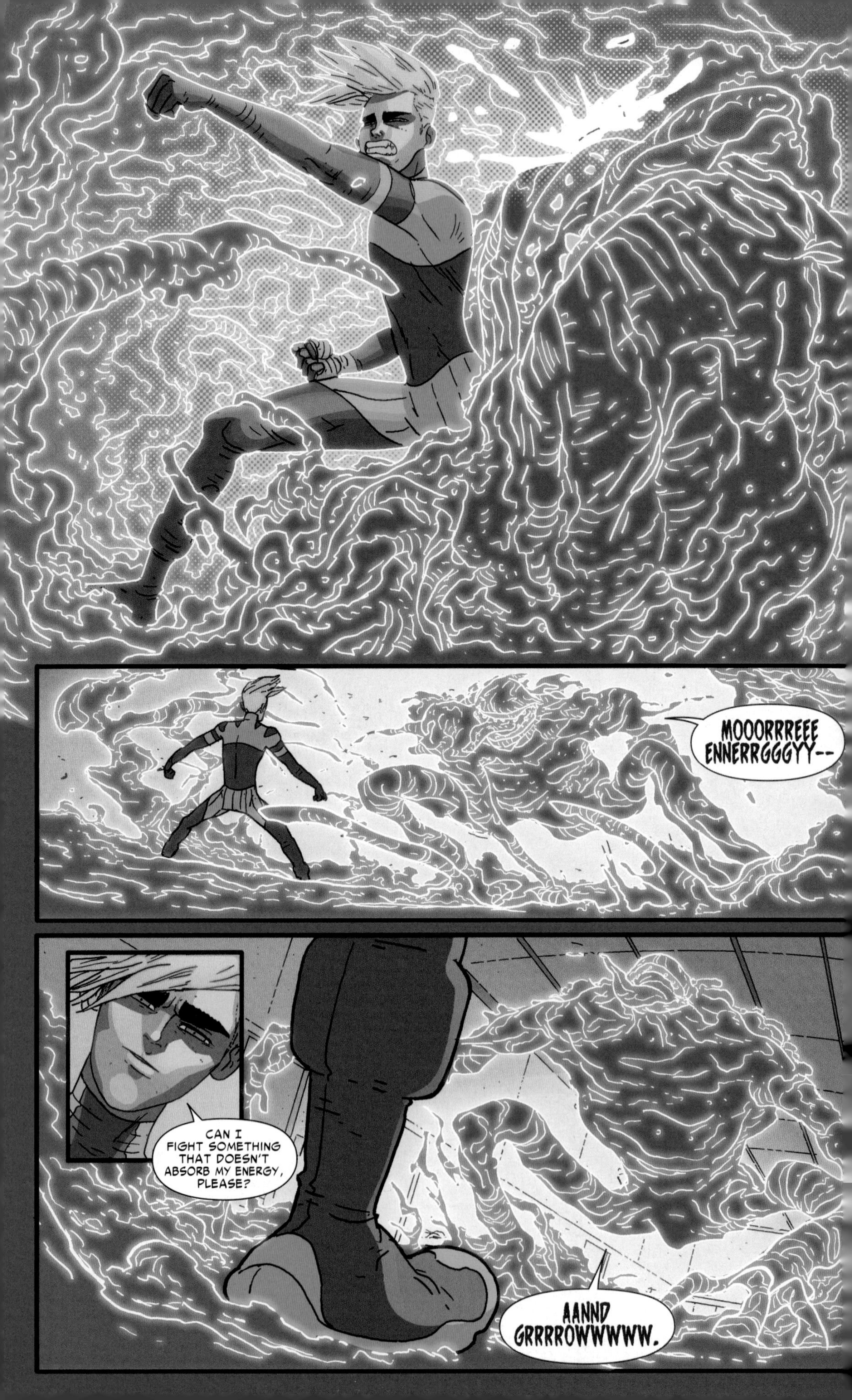
MOOORRREEE ENNERRGGGYY--
CAN I FIGHT SOMETHING THAT DOESN'T ABSORB MY ENERGY, PLEASE?
AANND GRRRROWWWWW.

ACK!

FEED!

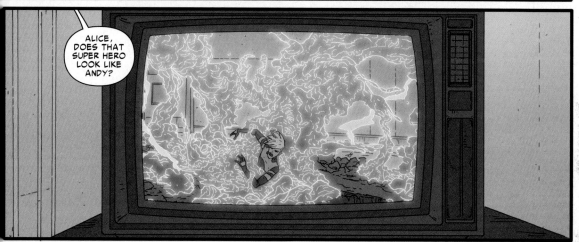

ALICE, DOES THAT SUPER HERO LOOK LIKE ANDY?

HUH? NO. HE DOESN'T HAVE HIS POWERS ANYMORE--

YOU SURE?

YEAH-- I...I KNOW! I MEAN, I AM HIS MOTHER--

KNOCK KNOCK

YES?

IS THIS ANDY MAGUIRE'S HOUSE?

WHAT'S THIS ABOUT?

IS HE HERE?

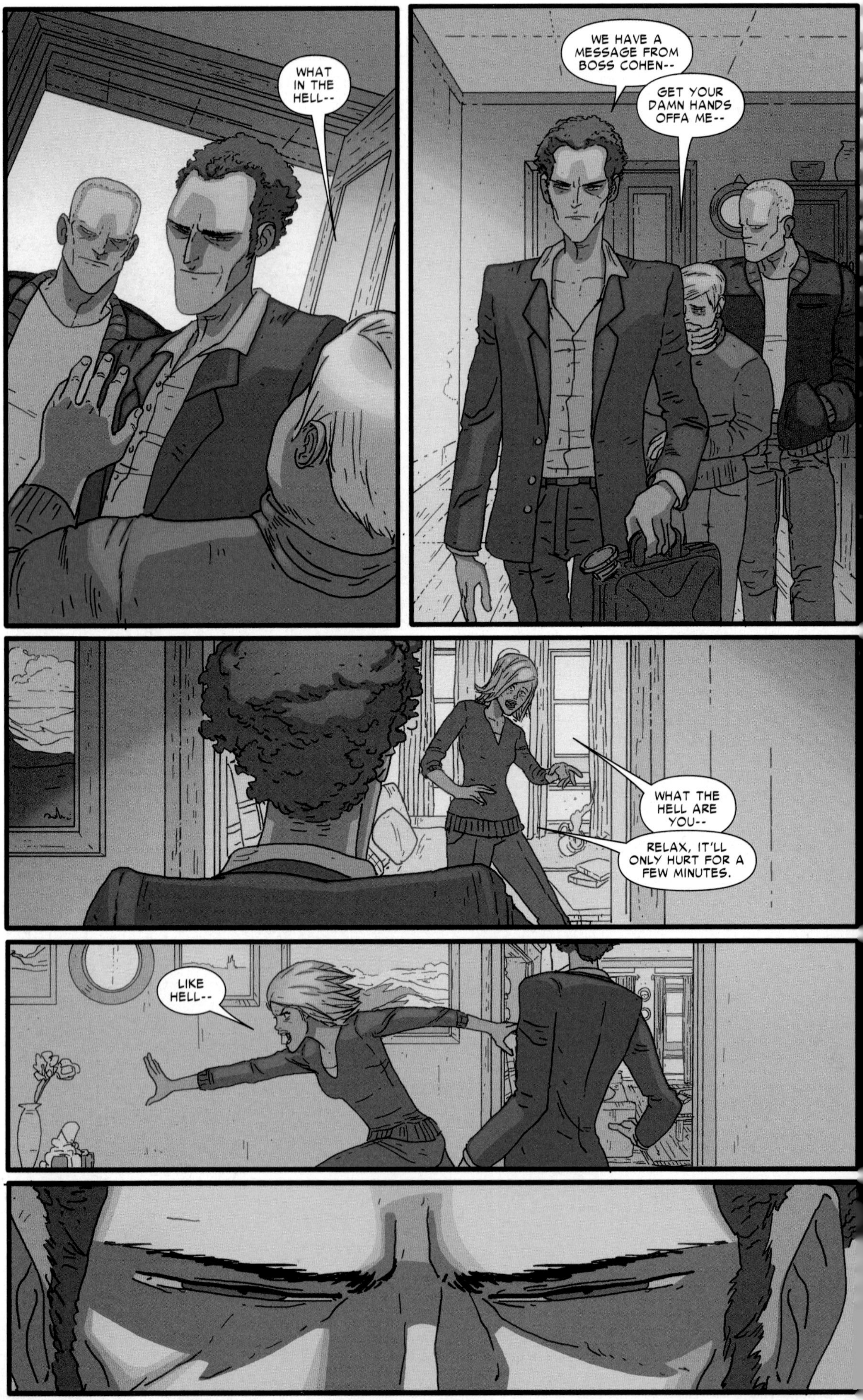
WHAT IN THE HELL--
WE HAVE A MESSAGE FROM BOSS COHEN--
GET YOUR DAMN HANDS OFFA ME--
WHAT THE HELL ARE YOU--
RELAX, IT'LL ONLY HURT FOR A FEW MINUTES.
LIKE HELL--

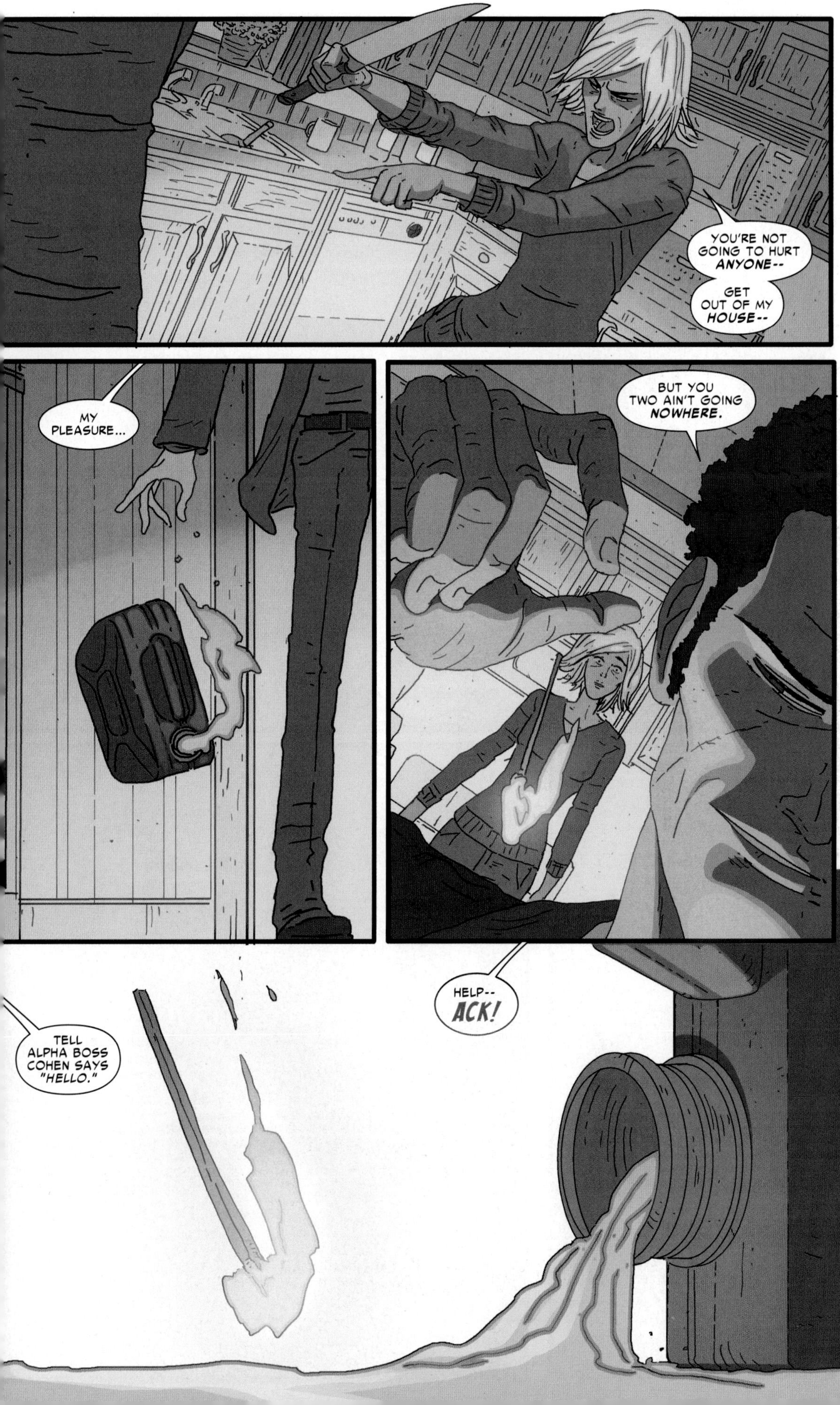
YOU'RE NOT GOING TO HURT ANYONE--
GET OUT OF MY HOUSE--
MY PLEASURE...
BUT YOU TWO AIN'T GOING NOWHERE.
TELL ALPHA BOSS COHEN SAYS "HELLO."
HELP-- ACK!

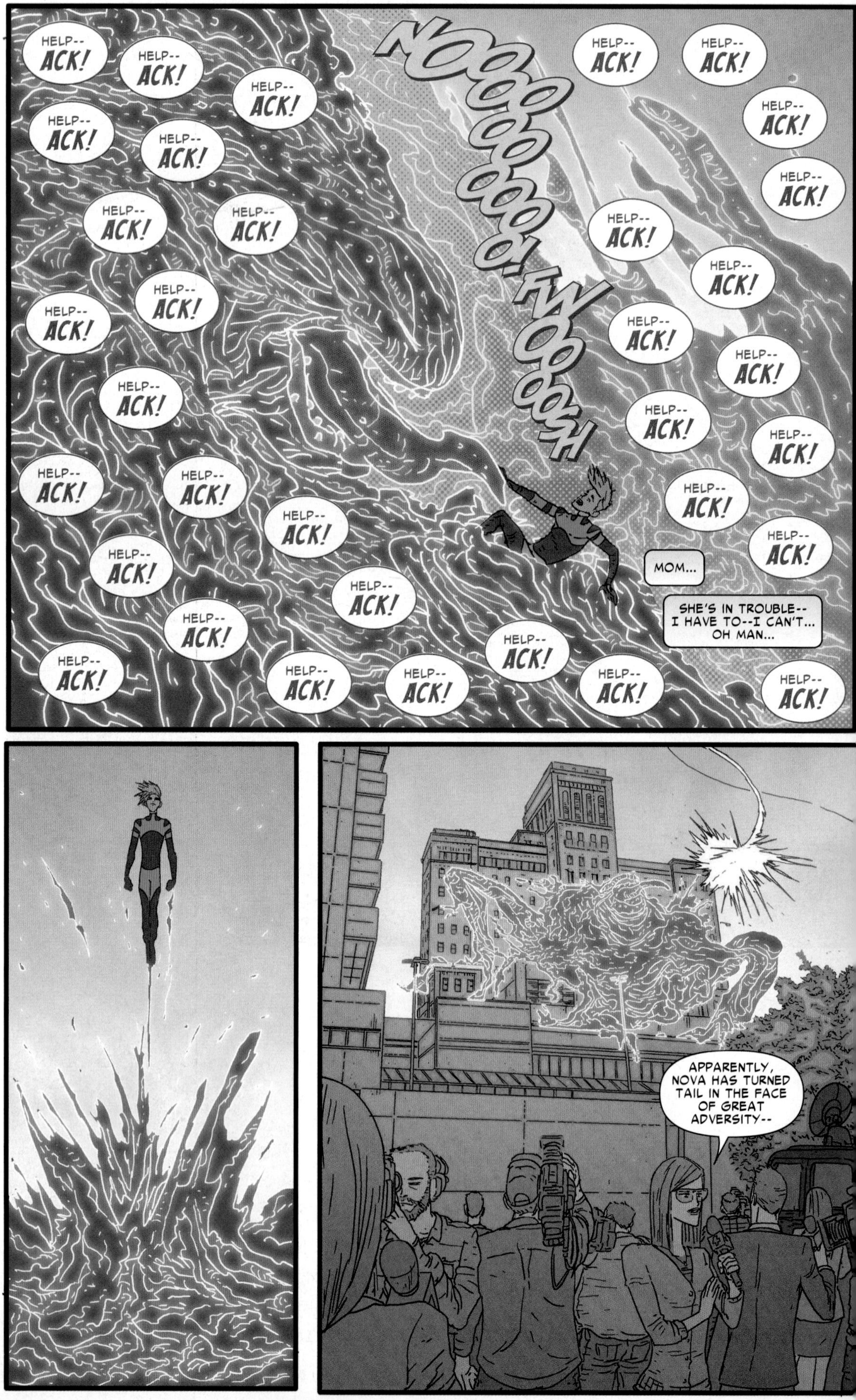
HELP-- ACK!
HELP-- ACK!
HELP-- ACK!
HELP-- ACK!
HELP-- ACK!
HELP-- ACK!
HELP-- ACK!
HELP-- ACK!
HELP-- ACK!
HELP-- ACK!
HELP-- ACK!
HELP-- ACK!
HELP-- ACK!
HELP-- ACK!
HELP-- ACK!
HELP-- ACK!
HELP-- ACK!
HELP-- ACK!
HELP-- ACK!
HELP-- ACK!
HELP-- ACK!
HELP-- ACK!
NOOOOOOOOOO!
FWOOOOOSH
HELP-- ACK!
HELP-- ACK!
HELP-- ACK!
HELP-- ACK!
HELP-- ACK!
HELP-- ACK!
HELP-- ACK!
HELP-- ACK!
HELP-- ACK!
HELP-- ACK!
HELP-- ACK!
HELP-- ACK!
MOM...
SHE'S IN TROUBLE-- I HAVE TO--I CAN'T... OH MAN...
APPARENTLY, NOVA HAS TURNED TAIL IN THE FACE OF GREAT ADVERSITY--

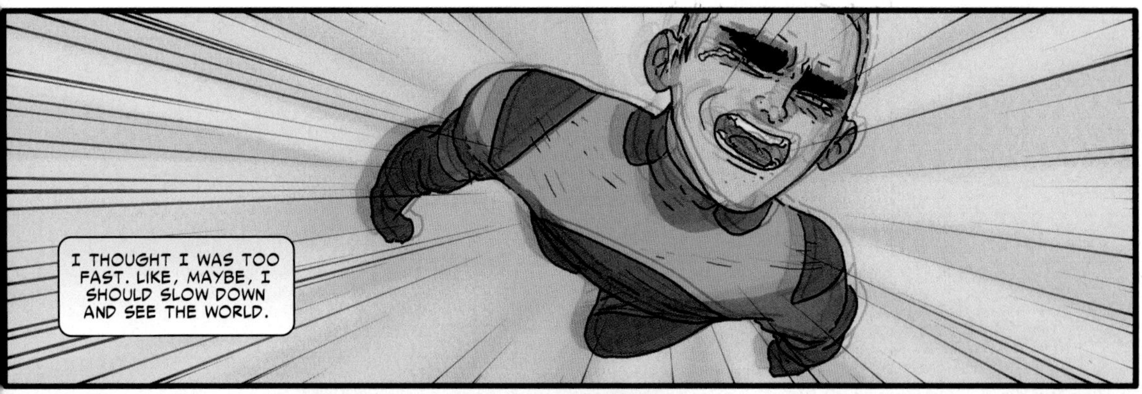
I THOUGHT I WAS TOO FAST. LIKE, MAYBE, I SHOULD SLOW DOWN AND SEE THE WORLD.

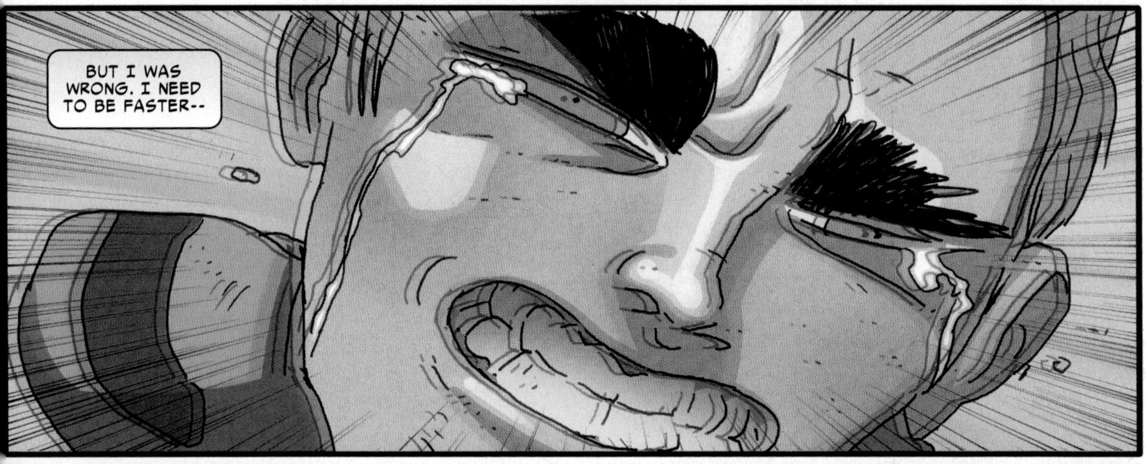
BUT I WAS WRONG. I NEED TO BE FASTER--

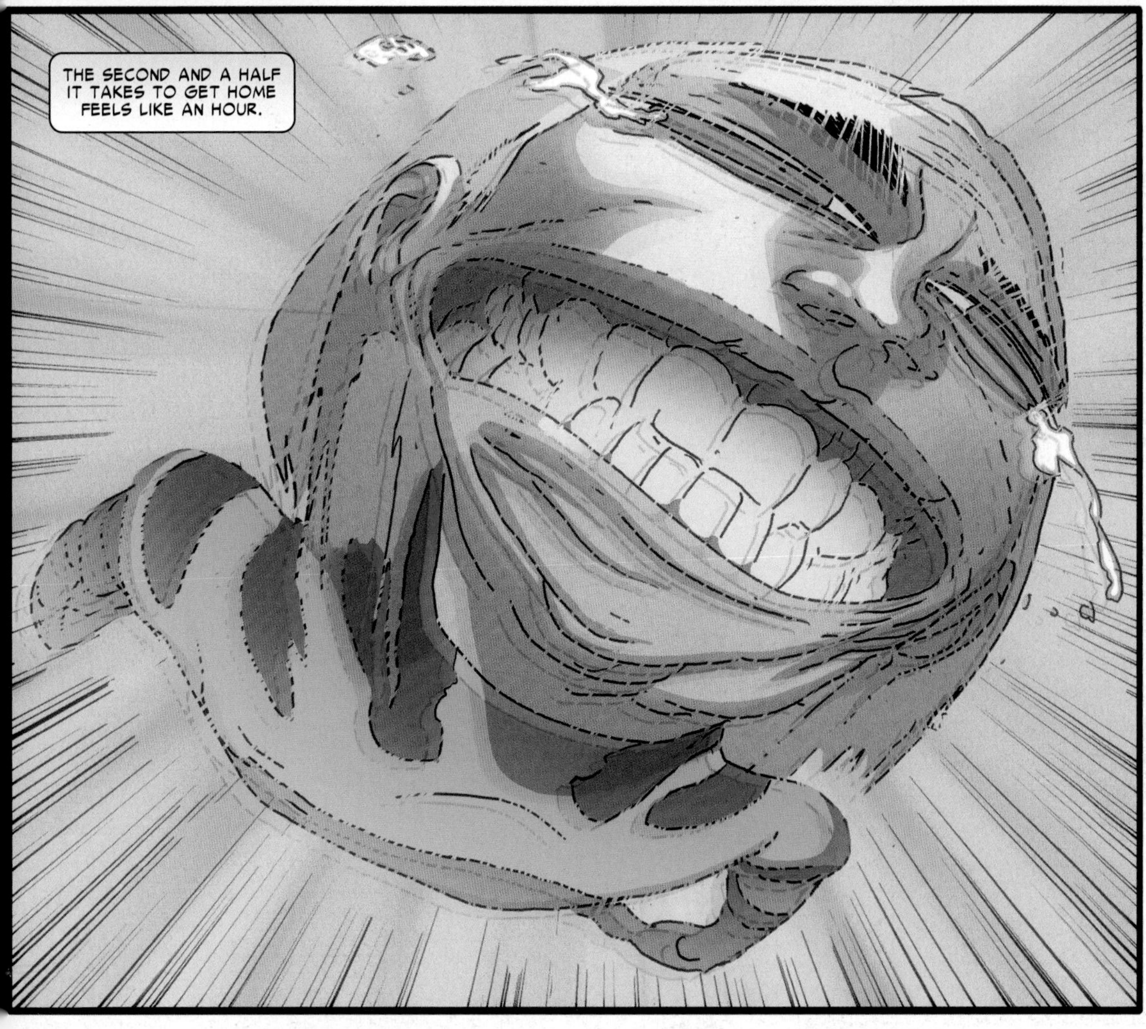
THE SECOND AND A HALF IT TAKES TO GET HOME FEELS LIKE AN HOUR.

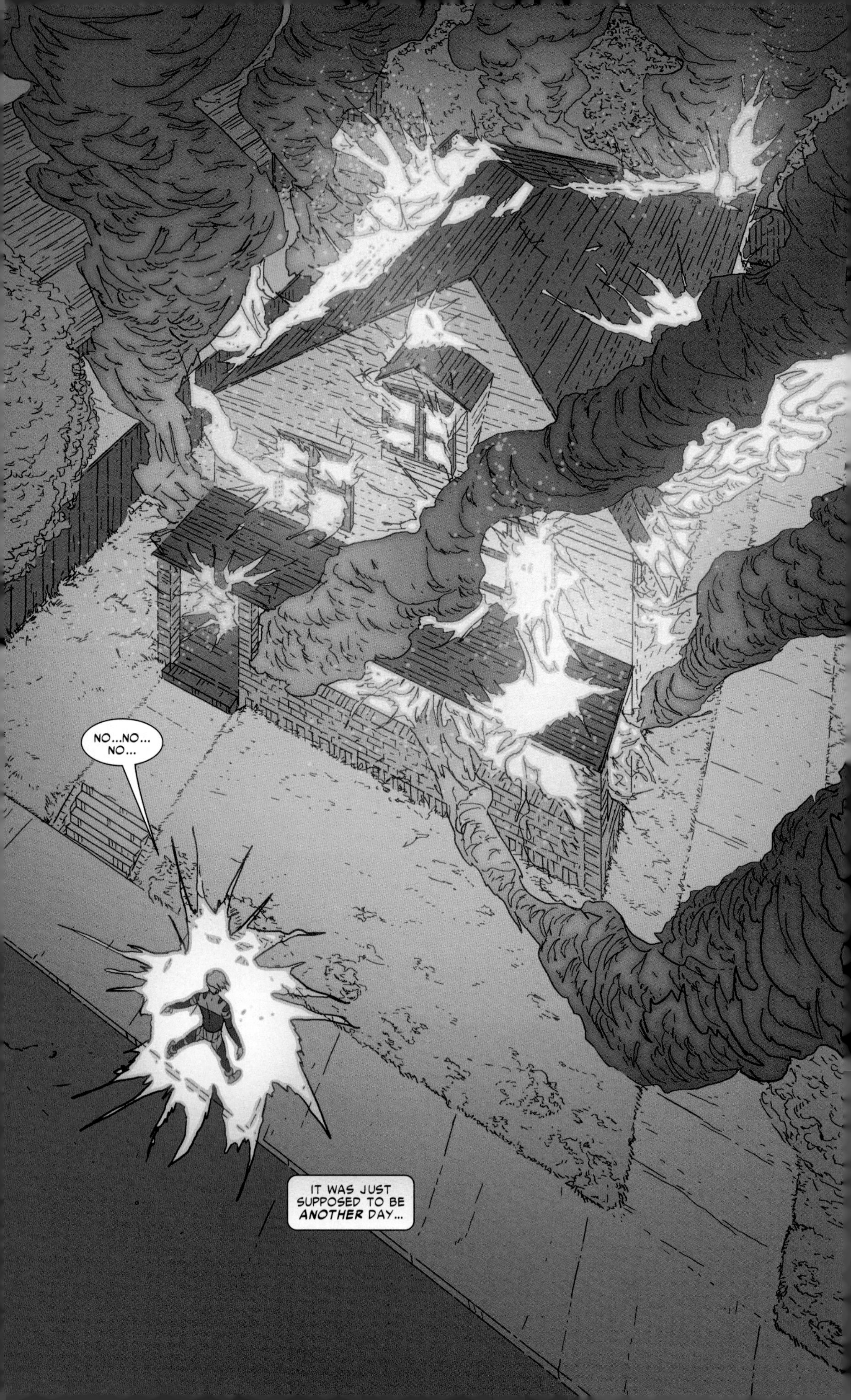
NO...NO... NO...
IT WAS JUST SUPPOSED TO BE ANOTHER DAY...

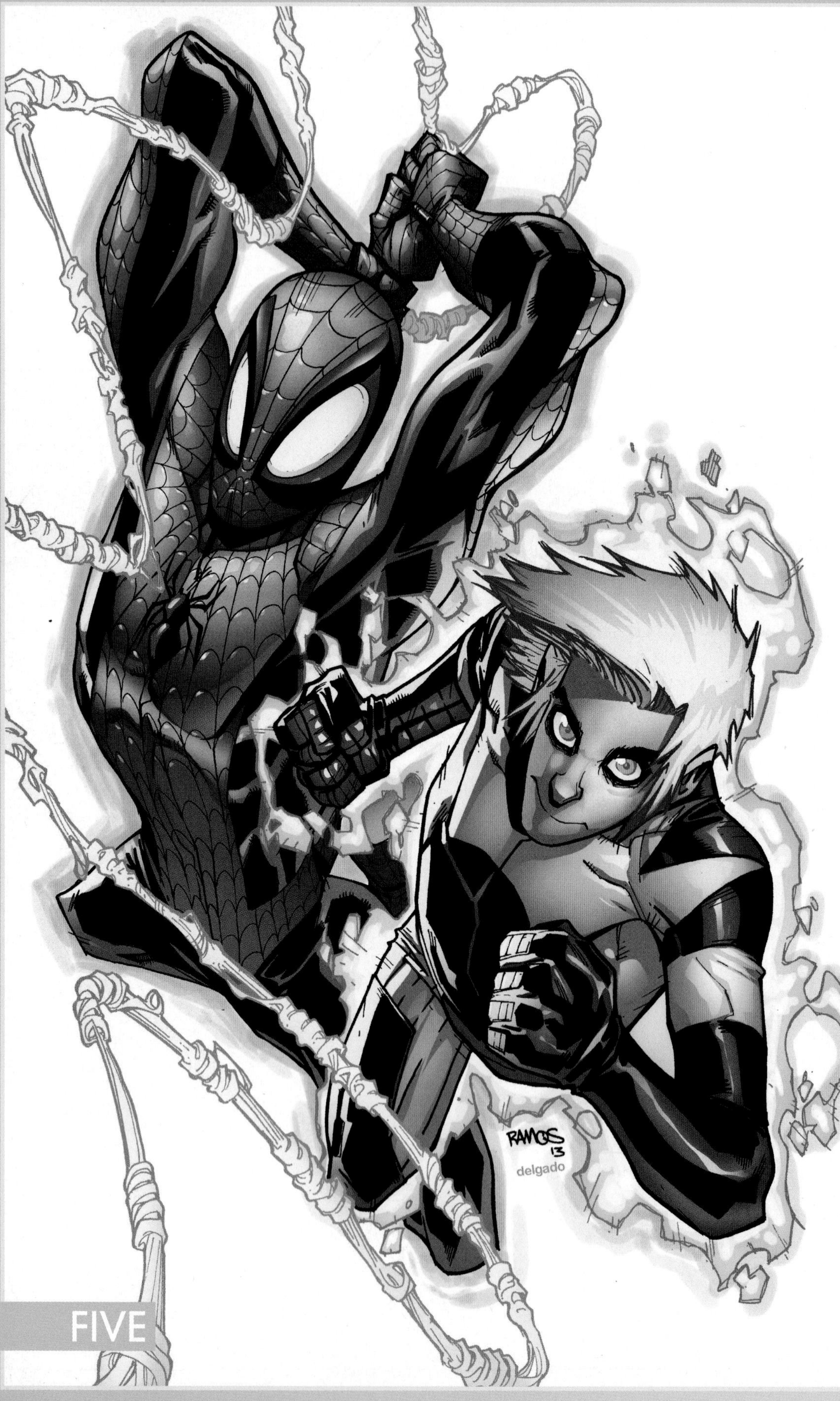
RAMOS
'13
delgado

FIVE

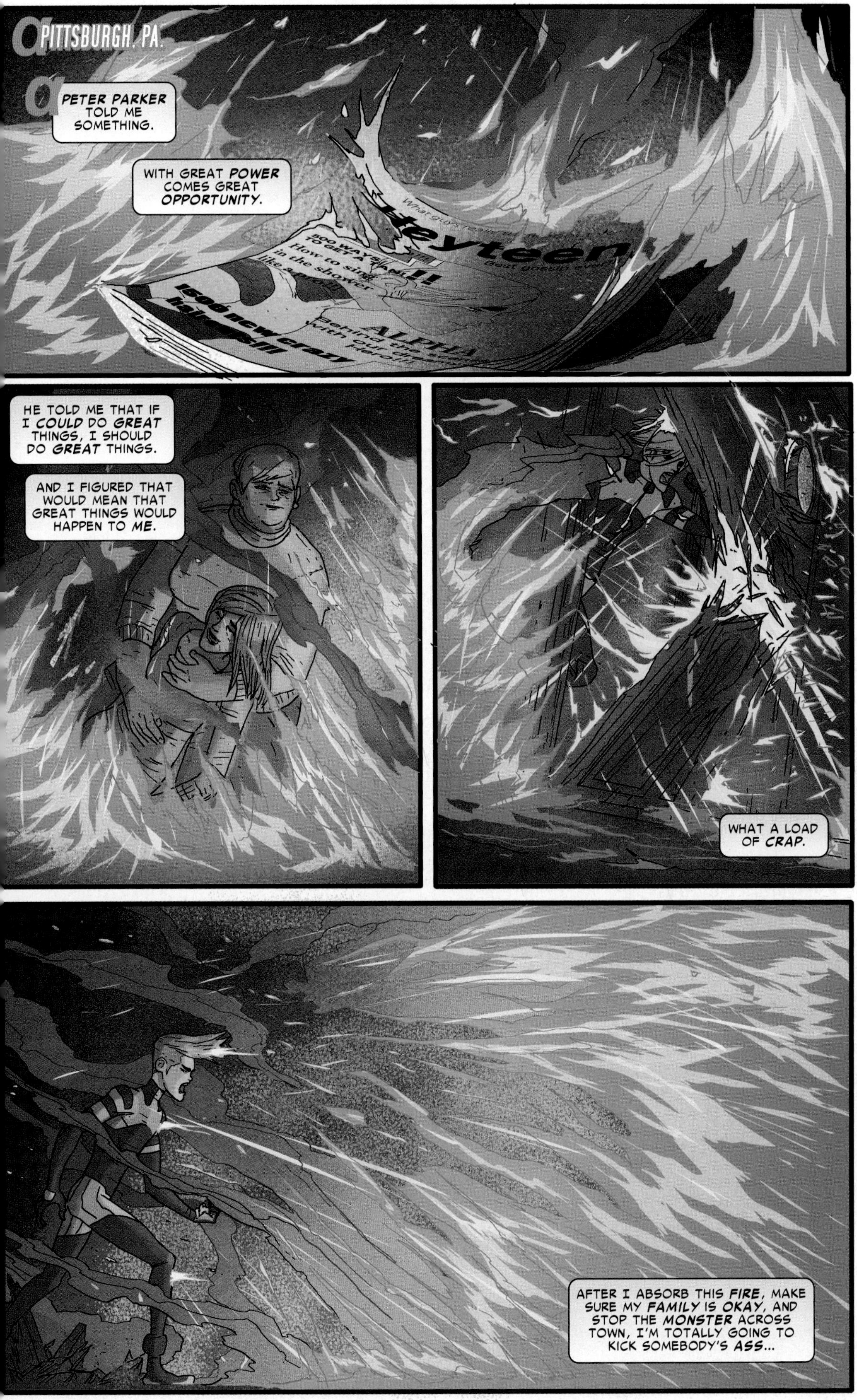
PITTSBURGH, PA.
PETER PARKER TOLD ME SOMETHING.
WITH GREAT POWER COMES GREAT OPPORTUNITY.
Heyteen
How to sing in the shower
ALPHA
HE TOLD ME THAT IF I COULD DO GREAT THINGS, I SHOULD DO GREAT THINGS.
AND I FIGURED THAT WOULD MEAN THAT GREAT THINGS WOULD HAPPEN TO ME.
WHAT A LOAD OF CRAP.
AFTER I ABSORB THIS FIRE, MAKE SURE MY FAMILY IS OKAY, AND STOP THE MONSTER ACROSS TOWN, I'M TOTALLY GOING TO KICK SOMEBODY'S ASS...

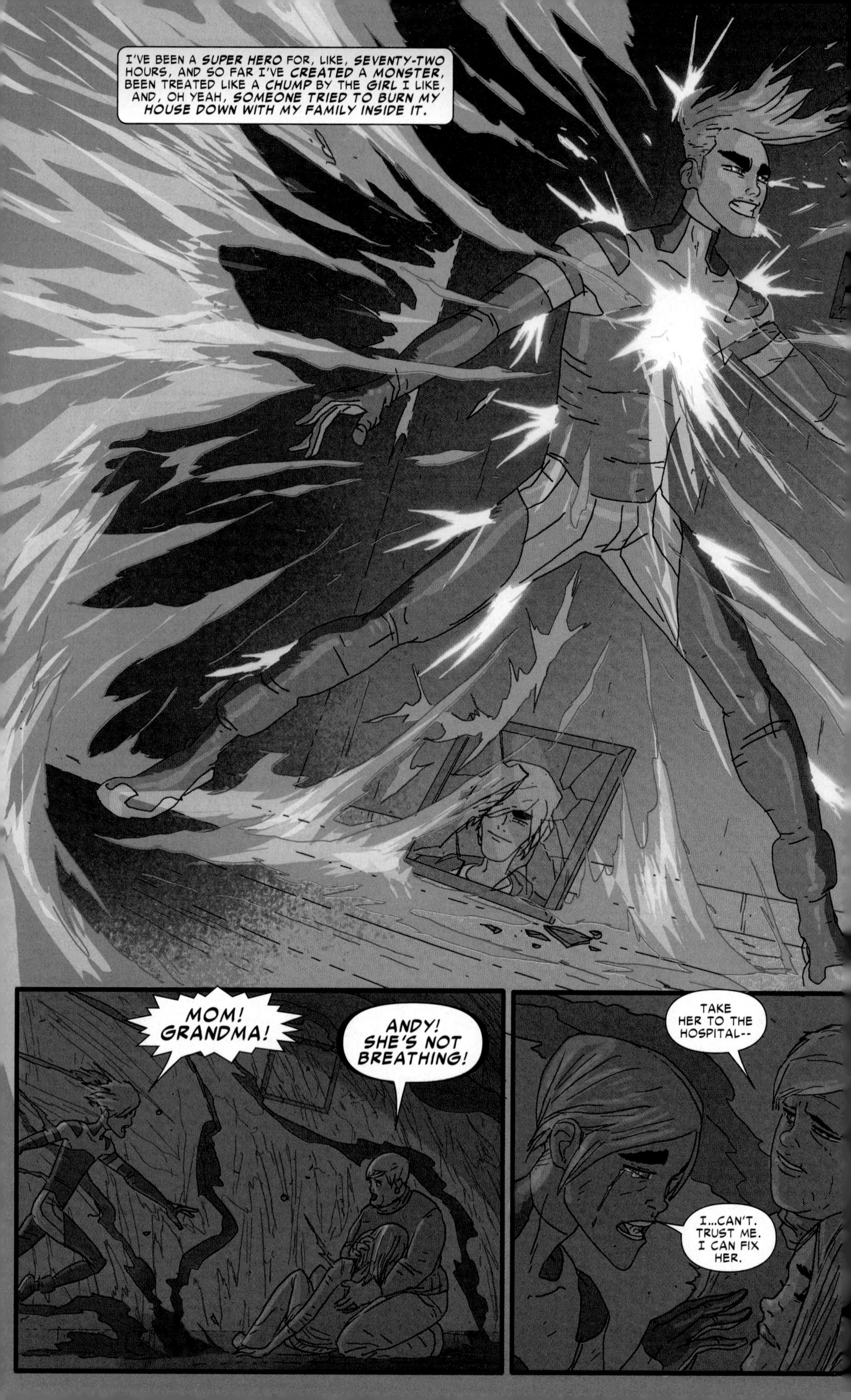
I'VE BEEN A SUPER HERO FOR, LIKE, SEVENTY-TWO HOURS, AND SO FAR I'VE CREATED A MONSTER, BEEN TREATED LIKE A CHUMP BY THE GIRL I LIKE, AND, OH YEAH, SOMEONE TRIED TO BURN MY HOUSE DOWN WITH MY FAMILY INSIDE IT.
MOM! GRANDMA!
ANDY! SHE'S NOT BREATHING!
TAKE HER TO THE HOSPITAL--
I...CAN'T. TRUST ME. I CAN FIX HER.

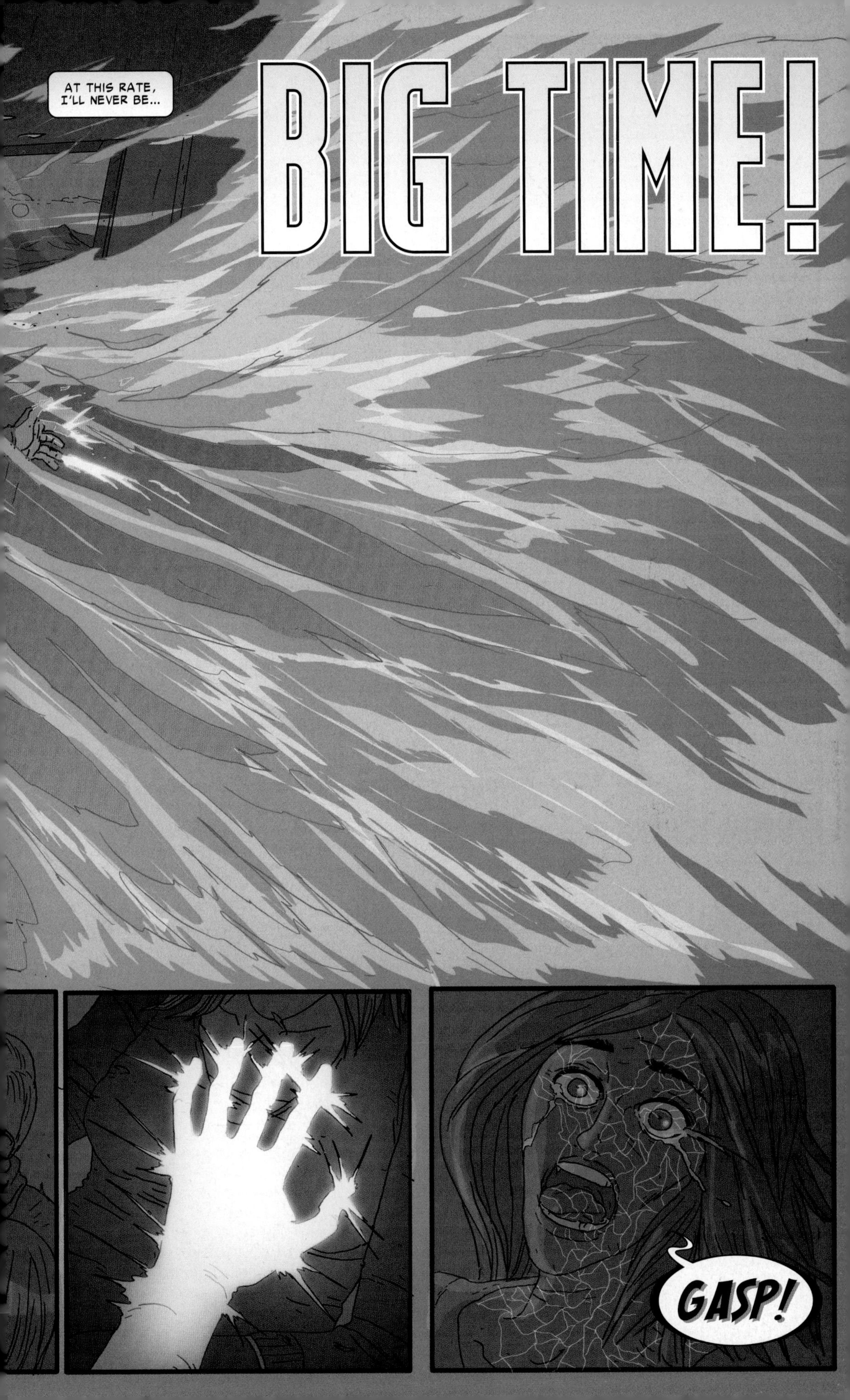
AT THIS RATE, I'LL NEVER BE...
BIG TIME!
GASP!

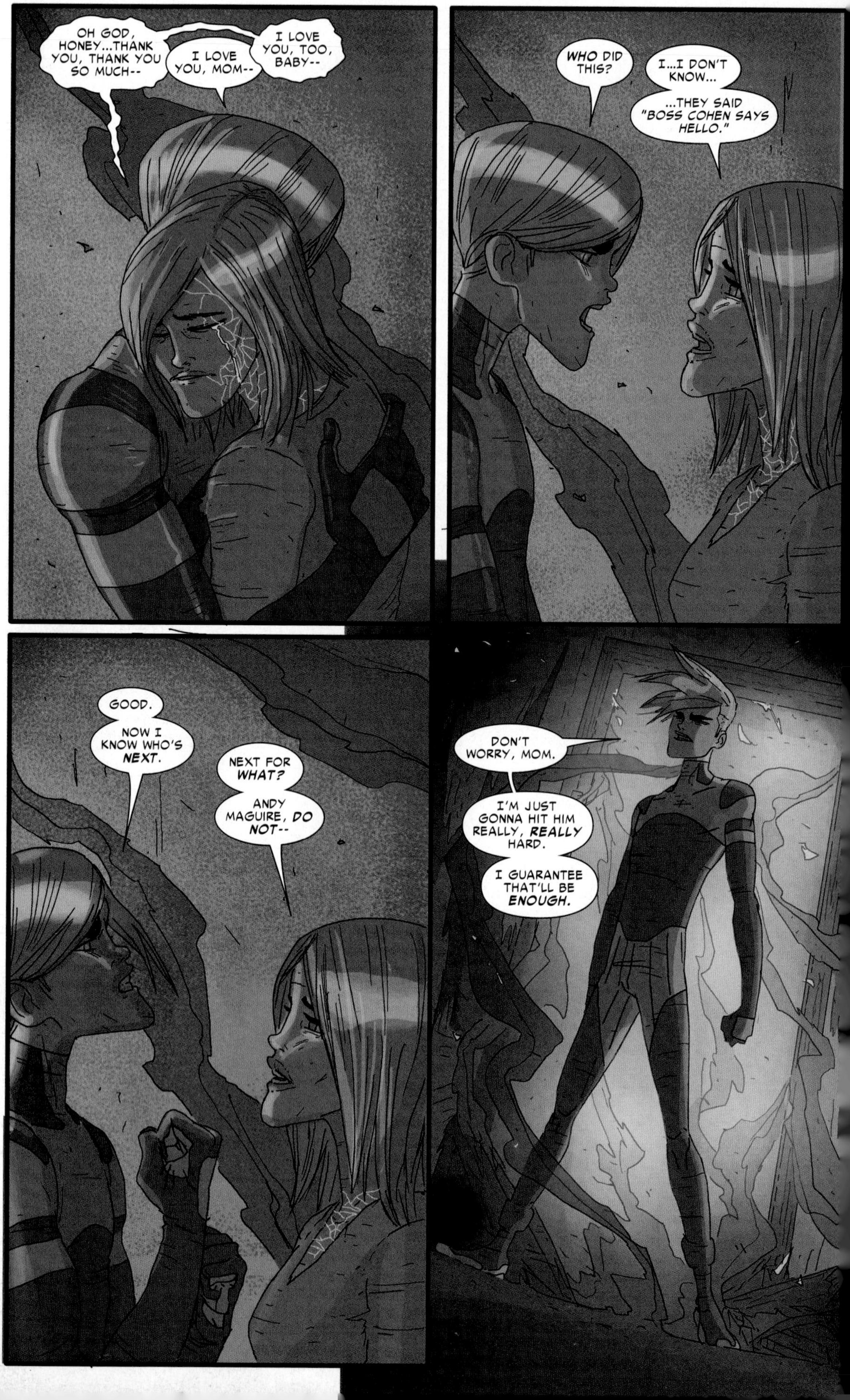
OH GOD, HONEY...THANK YOU, THANK YOU SO MUCH--
I LOVE YOU, MOM--
I LOVE YOU, TOO, BABY--
WHO DID THIS?
I...I DON'T KNOW...
...THEY SAID "BOSS COHEN SAYS HELLO."
GOOD.
NOW I KNOW WHO'S NEXT.
NEXT FOR WHAT?
ANDY MAGUIRE, DO NOT--
DON'T WORRY, MOM.
I'M JUST GONNA HIT HIM REALLY, REALLY HARD.
I GUARANTEE THAT'LL BE ENOUGH.

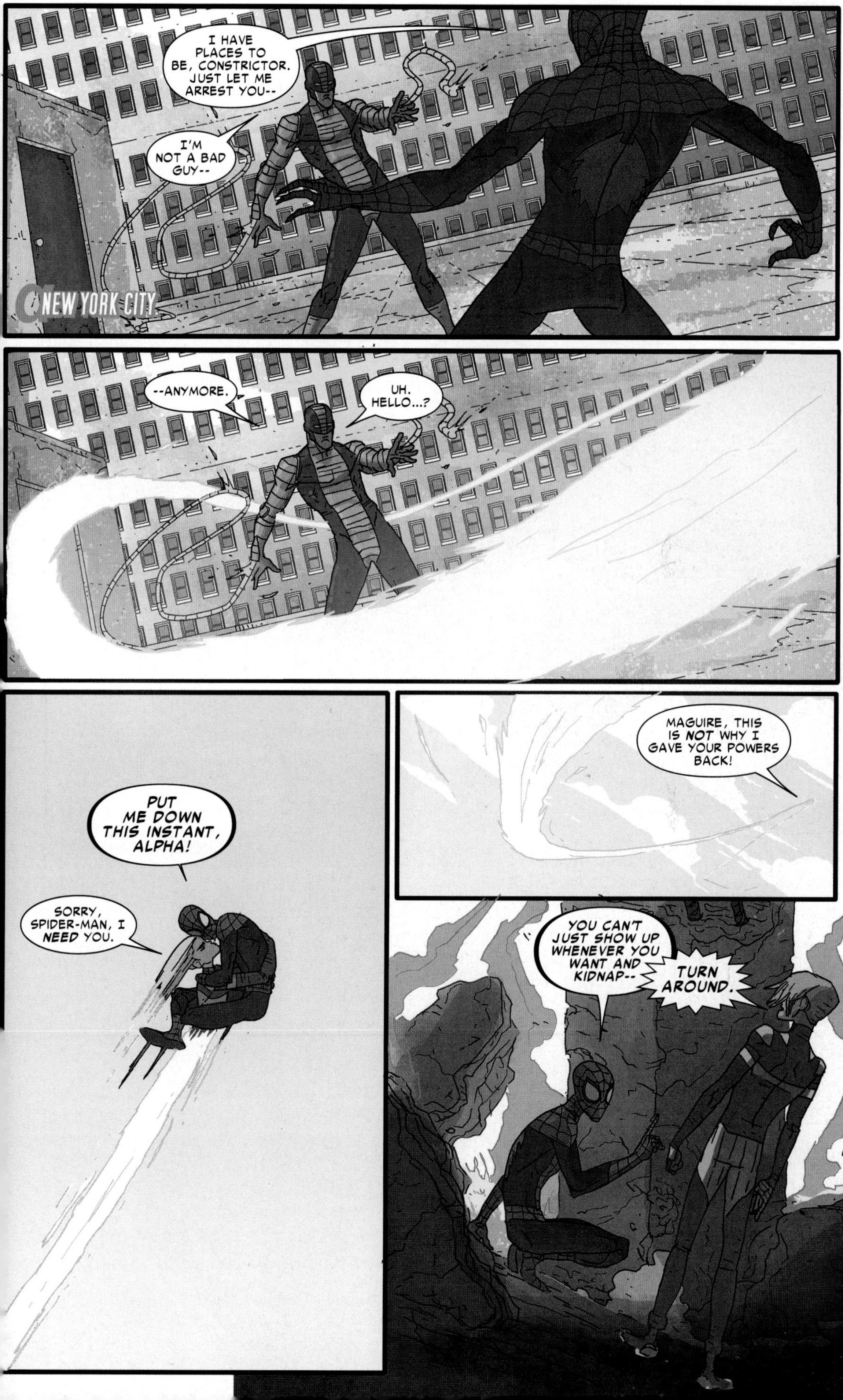
I HAVE PLACES TO BE, CONSTRICTOR. JUST LET ME ARREST YOU--
I'M NOT A BAD GUY--
NEW YORK CITY.
--ANYMORE.
UH. HELLO...?
PUT ME DOWN THIS INSTANT, ALPHA!
SORRY, SPIDER-MAN, I NEED YOU.
MAGUIRE, THIS IS NOT WHY I GAVE YOUR POWERS BACK!
YOU CAN'T JUST SHOW UP WHENEVER YOU WANT AND KIDNAP--
TURN AROUND.

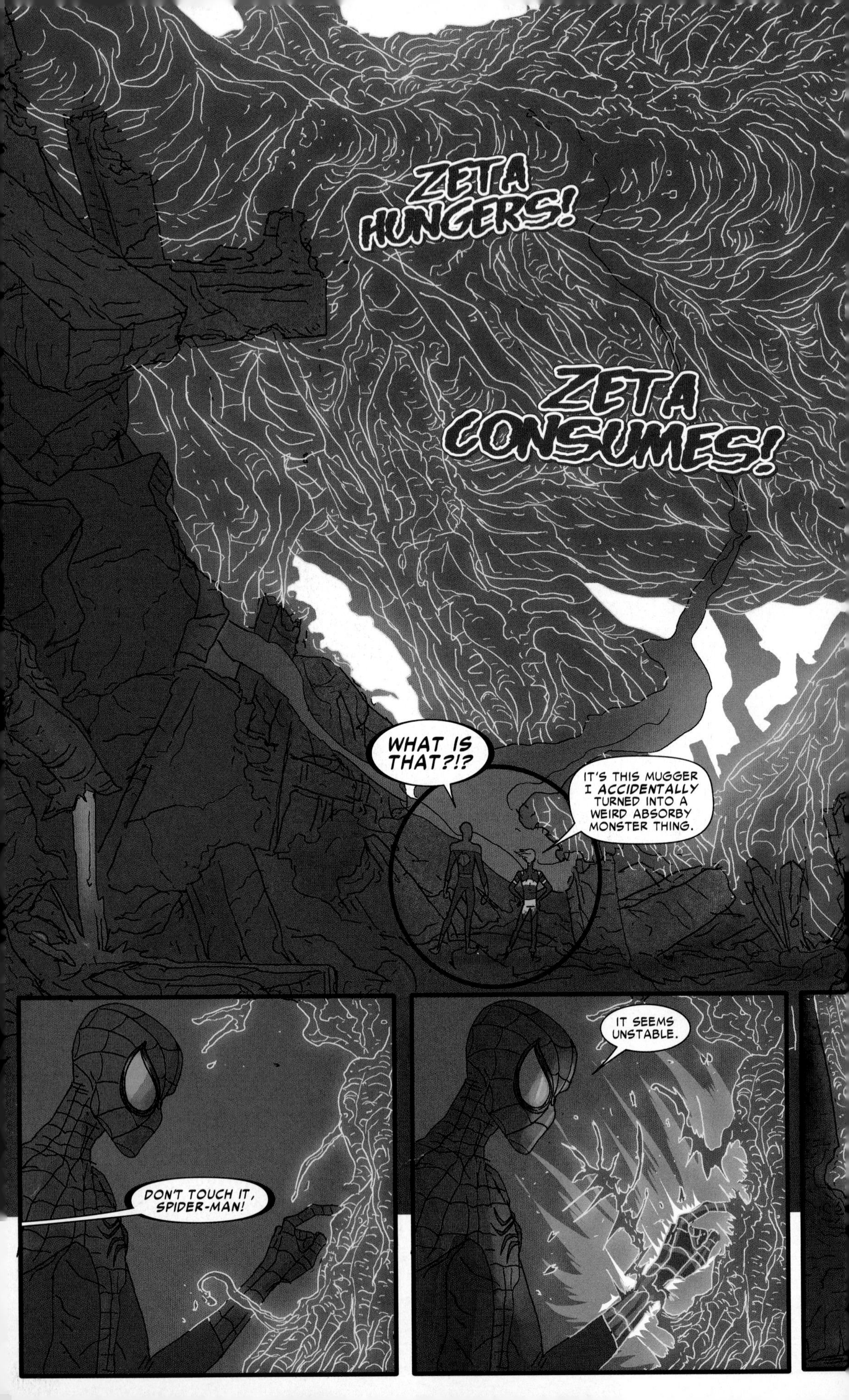
ZETA HUNGERS!
ZETA CONSUMES!
WHAT IS THAT?!?
IT'S THIS MUGGER I ACCIDENTALLY TURNED INTO A WEIRD ABSORBY MONSTER THING.
DON'T TOUCH IT, SPIDER-MAN!
IT SEEMS UNSTABLE.

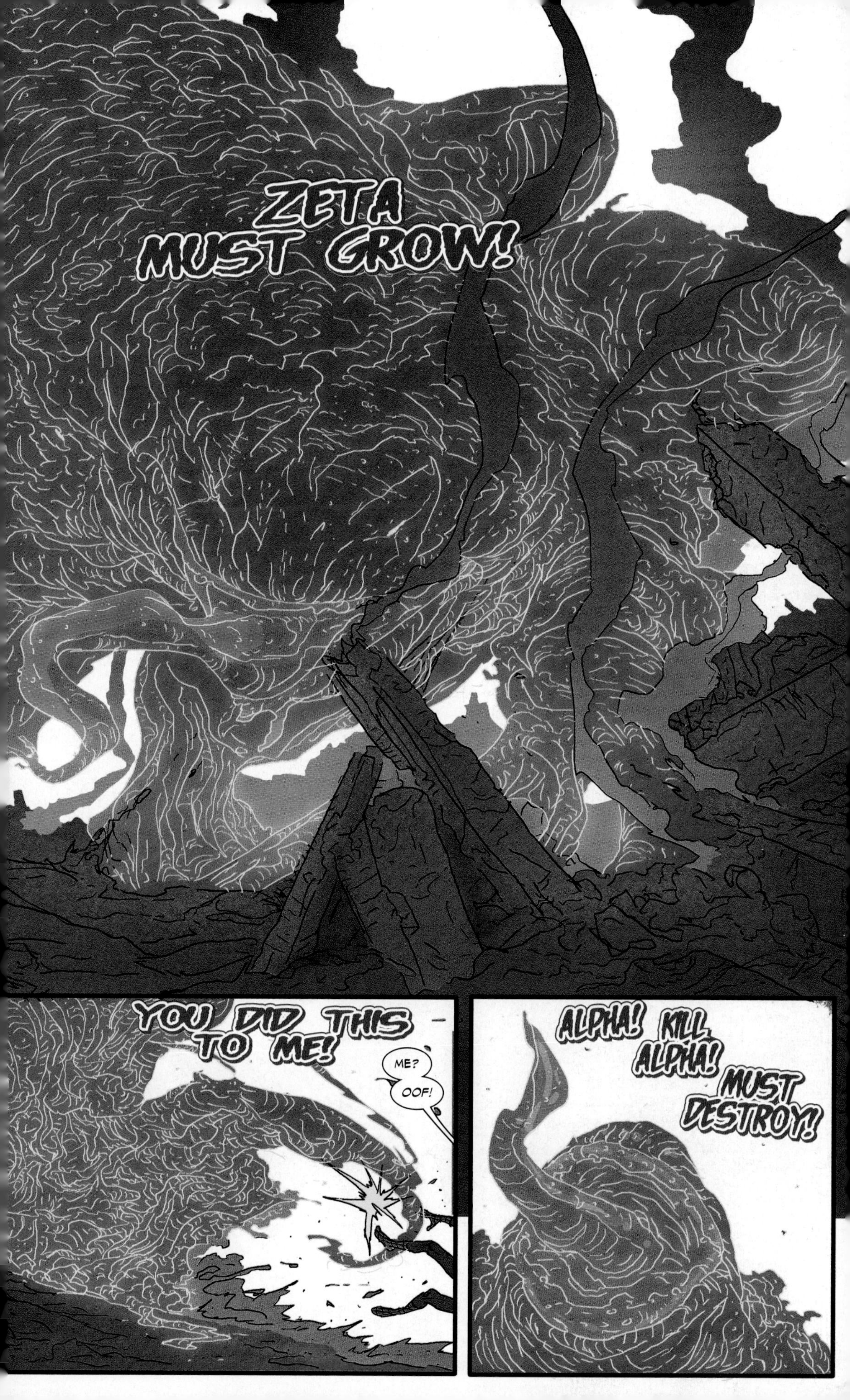
ZETA MUST GROW!
YOU DID THIS TO ME!
ME?
OOF!
ALPHA! KILL ALPHA!
MUST DESTROY!

KA-THOOOOOM

INCREDIBLE. HE'S MERGED WITH...HOW MANY PEOPLE?

THEY SAID HUNDREDS--

REMARKABLE!

KILL ALPHA AND HIS AMAZING FRIEND!

NOT AMAZING, NO--

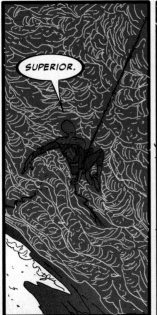

SUPERIOR.

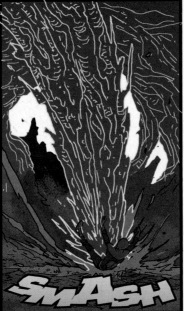

SMASH

...OUCH.

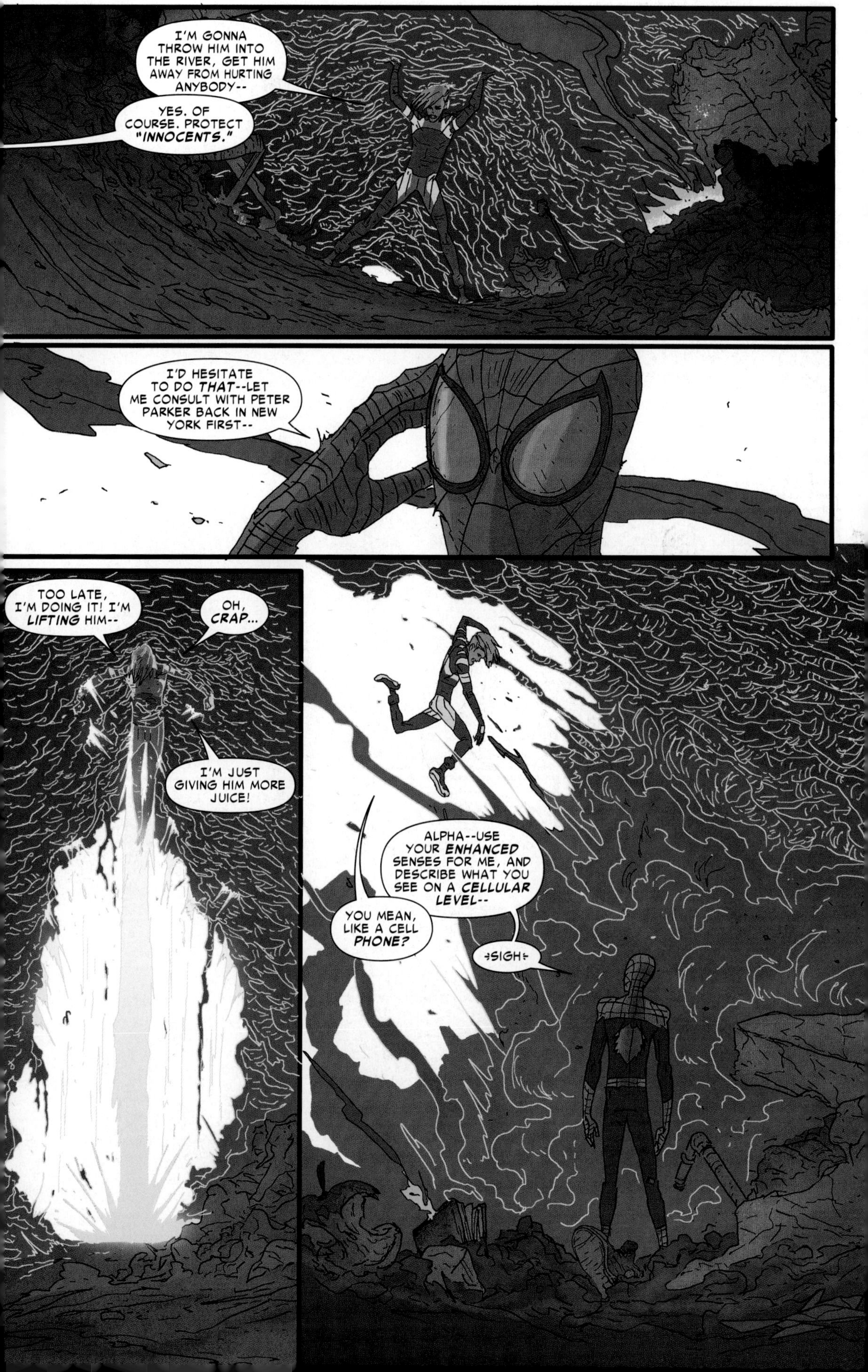
I'M GONNA THROW HIM INTO THE RIVER, GET HIM AWAY FROM HURTING ANYBODY--
YES. OF COURSE. PROTECT "INNOCENTS."
I'D HESITATE TO DO THAT--LET ME CONSULT WITH PETER PARKER BACK IN NEW YORK FIRST--
TOO LATE, I'M DOING IT! I'M LIFTING HIM--
OH, CRAP...
I'M JUST GIVING HIM MORE JUICE!
ALPHA--USE YOUR ENHANCED SENSES FOR ME, AND DESCRIBE WHAT YOU SEE ON A CELLULAR LEVEL--
YOU MEAN, LIKE A CELL PHONE?
SIGH

LOOK AT HIM. REALLY, REALLY HARD.

UH...

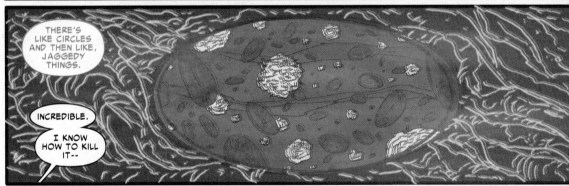

OKAY.

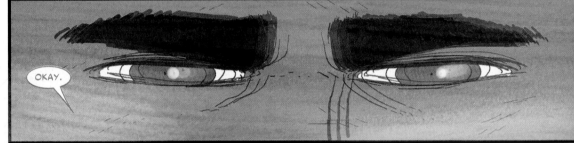

THERE'S LIKE CIRCLES AND THEN LIKE, JAGGEDY THINGS.

INCREDIBLE.

I KNOW HOW TO KILL IT--

DUDE, THAT'S A *LOT* OF INNOCENT PEOPLE.

--

FINE.

I CAN SAVE THEM ALL.

YOU NEED TO USE YOUR POWERS TO *RADIATE* THE CELLS, CAUSE THE CORRUPTED CELLS TO *DIE.* CAN YOU DO THAT?

BUT ONLY THE CORRUPTED CELLS!

UH...

...COOL.

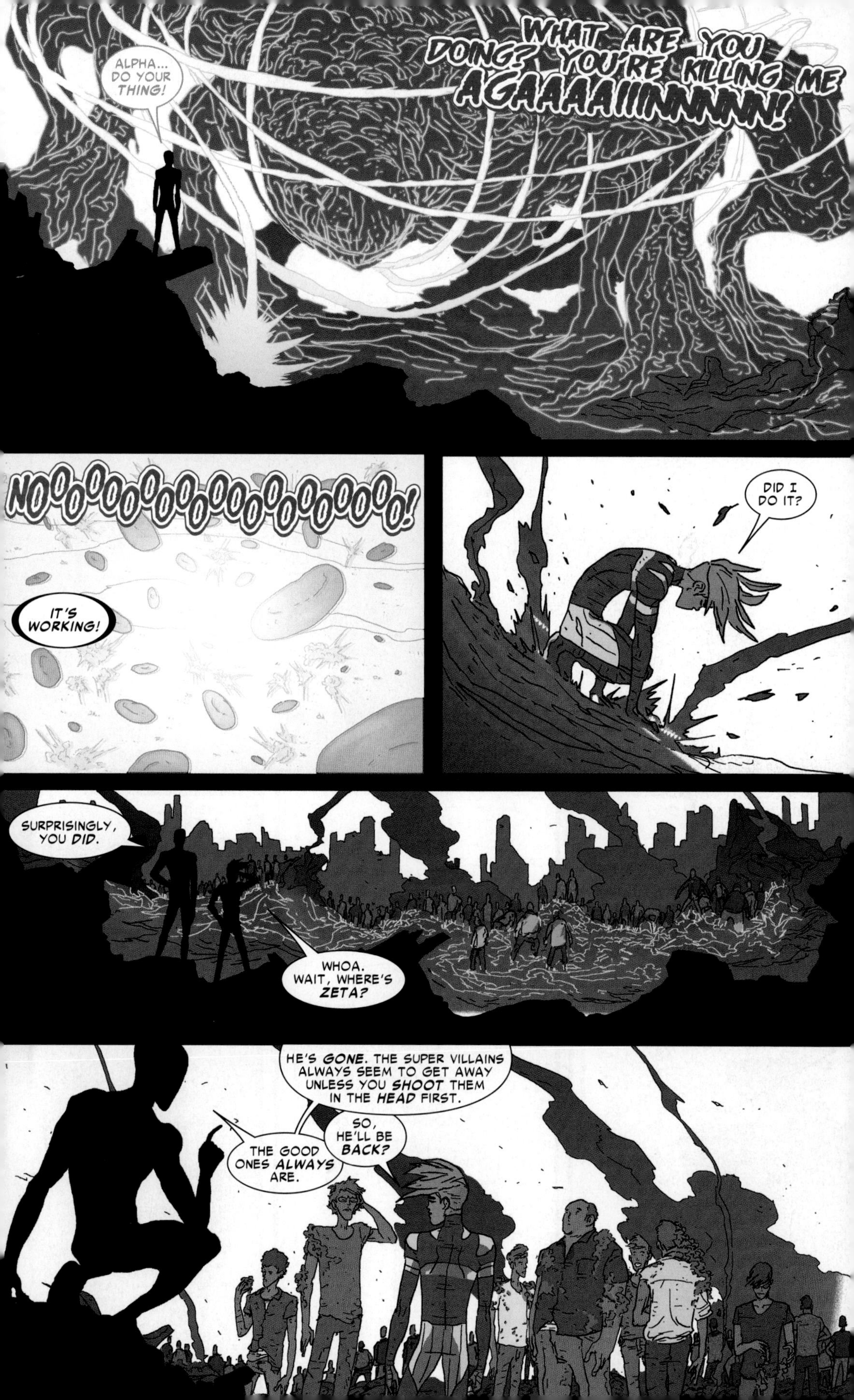
ALPHA... DO YOUR THING!
WHAT ARE YOU DOING? YOU'RE KILLING ME AGAAAAIIINNNNN!
NOOOOOOOOOOOOOOOOOOOOOO!
IT'S WORKING!
DID I DO IT?
SURPRISINGLY, YOU DID.
WHOA. WAIT, WHERE'S ZETA?
HE'S GONE. THE SUPER VILLAINS ALWAYS SEEM TO GET AWAY UNLESS YOU SHOOT THEM IN THE HEAD FIRST.
SO, HE'LL BE BACK?
THE GOOD ONES ALWAYS ARE.

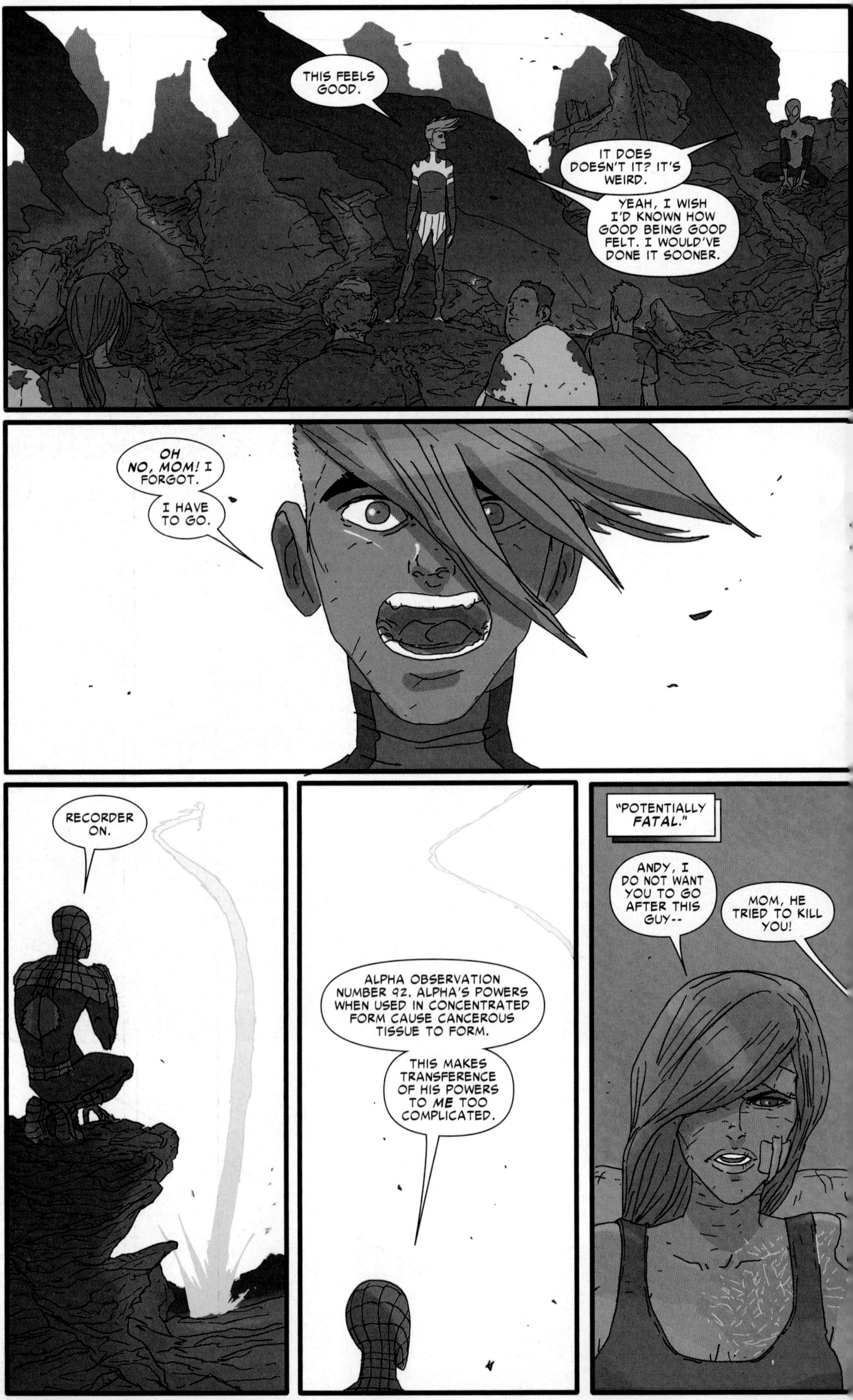
THIS FEELS GOOD.
IT DOES DOESN'T IT? IT'S WEIRD.
YEAH, I WISH I'D KNOWN HOW GOOD BEING GOOD FELT. I WOULD'VE DONE IT SOONER.
OH NO, MOM! I FORGOT.
I HAVE TO GO.
RECORDER ON.
ALPHA OBSERVATION NUMBER 92. ALPHA'S POWERS WHEN USED IN CONCENTRATED FORM CAUSE CANCEROUS TISSUE TO FORM.
THIS MAKES TRANSFERENCE OF HIS POWERS TO ME TOO COMPLICATED.
"POTENTIALLY FATAL."
ANDY, I DO NOT WANT YOU TO GO AFTER THIS GUY--
MOM, HE TRIED TO KILL YOU!

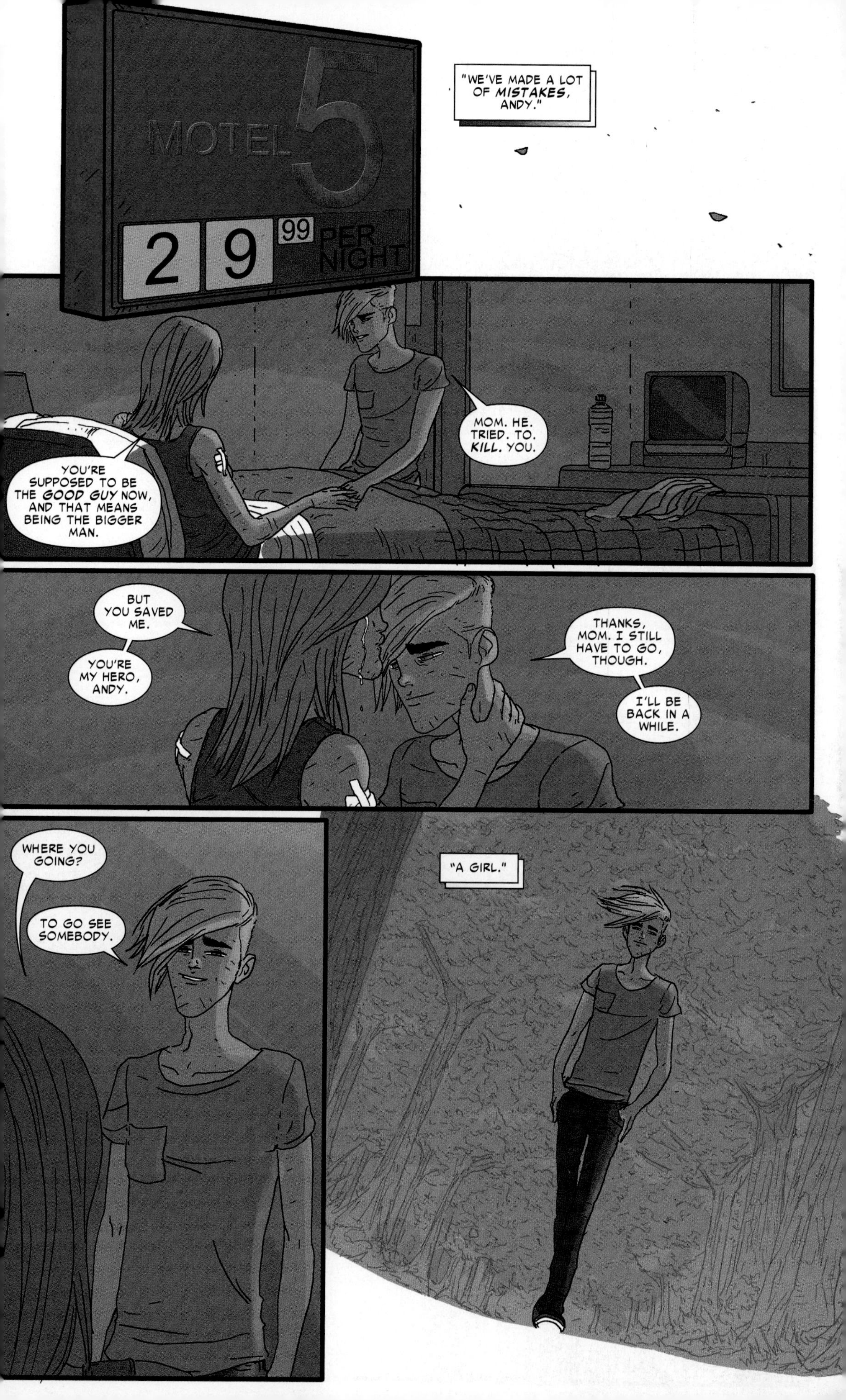
MOTEL 5
29 99 PER NIGHT
"WE'VE MADE A LOT OF MISTAKES, ANDY."
YOU'RE SUPPOSED TO BE THE GOOD GUY NOW, AND THAT MEANS BEING THE BIGGER MAN.
MOM. HE. TRIED. TO. KILL. YOU.
BUT YOU SAVED ME.
YOU'RE MY HERO, ANDY.
THANKS, MOM. I STILL HAVE TO GO, THOUGH.
I'LL BE BACK IN A WHILE.
WHERE YOU GOING?
TO GO SEE SOMEBODY.
"A GIRL."

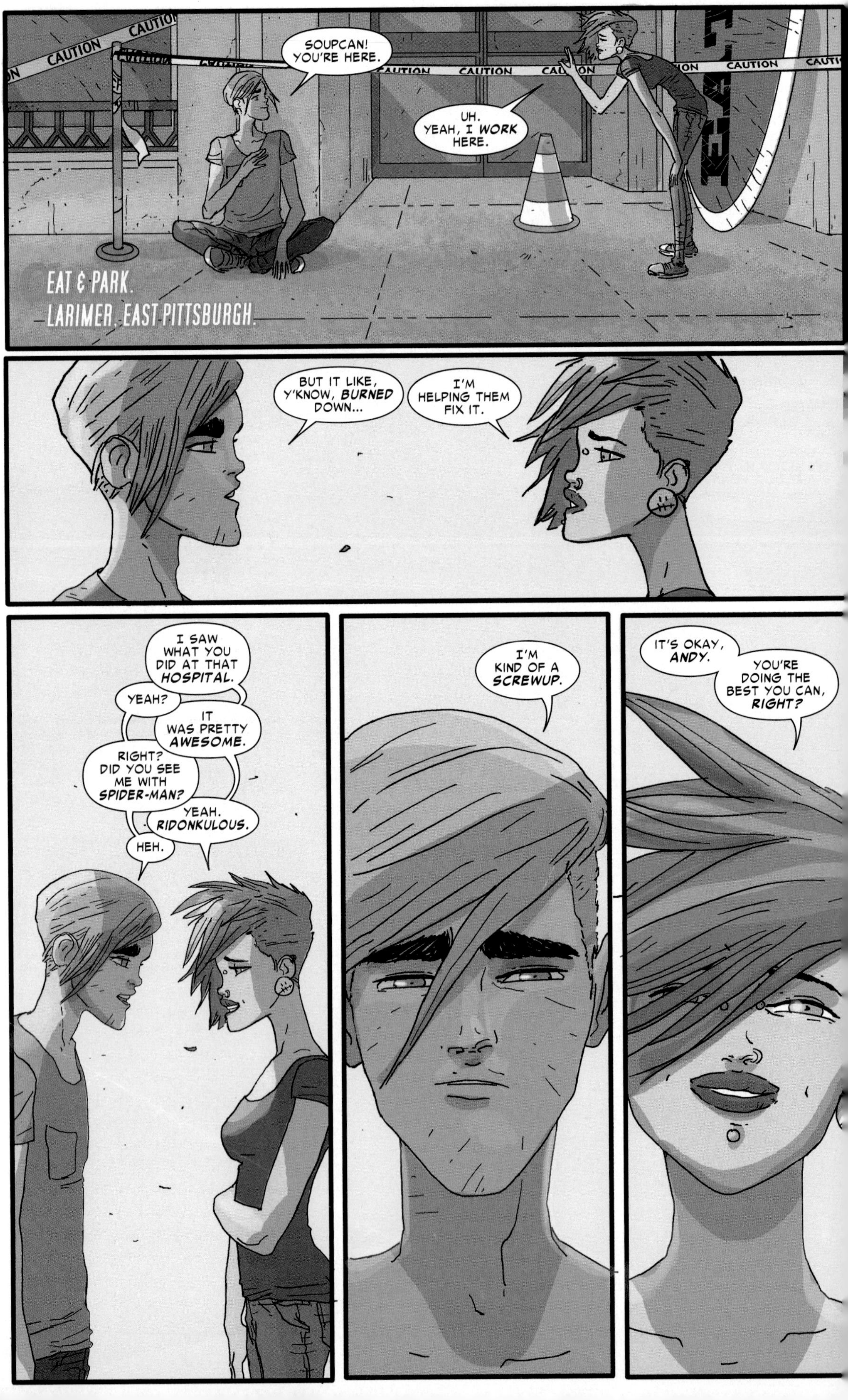
SOUPCAN! YOU'RE HERE.
UH. YEAH, I WORK HERE.
EAT & PARK.
LARIMER, EAST PITTSBURGH.
BUT IT LIKE, Y'KNOW, BURNED DOWN...
I'M HELPING THEM FIX IT.
I SAW WHAT YOU DID AT THAT HOSPITAL.
YEAH?
IT WAS PRETTY AWESOME.
RIGHT? DID YOU SEE ME WITH SPIDER-MAN?
YEAH. RIDONKULOUS.
HEH.
I'M KIND OF A SCREWUP.
IT'S OKAY, ANDY.
YOU'RE DOING THE BEST YOU CAN, RIGHT?

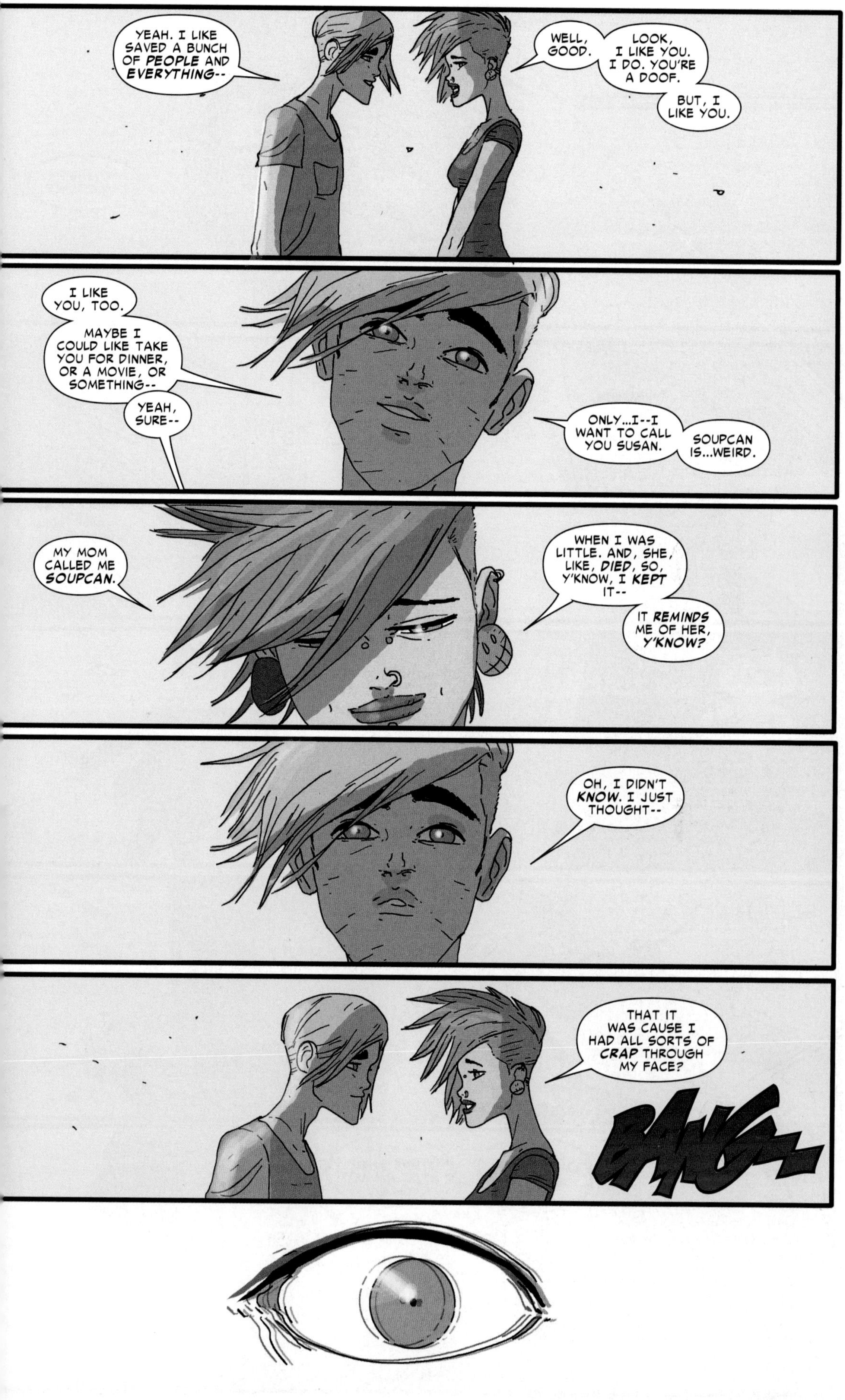
YEAH. I LIKE SAVED A BUNCH OF PEOPLE AND EVERYTHING--
WELL, GOOD.
LOOK, I LIKE YOU. I DO. YOU'RE A DOOF.
BUT, I LIKE YOU.
I LIKE YOU, TOO.
MAYBE I COULD LIKE TAKE YOU FOR DINNER, OR A MOVIE, OR SOMETHING--
YEAH, SURE--
ONLY...I--I WANT TO CALL YOU SUSAN.
SOUPCAN IS...WEIRD.
MY MOM CALLED ME SOUPCAN.
WHEN I WAS LITTLE. AND, SHE, LIKE, DIED, SO, Y'KNOW, I KEPT IT--
IT REMINDS ME OF HER, Y'KNOW?
OH, I DIDN'T KNOW. I JUST THOUGHT--
THAT IT WAS CAUSE I HAD ALL SORTS OF CRAP THROUGH MY FACE?
BANG

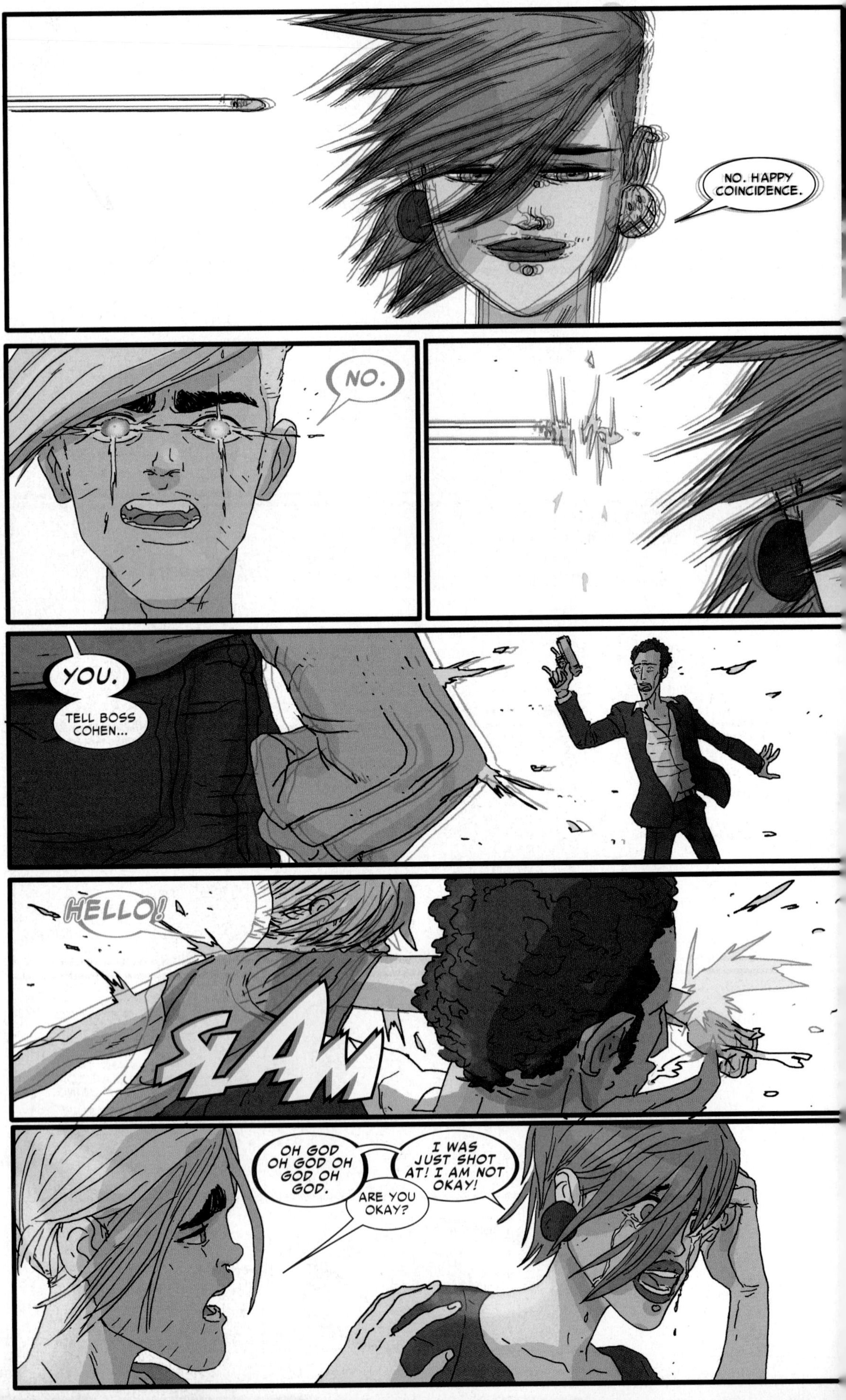
NO. HAPPY COINCIDENCE.
NO.
YOU.
TELL BOSS COHEN...
HELLO!
SLAM
OH GOD OH GOD OH GOD OH GOD.
I WAS JUST SHOT AT! I AM NOT OKAY!
ARE YOU OKAY?

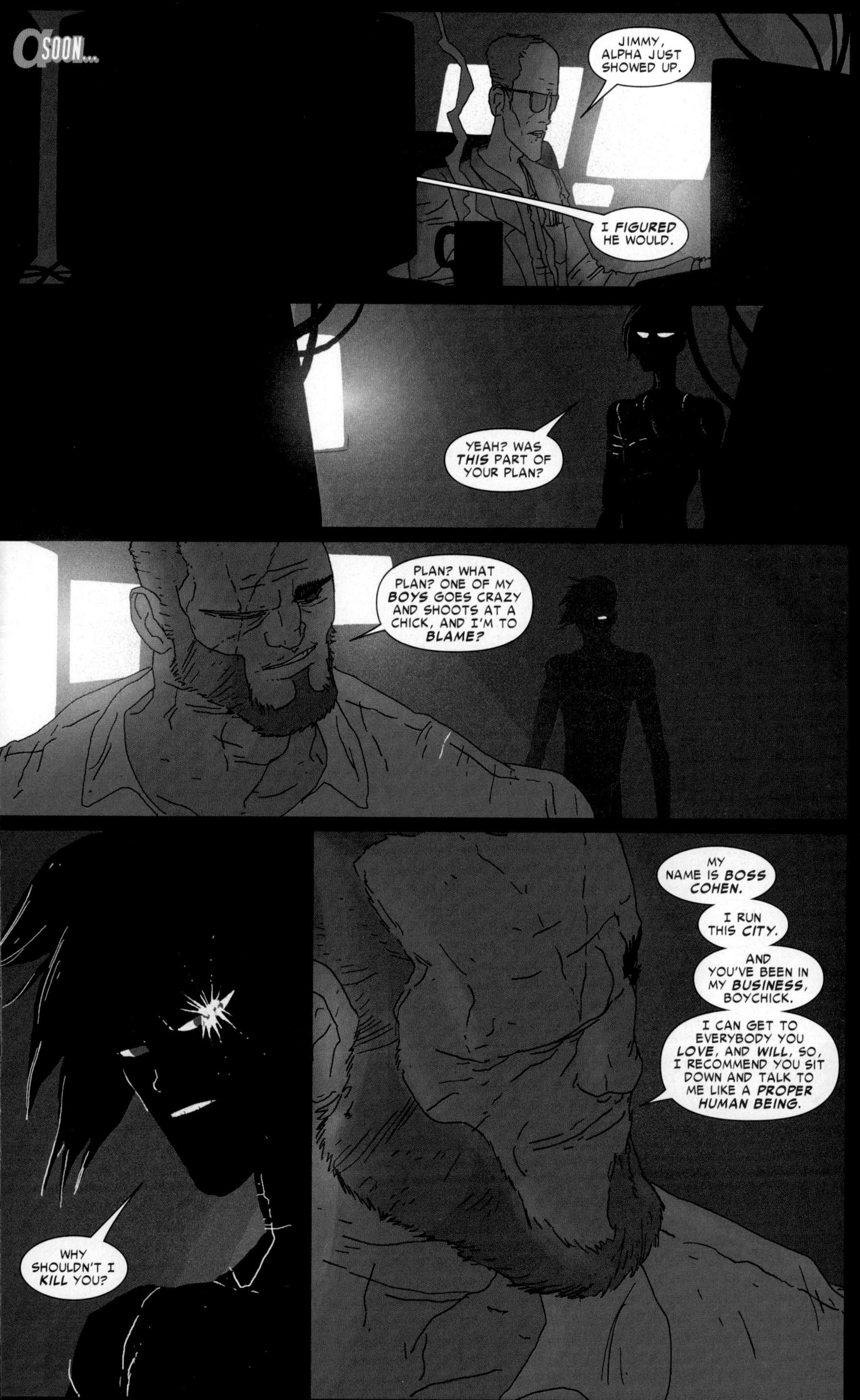
SOON...
JIMMY, ALPHA JUST SHOWED UP.
I FIGURED HE WOULD.
YEAH? WAS THIS PART OF YOUR PLAN?
PLAN? WHAT PLAN? ONE OF MY BOYS GOES CRAZY AND SHOOTS AT A CHICK, AND I'M TO BLAME?
MY NAME IS BOSS COHEN.
I RUN THIS CITY.
AND YOU'VE BEEN IN MY BUSINESS, BOYCHICK.
I CAN GET TO EVERYBODY YOU LOVE, AND WILL, SO, I RECOMMEND YOU SIT DOWN AND TALK TO ME LIKE A PROPER HUMAN BEING.
WHY SHOULDN'T I KILL YOU?

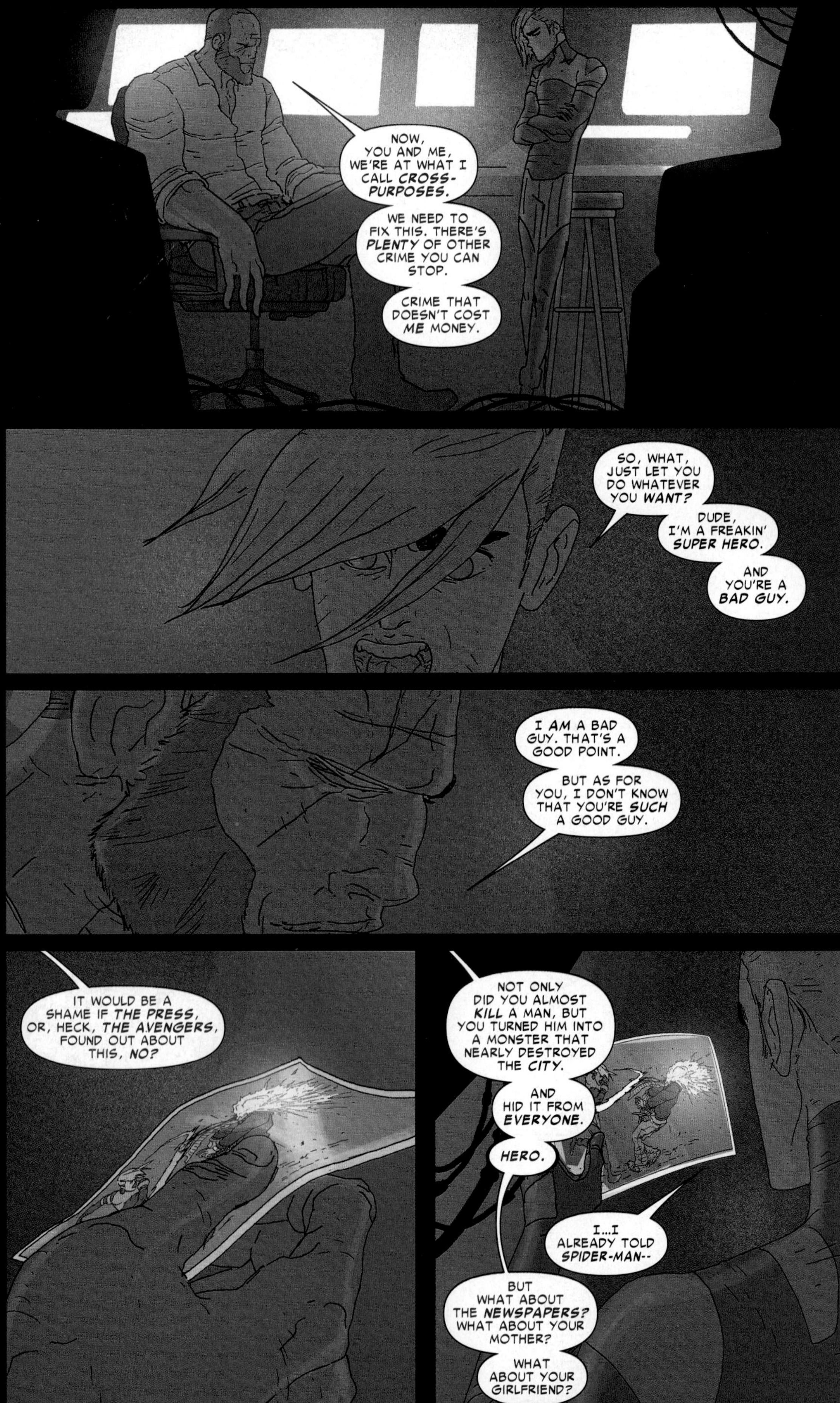
NOW, YOU AND ME, WE'RE AT WHAT I CALL CROSS-PURPOSES.
WE NEED TO FIX THIS. THERE'S PLENTY OF OTHER CRIME YOU CAN STOP.
CRIME THAT DOESN'T COST ME MONEY.
SO, WHAT, JUST LET YOU DO WHATEVER YOU WANT?
DUDE, I'M A FREAKIN' SUPER HERO.
AND YOU'RE A BAD GUY.
I AM A BAD GUY. THAT'S A GOOD POINT.
BUT AS FOR YOU, I DON'T KNOW THAT YOU'RE SUCH A GOOD GUY.
IT WOULD BE A SHAME IF THE PRESS, OR, HECK, THE AVENGERS, FOUND OUT ABOUT THIS, NO?
NOT ONLY DID YOU ALMOST KILL A MAN, BUT YOU TURNED HIM INTO A MONSTER THAT NEARLY DESTROYED THE CITY.
AND HID IT FROM EVERYONE.
HERO.
I...I ALREADY TOLD SPIDER-MAN--
BUT WHAT ABOUT THE NEWSPAPERS? WHAT ABOUT YOUR MOTHER?
WHAT ABOUT YOUR GIRLFRIEND?

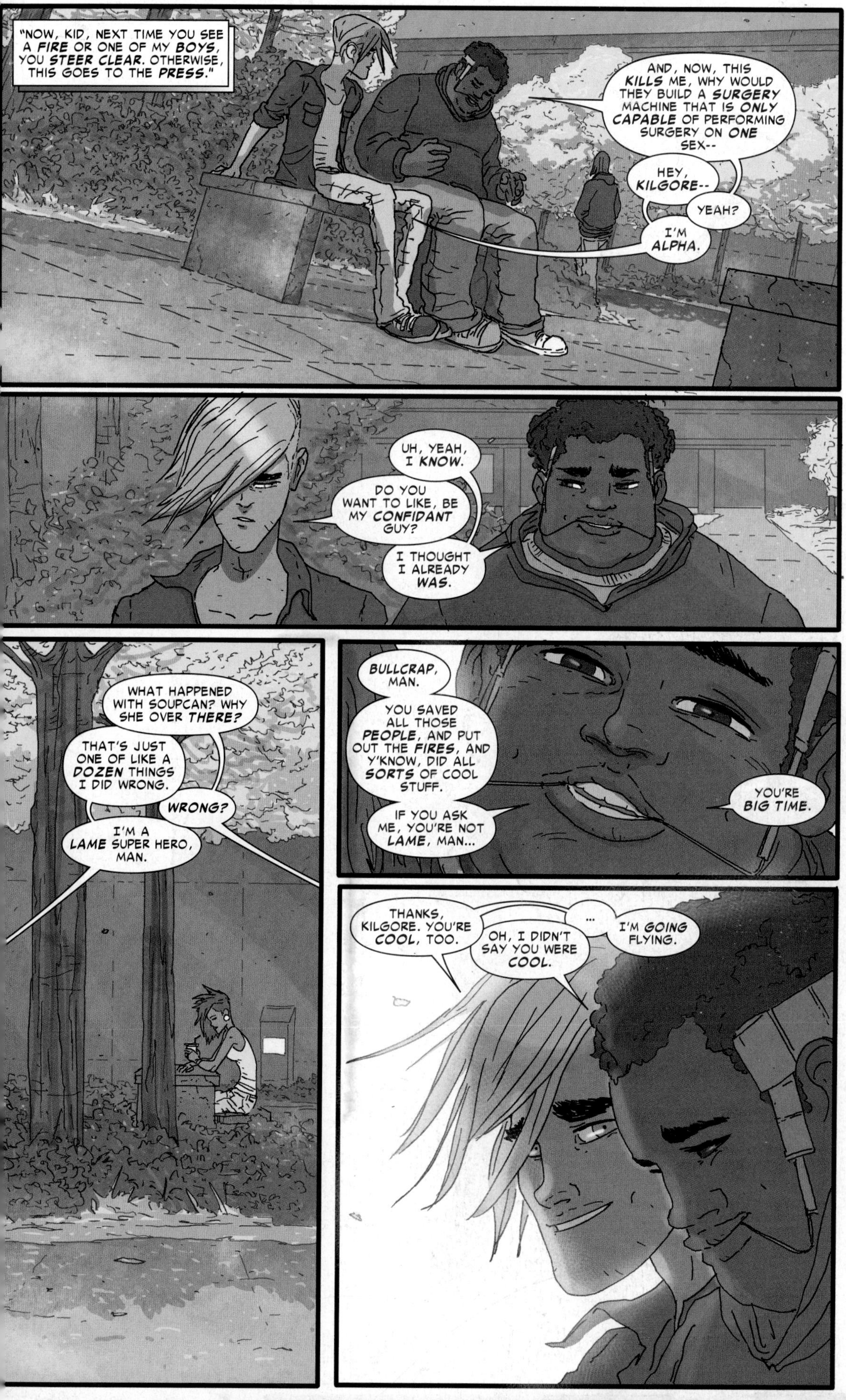
"NOW, KID, NEXT TIME YOU SEE A FIRE OR ONE OF MY BOYS, YOU STEER CLEAR. OTHERWISE, THIS GOES TO THE PRESS."
AND, NOW, THIS KILLS ME, WHY WOULD THEY BUILD A SURGERY MACHINE THAT IS ONLY CAPABLE OF PERFORMING SURGERY ON ONE SEX--
HEY, KILGORE--
YEAH?
I'M ALPHA.
UH, YEAH, I KNOW.
DO YOU WANT TO LIKE, BE MY CONFIDANT GUY?
I THOUGHT I ALREADY WAS.
WHAT HAPPENED WITH SOUPCAN? WHY SHE OVER THERE?
THAT'S JUST ONE OF LIKE A DOZEN THINGS I DID WRONG.
WRONG?
I'M A LAME SUPER HERO, MAN.
BULLCRAP, MAN.
YOU SAVED ALL THOSE PEOPLE, AND PUT OUT THE FIRES, AND Y'KNOW, DID ALL SORTS OF COOL STUFF.
IF YOU ASK ME, YOU'RE NOT LAME, MAN...
YOU'RE BIG TIME.
THANKS, KILGORE. YOU'RE COOL, TOO.
OH, I DIDN'T SAY YOU WERE COOL.
...
I'M GOING FLYING.

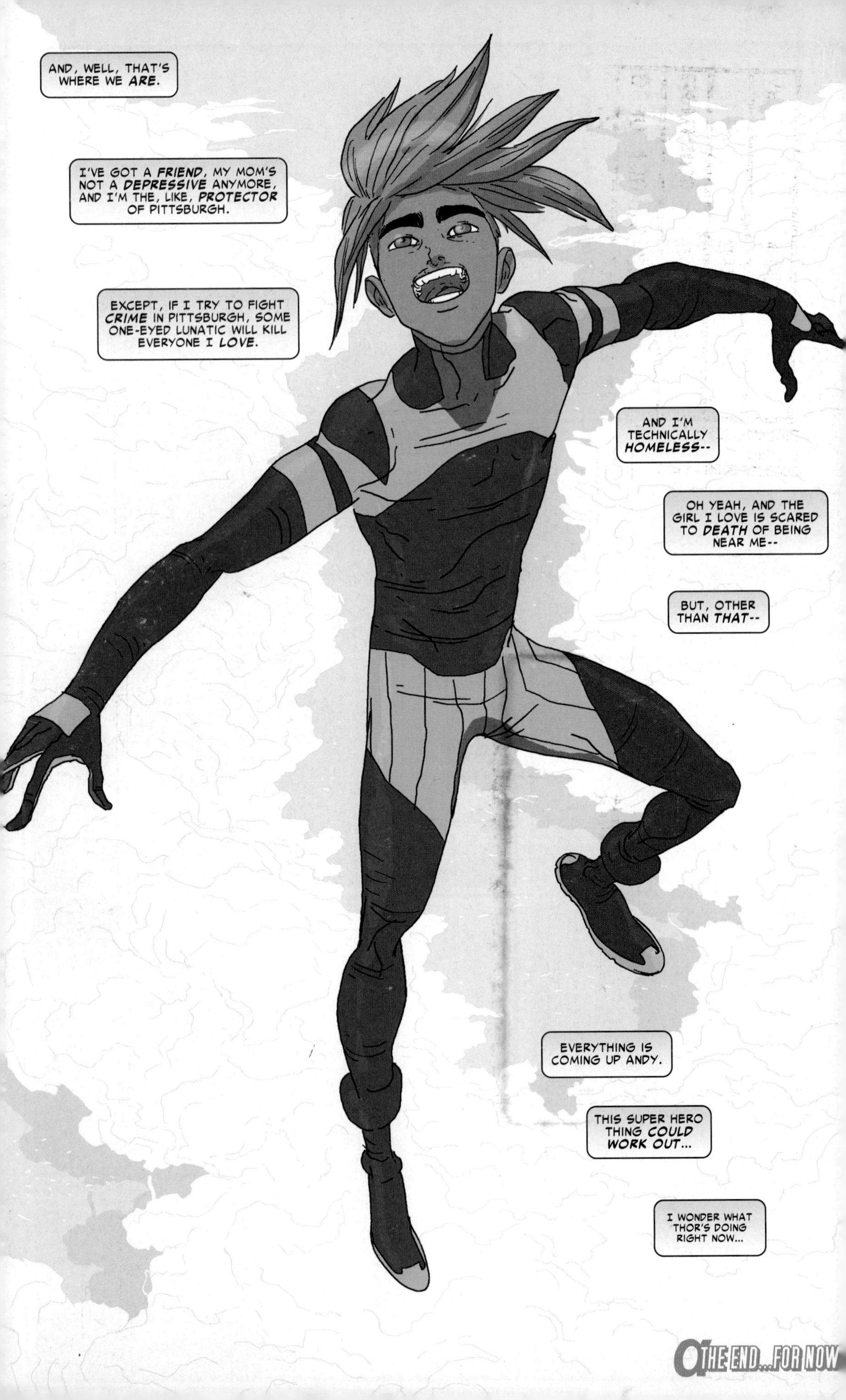
AND, WELL, THAT'S WHERE WE *ARE*.
I'VE GOT A *FRIEND*, MY MOM'S NOT A *DEPRESSIVE* ANYMORE, AND I'M THE, LIKE, *PROTECTOR* OF PITTSBURGH.
EXCEPT, IF I TRY TO FIGHT *CRIME* IN PITTSBURGH, SOME ONE-EYED LUNATIC WILL KILL EVERYONE I *LOVE*.
AND I'M TECHNICALLY *HOMELESS*--
OH YEAH, AND THE GIRL I LOVE IS SCARED TO *DEATH* OF BEING NEAR ME--
BUT, OTHER THAN *THAT*--
EVERYTHING IS COMING UP ANDY.
THIS SUPER HERO THING *COULD WORK OUT*...
I WONDER WHAT THOR'S DOING RIGHT NOW...
THE END...FOR NOW